Quantitative Data Analysis with SPSS 12 and 13

This new edition has been completely updated to accommodate the needs of users of SPSS Releases 12 and 13 for Windows, whilst still being applicable to those using SPSS Releases 11 and 10.

Alan Bryman and Duncan Cramer provide a non-technical approach to quantitative data analysis and a user-friendly introduction to the widely used SPSS. No previous familiarity with computing or statistics is required to benefit from this step-by-step guide to techniques including:

- non-parametric tests
- correlation
- simple and multiple regression
- multivariate analysis of variance and covariance
- factor analysis

The authors discuss key issues facing the newcomer to research, such as how to decide which statistical procedure is suitable, and how to interpret the subsequent results. Each chapter contains worked examples to illustrate the points raised and ends with a comprehensive range of exercises which allow the reader to test their understanding of the topic.

This new edition of this hugely successful textbook will guide the reader through the basics of quantitative data analysis and become an essential reference tool for both students and researchers in the social sciences.

The data sets used in *Quantitative Data Analysis for SPSS 12 and 13* are available via the Internet at:

http://www.psypress.co.uk/brymancramer

Alan Bryman and **Duncan Cramer** both teach at Loughborough University and have written several books on statistical analysis with both SPSS and Minitab.

Quantitative Data Analysis with SPSS 12 and 13

A Guide for Social Scientists

- Alan Bryman and Duncan Cramer

Routledge
Taylor & Francis Group

LONDON AND NEW YORK

First published 2005 by Routledge
27 Church Road, Hove, East Sussex, BN3 2FA

Simultaneously published in the USA and Canada
by Routledge
270 Madison Avenue, New York, NY 10016

Routledge is an imprint of the Taylor & Francis Group

Copyright © 2005 Psychology Press

Typeset in Times by RefineCatch Limited, Bungay, Suffolk
Printed and bound in Great Britain by
TJ International Ltd, Padstow, Cornwall

Cover design by Hybert Design

British Library Cataloguing in Publication Data
A catalogue record for this book is available from the British Library

Library of Congress Cataloging-in-Publication Data
Applied for

ISBN 0-415-34081-0 (hbk)
ISBN 0-415-34080-2 (pbk)

For Sue, Sarah and Stella

Contents

CONTENTS

Figures

Tables

Boxes
(screenshots)

Preface

In this book, we introduce readers to the main techniques of statistical analysis employed by psychologists and sociologists. However, we do not see the book as a standard introduction to statistics. We see the book as distinctively different because we are not concerned to introduce the often complex formulae that underlie the statistical methods covered. Students often find these formulae and the calculations that are associated with them extremely daunting, especially when their background in mathematics is weak. Moreover, in these days of powerful computers and packages of statistical programs, it seems gratuitous to put students through the anxiety of confronting complex calculations when machines can perform the bulk of the work. Indeed, most practitioners employ statistical packages that are run on computers to perform their calculations, so there seems little purpose in treating formulae and their application as a *rite de passage* for social scientists. Moreover, few students would come to understand fully the rationale for the formulae that they would need to learn. Indeed, we prefer the term 'quantitative data analysis' to 'statistics' because of the adverse image that the latter term has in the minds of many prospective readers.

In view of the widespread availability of statistical packages and computers, we feel that the two areas that students need to get to grips with are how to decide which statistical procedures are suitable for which purpose and how to interpret the ensuing results. We try to emphasise these two elements in this book.

In addition, the student needs to get to know how to operate the computer and in particular how to use computer software needed to perform the statistical procedures described in this book. To this end, we introduce students to what is probably the most widely used suite of programs for statistical analysis in the social sciences – the Statistical Package for the Social Sciences (SPSS). This package was first developed in the 1960s and was the first major attempt to provide software for the social scientist. It has since undergone numerous revisions and refinements. The first two editions of this book (Bryman and Cramer, 1990, 1994) dealt with versions of SPSS that were designed for mainframe computers or for the Microsoft operating system MS-DOS. A few years ago, a version of SPSS was developed to operate within the widely used Microsoft Windows environment. This too has undergone a number of revisions. The next edition of this book (Bryman and Cramer, 1997) was concerned with Release 6 for Windows which was designed for Microsoft Windows 3.11. After the introduction of Windows 95, a new release of SPSS (Release 7) was designed to run on this operating system. Subsequent books described Releases 8 and 9 (Bryman and Cramer, 1999) and Release 10 (Bryman and Cramer, 2001). The latest version of SPSS is Release 13. The present book describes the use of this version, which we shall refer to as SPSS for short unless otherwise indicated. As Release 13 is very similar to Releases 12, 11 and 10, this book can also be used for these earlier versions. The main difference is in the way the Chart Editor works. The Chart Editor in Releases 12 and 13 operates differently from that in previous versions. However, as only a few pages of this book deal with the Chart Editor, this difference is unlikely to affect users of this book.

In order to distinguish methods of quantitative data analysis from SPSS commands, the latter are always in **bold**. We also present some data that students can work on and the names of the variables are also in bold (e.g. **income**). The data sets can be copied from the Psychology Press website on the Internet at the following address: http://www.psypress.co.uk/brymancramer.

There are exercises at the end of each chapter and the answers are provided for all exercises at the end of the book. We hope that students and instructors alike find these useful; they can easily be adapted to provide further exercises.

The case for combining methods of quantitative data analysis used by both psychologists and sociologists in part derives from our belief that the requirements of students of the two subjects often overlap substantially. None the less, instructors can omit particular techniques as they wish.

We wish to thank David Stonestreet, formerly of Routledge, for his support of the earlier editions of this book and our current editor Lucy Farr for her support of the present book. We also wish to thank Louis Cohen, Max Hunt and Tony Westaway for reading the manuscript for the first edition of this book and for making useful suggestions for improvement. We accept that they cannot be held liable for any errors in that or the present edition. Such errors are entirely of our own making, though we will undoubtedly blame each other for them.

ALAN BRYMAN AND DUNCAN CRAMER
Loughborough University

Data analysis and the research process

THIS BOOK LARGELY covers the field that is generally referred to as 'statistics', but as our Preface has sought to establish, we have departed in a number of respects from the way in which this subject is conventionally taught to under- and post-graduates. In particular, our preferences are for integrating data analysis with computing skills and for not burdening the student with formulae. These predilections constitute a departure from many, if not most, treatments of this subject. We prefer the term 'quantitative data analysis' because the emphasis is on the understanding and analysis of data rather than on the precise nature of the statistical techniques themselves.

Why should social science students have to study quantitative data analysis, especially at a time when qualitative research is coming increasingly to the fore (Bryman, 1988a)? After all, everyone has heard of the ways in which statistical materials can be distorted, as indicated by Disraeli's often-quoted dictum: 'There are lies, damn lies and statistics.' Why should serious researchers and students be prepared to get involved in such a potentially unworthy activity? If we take the first issue – why should social science students study quantitative data analysis – it is necessary to remember that an extremely large proportion of the empirical research undertaken by social scientists is designed to generate or draws upon quantitative data. In order to be able to appreciate the kinds of analyses that are conducted in relation to such data and possibly to analyse their own data (especially since many students are required to carry out projects), an acquaintance with the appropriate methods of analysis is highly desirable for social science students. Further, although qualitative research has quite properly become a prominent strategy in sociology and some other areas of the social sciences, it is by no means as pervasive as quantitative research, and in any case many writers recognise that there is much to be gained from a fusion of the two research traditions (Bryman, 1988a).

On the question of the ability of statisticians to distort the analyses that they carry out, the prospects for which are substantially enhanced in many people's eyes by books with such disconcerting titles as *How to Lie with Statistics* (Huff, 1973), it should be recognised that an understanding of the techniques to be covered in our book will greatly enhance the ability to see through the misrepresentations about which many people are concerned. Indeed, the inculcation of a sceptical appreciation of quantitative data analysis is beneficial in the light of the pervasive use of statistical data in everyday life. We are deluged with such data in the form of the results of opinion polls, market research findings, attitude surveys, health and crime statistics, and so on. An awareness of quantitative data analysis greatly enhances the ability to recognise faulty conclusions or potentially biased manipulations of the information. There is even a fair chance that a substantial proportion of the readers of this book will get jobs in which at some point they will have to think about the question of how to analyse and present statistical material. Moreover, quantitative data analysis does not comprise a mechanical application of predetermined techniques by statisticians and others; it is a subject with its own controversies and debates, just like the social sciences themselves. Some of these areas of controversy will be brought to the reader's attention where appropriate.

Quantitative data analysis and the research process

In this section, the way in which quantitative data analysis fits into the research process – specifically the process of quantitative research – will be explored. As we will see, the area covered by this book does not solely address the question of how to deal with quantitative data, since it is also concerned with other aspects of the research process that impinge on data analysis.

Figure 1.1 provides an illustration of the chief steps in the process of quantitative research. Although there are grounds for doubting whether research always conforms to a neat linear sequence (Bryman, 1988a, 1988b), the components depicted in Figure 1.1 provide a useful model. The following stages are delineated by the model.

Theory

The starting point for the process is a theoretical domain. Theories in the social sciences can vary between abstract general approaches (such as functionalism) and fairly low-level theories to explain specific phenomena (such as voting behaviour, delinquency, aggressiveness). By and large, the theories that are most likely to receive direct empirical attention are those which are at a fairly low level of generality. Merton (1967) referred to these as theories of the middle range, to denote theories that stood between general, abstract theories and empirical findings. Thus, Hirschi (1969), for example, formulated a

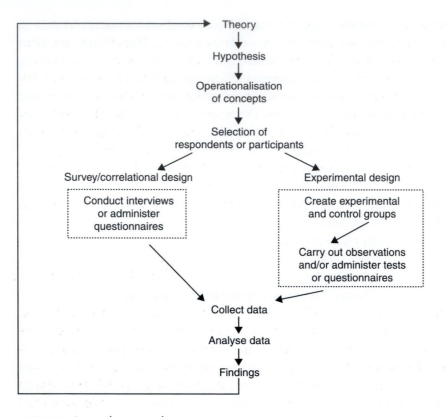

FIGURE 1.1 The research process

'control theory' of juvenile delinquency which proposes that delinquent acts are more likely to occur when the child's bonds to society are breached. This theory in large part derived from other theories and also from research findings relating to juvenile delinquency.

Hypothesis

Once a theory has been formulated, it is likely that researchers will want to test it. Does the theory hold water when faced with empirical evidence? However, it is rarely possible to test a theory as such. Instead, we are more likely to find that a hypothesis, which relates to a limited facet of the theory, will be deduced from the theory and submitted to a searching enquiry. For example, Hirschi, drawing upon his control theory, stipulates that children who are tied to conventional society (in the sense of adhering to conventional values and participating or aspiring to participate in conventional values) will be less likely to commit delinquent acts than those not so tied. Hypotheses very often take the form of relationships between two or more entities – in this case commitment to conventional society and juvenile delinquency. These 'entities' are usually referred to as 'concepts', that is, categories in which are stored our ideas and observations about common elements in the world. The nature of concepts is discussed in greater detail in Chapter 4. Although hypotheses have the advantage that they force researchers to think systematically about what they want to study and to structure their research plans accordingly, they exhibit a potential disadvantage in that they may divert a researcher's attention too far away from other interesting facets of the data he or she has amassed.

Operationalisation of concepts

In order to assess the validity of a hypothesis it is necessary to develop measures of the constituent concepts. This process is often referred to as *operationalisation*, following expositions of the measurement process in physics (Bridgman, 1927). In effect, what is happening here is the translation of the concepts into variables, that is, attributes on which relevant objects (individuals, firms, nations, or whatever) differ. Hirschi operationalised the idea of commitment to conventional society in a number of ways. One route was through a question on a questionnaire asking the children to whom it was to be administered whether they liked school. Delinquency was measured in one of two ways, of which one was to ask about the number of delinquent acts to which children admitted (i.e. self-reported delinquent acts). In much experimental research in psychology, the measurement of concepts is achieved through the observation of people, rather than through the administration of questionnaires. For example, if the researcher is interested in aggression, a laboratory situation may be set up in which variations in aggressive behaviour are observed. Another way in which concepts may be operationalised is through the analysis of existing statistics, of which Durkheim's (1952 [1898]) classic analysis of suicide rates is an example. A number of issues to do with the process of devising measures of concepts and some of the properties that measures should possess are discussed in Chapter 4.

Selection of respondents or subjects

If a survey investigation is being undertaken, the researcher must find relevant people to whom the research instrument that has been devised (e.g. self-administered questionnaire, interview schedule) should be administered. Hirschi, for example, randomly selected over 5,500 school children from an area in California. The fact of random selection is important here because it reflects a commitment to the production of findings that can be generalised beyond the confines of those who participate in a study. It is rarely possible to contact all units in a population, so that a *sample* invariably has to be selected. In order to be able to generalise to a wider population, a *representative sample*, such as one that can be achieved through random sampling, will be required. Moreover, many of the statistical techniques to be covered in this book are *inferential statistics*, which allow the researcher to demonstrate the probability that the results deriving from a sample are likely to be found in the population from which the sample was taken, but only if a random sample has been selected. These issues are examined in Chapter 6.

Setting up a research design

There are two basic types of research design that are employed by psychologists and sociologists. The former tend to use *experimental* designs in which the researcher actively manipulates aspects of a setting, either in the laboratory or in a field situation, and observes the effects of that manipulation on experimental subjects. There must also be a 'control group' which acts as a point of comparison with the group of subjects who receive the experimental manipulation. With a *survey/correlational* design, the researcher does not manipulate any of the variables of interest and data relating to all variables are collected simultaneously. The term *correlation* also refers to a technique for analysing relationships between variables (see Chapter 8), but is used in the present context to denote a type of research design. The researcher does not always have a choice regarding which of the two designs can be adopted. For example, Hirschi could not *make* some children committed to school and others less committed and observe the effects on their propensity to commit delinquent acts. Some variables, like most of those studied by sociologists, are not capable of manipulation. However, there are areas of research in which topics and hypotheses are addressed with both types of research design (e.g. the study of the effects of participation at work on job satisfaction and performance – see Bryman, 1986; Locke and Schweiger, 1979). It should be noted that in most cases, therefore, the nature of the research design – whether experimental or survey/correlational – is known at the outset of the sequence signified by Figure 1.1, so that research design characteristics permeate and inform a number of stages of the research process. The nature of the research design has implications for the kinds of statistical manipulation that can be performed on the resulting data. The differences between the two designs are given greater attention in the next section.

Collect data

The researcher collects data at this stage, by interview, questionnaire, observation, or whatever. The technicalities of the issues pertinent to this stage are not usually associated with a book such as this. Readers should consult a textbook concerned with social and psychological research methods if they are unfamiliar with the relevant issues.

Analyse data

This stage connects very directly with the material covered in this book. At a minimum, the researcher is likely to want to describe his or her subjects in terms of the variables deriving from the study. For example, the researcher might be interested in the proportion of children who claim to have committed no, just one, or two or more delinquent acts. The various ways of analysing and presenting the information relating to a single variable (sometimes called *univariate analysis*) are examined in Chapter 5. However, the analysis of a single variable is unlikely to suffice and the researcher will probably be interested in the connection between that variable and each of a number of other variables, that is, *bivariate analysis*. The examination of connections among variables can take either of two forms. A researcher who has conducted an experiment may be interested in the extent to which experimental and control groups differ in some respect. For example, the researcher might be interested in examining whether watching violent films increases aggressiveness. The experimental group (which watches the violent films) and the control group (which does not) can then be compared to see how far they differ. The techniques for examining differences are explored in Chapter 7. The researcher may be interested in relationships between variables – are two variables connected with each other so that they tend to vary together? For example, Hirschi (1969: 121) presents a table which shows how liking school and self-reported delinquent acts are interconnected. He found that whereas only 9 per cent of children who say they like school have committed two or more delinquent acts, 49 per cent of those who say they dislike school have committed as many delinquent acts. The ways in which relationships among pairs of variables can be elucidated can be found in Chapter 8. Very often the researcher will be interested in exploring connections among more than two variables, that is, *multivariate analysis*. Chapter 9 examines such analysis in the context of the exploration of differences, while Chapter 10 looks at the multivariate analysis of relationships among more than two variables. The distinction between studying differences and studying relationships is not always clear-cut. We might find that boys are more likely than girls to commit delinquent acts. This finding could be taken to mean that boys and girls differ in terms of propensity to engage in delinquent acts or that there is a relationship between gender and delinquency.

Findings

If the analysis of data suggests that a hypothesis is confirmed, this result can be fed back into the theory that prompted it. Future researchers can then concern themselves either with seeking to replicate the finding or with other ramifications of the theory. However, the refutation of a hypothesis can be just as important in that it may suggest that the theory is faulty or at the very least in need of revision. Sometimes, the hypothesis may be confirmed in some respects only. For example, a multivariate analysis may suggest that a relationship between two variables pertains only to some members of a sample, but not others (e.g. women but not men, or younger but not older people). Such a finding will require a reformulation of the theory. Not all findings will necessarily relate directly to a hypothesis. With a social survey, for example, the researcher may collect data on topics whose relevance only becomes evident at a later juncture.

As suggested above, the sequence depicted in Figure 1.1 constitutes a model of the research process, which may not always be reproduced in reality. None the less, it does serve to pinpoint the importance to the process of quantitative research of developing measures of concepts and the thorough analysis of subsequent data. One point that was not mentioned in the discussion is the *form* that the hypotheses and findings tend to assume. One of the main aims of much quantitative research in the social sciences is the demonstration of *causality* – that one variable has an impact upon another. The terms *independent variable* and *dependent variable* are often employed in this context. The former denotes a variable that has an impact upon the dependent variable. The latter, in other words, is deemed to be an effect of the independent variable. This causal imagery is widespread in the social sciences and a major role of multivariate analysis is the elucidation of such causal relationships (Bryman, 1988a). The ease with which a researcher can establish cause and effect relationships is strongly affected by the nature of the research design and it is to this topic that we shall now turn.

Causality and research design

As suggested in the last paragraph, one of the chief preoccupations among quantitative researchers is to establish causality. This preoccupation in large part derives from a concern to establish findings similar to those of the natural sciences, which often take a causal form. Moreover, findings which establish cause and effect can have considerable practical importance: if we know that one thing affects another, we can manipulate the cause to produce an effect. In much the same way that our knowledge that smoking may cause a number of illnesses, such as lung cancer and heart disease, the social scientist is able to provide potentially practical information by demonstrating causal relationships in appropriate settings.

To say that something causes something else is not to suggest that the dependent variable (the effect) is totally influenced by the independent variable (the cause). You do not necessarily contract a disease if you smoke and many of the diseases contracted by people who smoke afflict those who never smoke. 'Cause' here should be taken to mean that variation in the dependent variable is affected by variation in the independent variable. Those who smoke a lot are more likely than those who smoke less, who in turn are more likely than those who do not smoke at all, to contract a variety of diseases that are associated with smoking. Similarly, if we find that watching violence on television induces aggressive behaviour, we are not saying that only people who watch televised violence will behave aggressively, nor that only those people who behave aggressively watch violent television programmes. Causal relationships are invariably about the likelihood of an effect occurring in the light of particular levels of the cause: aggressive behaviour may be more likely to occur when a lot of television violence is watched and people who watch relatively little television violence may be less likely to behave aggressively.

Establishing causality

In order to establish a causal relationship, three criteria have to be fulfilled. First, it is necessary to establish that there is an apparent relationship between two variables. This means that it is necessary to demonstrate that the distribution of values of one variable corresponds to the distribution of values of another variable. Table 1.1 provides information for ten children on the number of aggressive acts they exhibit when they play in two groups of five for two hours per group. The point to note is that there is a relationship between the two variables in that the distribution of values for number of aggressive acts coincides with the distribution for the amount of televised violence watched – children who watch more violence exhibit more aggression than those who watch little violence. The relationship is not perfect: three pairs of children – 3 and 4, 6 and 7 and 9 and 10 – record the same number of aggressive acts, even though they watch different amounts of television violence. Moreover, 8 exhibits more aggression than 6 or 7, even though the latter watch more violence. None the less, a clear pattern is evident which suggests that there is a relationship between the two variables.

Second, it is necessary to demonstrate that the relationship is *non-spurious*. A spurious relationship occurs when there is not a 'true' relationship between two variables that appear to be connected. The variation exhibited by each variable is affected by a common variable. Imagine that the first five

TABLE 1.1 Data on television violence and aggression

Child	Number of hours of violence watched on television per week	Number of aggressive acts recorded
1	9.50	9
2	9.25	8
3	8.75	7
4	8.25	7
5	8.00	6
6	5.50	4
7	5.25	4
8	4.75	5
9	4.50	3
10	4.00	3

children are boys and the second five are girls. This would suggest that gender has a considerable impact on both variables. Boys are more likely than girls both to watch more television violence *and* to exhibit greater aggressiveness. There is still a slight tendency for watching more violence and aggression to be related for both boys and girls, but these tendencies are far less pronounced than for the ten children as a whole. In other words, gender affects each of the two variables. It is because boys are much more likely than girls both to watch more television violence and to behave aggressively that Figure 1.2 illustrates the nature of such a spurious relationship.

Third, it is necessary to establish that the cause precedes the effect, that is, the *time order* of the two related variables. In other words, we must establish that aggression is a consequence of watching televised violence and not the other way around. An effect simply cannot come before a cause. This may seem an extremely obvious criterion that is easy to demonstrate, but as we will see, it constitutes a very considerable problem for non-experimental research designs.

Causality and experimental designs

A research design provides the basic structure within which an investigation takes place. While a number of different designs can be found, a basic distinction is that between experimental and non-experimental research designs of which the survey/correlational is the most prominent. In an experiment, the elucidation of cause and effect is an explicit feature of the framework. The term *internal validity* is often employed as an attribute of research and indicates whether the causal findings deriving from an investigation are relatively unequivocal. An internally valid study is one which provides firm

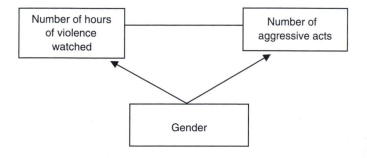

FIGURE 1.2   A spurious relationship

evidence of cause and effect. Experimental designs are especially strong in respect of internal validity; this attribute is scarcely surprising in view of the fact that they have been developed specifically in order to generate findings which indicate cause and effect.

Imagine that we wanted to establish that watching violence on television enhances aggression in children, we might conceive of the following study. We bring together a group of ten children. They are allowed to interact and play for two hours, during which the number of aggressive acts committed by each child is recorded by observers, and the children are then exposed to a television programme with a great deal of violence. Such exposure is often called the experimental treatment. They are then allowed a further two-hour period of play and interaction. Aggressive behaviour is recorded in exactly the same way. What we have here is a sequence which runs

$$\text{Obs}_1 \quad \text{Exp} \quad \text{Obs}_2$$

where Obs_1 is the initial measurement of aggressive behaviour (often called the *pre-test*), Exp is the experimental treatment which allows the independent variable to be introduced, and Obs_2 is the subsequent measurement of aggression (often called the *post-test*).

Let us say that Obs_2 is 30 per cent higher than Obs_1, suggesting that aggressive behaviour has increased substantially. Does this mean that we can say that the increase in aggression was caused by the violence? We cannot make such an attribution because there are alternative explanations of the presumed causal connection. The children may well have become more aggressive over time simply as a consequence of being together and becoming irritated by each other. The researchers may not have given the children enough food or drink and this may have contributed to their bad humour. There is even the possibility that different observers were used for the pre- and post-tests who used different criteria of aggressiveness. So long as we cannot discount these alternative explanations, a definitive conclusion about causation cannot be proffered.

Anyone familiar with the natural sciences will know that an important facet of a properly conducted experiment is that it is controlled so that potentially contaminating factors are minimised. In order to control the contaminating factors that have been mentioned (and therefore to allow the alternative explanations to be rejected), a *control group* is required. This group has exactly the same cluster of experiences as the group which receives the first treatment – known as the *experimental group* – but it does not receive the experimental treatment. In the context of our imaginary television study, we now have two groups of children who are exposed to exactly the same conditions, except that one group watches the violent films (the experimental group) and the second group has no experimental treatment (the control group). This design is illustrated in Figure 1.3. The two groups' experiences have to be as similar as possible, so that only the experimental group's exposure to the experimental treatment distinguishes them.

It is also necessary to ensure that the members of the two groups are as similar as possible. This is achieved by taking a sample of children and *randomly assigning* them to either the experimental or the control group. If random assignment is not carried out, there is always the possibility that differences between the two groups can be attributed to divergent personal or other characteristics. For example, there may be more boys than girls in one group, or differences in the ethnic composition of the two groups. Such differences in personal or background characteristics would mean that the ensuing findings could not be validly attributed to the independent variable, and to that factor alone.

Let us say that the difference between Obs_1 and Obs_2 is 30 per cent and between Obs_3 and Obs_4 is 28 per cent. If this were the case, we would conclude that the difference between the two groups is so small that it appears that the experimental treatment (Exp) has made no difference to the increase in aggression; in other words, aggression in the experimental group would probably have increased anyway. The frustration of being together too long or insufficient food or drink or some other factor probably accounts for the Obs_2–Obs_1 difference. However, if the difference between Obs_3 and Obs_4 was only 3 per cent, we would be much more prepared to say that watching violence has increased aggression in the experimental group. It would suggest that around 27 per cent of the increase in aggressive behaviour in the experimental group (i.e. 30 − 3) can be attributed to the experimental treatment.

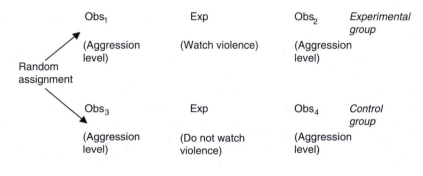

FIGURE 1.3 An experiment

Differences between experimental and control groups are not usually as clear-cut as in this illustration, since often the difference between the groups is fairly small. Statistical tests are necessary in this context to determine the probability of obtaining such a difference by chance. Such tests are described in Chapters 7 and 9.

In this imaginary investigation, the three criteria of causality are met, and therefore if we did find that the increase in the dependent variable was considerably greater for the experimental group than the control group we could have considerable confidence in saying that watching television violence caused greater aggression. First, a relationship is established by demonstrating that subjects watching television violence exhibited greater aggression than those who did not. Second, the combination of a control group and random assignment allows the possibility of the relationship being spurious to be eliminated, since other factors which may impinge on the two variables would apply equally to the two groups. Third, the time order of the variables is demonstrated by the increase in aggressive behaviour succeeding the experimental group's exposure to the television violence. Precisely because the independent variable is manipulated by the researcher, time order can be easily demonstrated, since the effects of the manipulation can be directly gauged. Thus, we could say confidently that Watching television violence $\rightarrow$ Aggressive behaviour since the investigation exhibits a high degree of internal validity.

There is a variety of different types of experimental design. These are briefly summarised in Figure 1.4. In the first design, there is no pre-test, just a comparison between the experimental and control groups in terms of the dependent variable. With the second design, there is a number of groups. This is a frequent occurrence in the social sciences where one is more likely to be interested in different levels or types of the independent variable rather than simply its presence or absence. Thus, in the television violence context, we could envisage four groups consisting of different degrees of violence. The third design, a *factorial* design, occurs where the researcher is interested in the effects of more than one independent variable on the dependent variable. The researcher might be interested in whether the presence of adults in close proximity reduces children's propensity to behave aggressively. We might then have four possible combinations deriving from the manipulation of each of the two independent variables. For example, Exp_{1+A} would mean a combination of watching violence and adults in close proximity; Exp_{1+B} would be watching violence and no adults in close proximity.

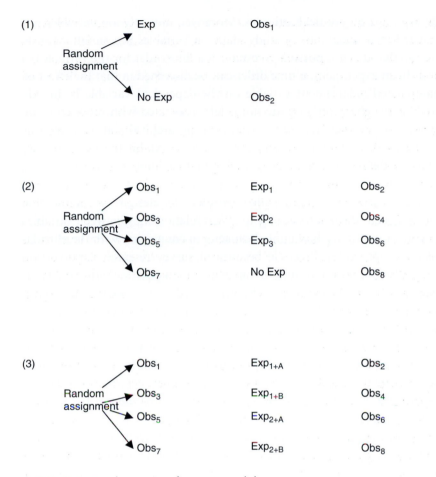

FIGURE 1.4 Three types of experimental design

Survey design and causality

When a social survey is carried out, the nature of the research design is very different from the experiment. The survey usually entails the collection of data on a number of variables at a single juncture. The researcher might be interested in the relationship between people's political attitudes and behaviour on the one hand, and a number of other variables such as each respondent's occupation, social background, race, gender, age, and various non-political attitudes. But none of these variables is manipulated as in the experiment. Indeed, many variables cannot be manipulated and their relationships with other variables can only be examined through a social survey. We cannot make some people old, others young, and still others middle-aged and then observe the effects of age on political attitudes. Moreover, not only are variables not manipulated in a social survey study, data on variables are simultaneously collected so that it is not possible to establish a time order for the variables in question. In an experiment, a time order can be discerned in that the effect of the manipulated independent variable on the dependent variable is directly observed. These characteristics are not solely associated with research using interviews or questionnaires. Many studies using archival statistics, such as those collected by governments and organisations, exhibit the same characteristics, since data are often available in relation to a number of variables for a particular year.

Survey designs are often called *correlational* designs to denote the tendency for such research to be able to reveal relationships between variables and to draw attention to their limited capacity in connection with the elucidation of causal processes. Precisely because in survey research variables are not manipulated (and often are not capable of manipulation), the ability of the researcher to impute cause and effect is limited. Let us say that we collect data on manual workers' levels of job satisfaction and productivity in a firm. We may find, through the kinds of techniques examined in Chapter 8 of this book, that there is a strong relationship between the two, suggesting that workers who exhibit high levels of job satisfaction also have high levels of productivity. We can say that there is a relationship between the two variables (see Figure 1.5), but as we have seen, this is only a first step in the demonstration of causality. It is also necessary to confirm that the relationship is non-spurious. For example, could it be that workers who have been with the firm a long time are both more satisfied and more productive (see Figure 1.6)?

FIGURE 1.5 A relationship between two variables

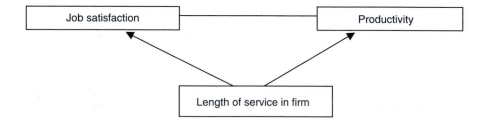

FIGURE 1.6 Is the relationship spurious?

The ways in which the possibility of non-spuriousness can be checked are examined in Chapter 10.

However, the third hurdle – establishing that the putative cause precedes the putative effect – is extremely difficult. The problem is that either of the two possibilities depicted in Figure 1.7 may be true. Job satisfaction may cause greater productivity, but it has long been recognised that the causal connection may work the other way around (i.e. if you are good at your job you often enjoy it more). Because data relating to each of the two variables have been simultaneously collected, it is not possible to arbitrate between the two versions of causality presented in Figure 1.7. One way of dealing with this problem is through a reconstruction of the likely causal order of the variables involved. Sometimes this process of inference can be fairly uncontroversial. For example, if we find a relationship between race and number of years spent in formal schooling, we can say that the former affects the latter. However, this modelling of likely causal connections is more fraught when it is not obvious which variable precedes the other, as with the relationship between job satisfaction and productivity. When such difficulties arise, it may be necessary to include a second wave of data collection in relation to the same respondents in order to see, for example, whether the impact of job satisfaction on subsequent productivity is greater than the impact of productivity on subsequent job satisfaction. Such a design is known as a *panel design* (Cramer, 1996), but is not very common in the social sciences. The bulk of the discussion in this book about non-experimental research will be concerned with the survey/correlational design in which data on variables are simultaneously collected.

The procedures involved in making causal inferences from survey data are examined in Chapter 10 in the context of the multivariate analysis of relationships among variables. The chief point to be gleaned from the preceding discussion is that the extraction of causal connections among variables can be undertaken with greater facility in the context of experimental research than when survey data are being analysed.

FIGURE 1.7   Two possible causal interpretations of a relationship

Exercises

1   What is the chief difference between univariate, bivariate and multivariate quantitative data analysis?

2   Why is random assignment crucial to a true experimental design?

3   A researcher collects data by interview on a sample of households to find out if people who read 'quality' daily newspapers are more knowledgeable about politics than people who read 'tabloid' newspapers daily. The hunch was confirmed. People who read the quality newspapers were twice as likely to respond accurately to a series of questions designed to test their political knowledge. The researcher concludes that the quality dailies induce higher levels of political knowledge than the tabloids. Assess this reasoning.

Analysing data with computers: first steps with SPSS 12 and 13

19

SINCE THE DIFFERENT kinds of statistics to be described in this book will be carried out with one of the, if not the, most widely used and comprehensive statistical programs in the social sciences, SPSS, we will begin by outlining what this entails. The abbreviation SPSS stands for *Statistical Package for the Social Sciences*. This package of programs is available for personal computers. These programs are being continuously updated and so there are various versions in existence. This book covers the latest version of SPSS, Release 13, which we shall refer to as SPSS for short unless otherwise indicated. Previous editions of this book have described earlier versions of SPSS (Bryman and Cramer, 1990, 1994, 1997, 1999, 2001). As Releases 12 and 13 are very similar to Releases 11 and 10, this book can also be used for these earlier versions. The main difference is in the way the **Chart Editor** works. The **Chart Editor** in Releases 12 and 13 operates differently from that in previous versions. However, as only a few pages of this book deal with the **Chart Editor**, this difference is unlikely to affect users of this book.

The great advantage of using a package like SPSS is that it will enable you to score and to analyse quantitative data very quickly and in many different ways once you have learned how. In other words, it will help you to eliminate those long hours spent working out scores, carrying out involved calculations, and making those inevitable mistakes that so frequently occur while doing this. It will also provide you with the opportunity for using more complicated and often more appropriate statistical techniques which would not have dreamt of attempting otherwise.

There is, of course, what may seem to be a strong initial disadvantage in using computer programs to analyse data and that is you will have to learn how to run these programs. The time spent doing this, however, will be much less than doing these same calculations by hand. In addition, you will have picked up some knowledge which should be of value to you in a world where the use of computers has become common. The ability to do things quickly and with little effort is also much more fun and often easier than you might at first imagine.

When mastering a new skill, like SPSS, it is inevitable that you will make mistakes which can be frustrating and off-putting. While this is something we all do, it may seem that we make many more mistakes when learning to use a computer than we do carrying out other activities. The reason for this is that programs require instructions to be given in a very precise form and usually in a particular sequence in order for them to work. This precision may be less obvious or true of other everyday things that we do. It is worth remembering, however, that these errors will not harm the computer or its program in any way.

In order to make as few mistakes as possible, it is important at this stage to follow precisely the instructions laid down for the examples in this and subsequent chapters. Although 'bugs' do sometimes occur, errors are usually the result of something you have done and not the fault of the machine or the program. The program will tell you what the error is if there is something wrong with the form of the instructions you have given it, but not if you have told it to add up the wrong set of numbers. In other words, it questions the presentation but not the objectives of the instructions.

Gaining access to SPSS

To use SPSS, it is necessary to have access to it via a personal computer. A personal computer consists of a *keyboard* on which you type in your instructions, a *mouse* which provides an alternative way of moving about the screen and selecting instructions, and usually a video display unit (VDU) or television-like *screen* which displays information. While the amount of information shown at any one moment on the screen is necessarily limited, further information can be brought into view with the appropriate use of the keys or the mouse. A personal computer is usually connected to a printer which can be used to print out information stored in the computer and can be used to print out a record of what you have done. Keyboards are used to type or put in (hence the term *input*) the data that you want to analyse and also the names of variables and files you have created.

The Windows system allows commands to be selected from words or *icons* presented as a menu in a window on the screen. Commands can usually be selected by moving a pointer called a *cursor* onto them with either the keys or, more normally, the mouse, and then pressing the Return key or the left button on the mouse, or in Windows 2000 by simply selecting the next option. Choosing options with the mouse is generally easier than doing this with keys since it simply involves moving the mouse appropriately. With keys, however, some options are chosen by pressing the relevant cursor keys while others are selected by pressing up to two keys other than the cursor keys. The cursor keys are usually on the right-hand side of the keyboard and have arrows on them pointing in the direction in which the cursor is to be moved. You may prefer to use the mouse for some operations and the keys for others.

To access SPSS in the windows environment, select the 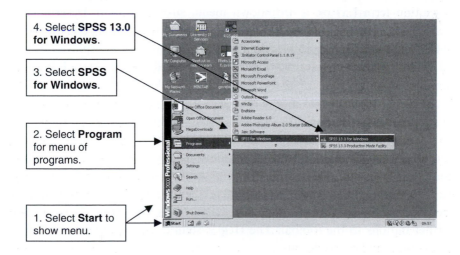Start button or icon at the bottom of the screen which presents the first column or menu on the left in Box 2.1.

Select **Programs** on this menu which displays the second menu (column 2) in Box 2.1.

Select **SPSS for Windows** from this menu which opens the third menu (in column 3) in Box 2.1.

Select **SPSS 13.0 for Windows** which produces the **Data Editor** window in Box 2.2. The **SPSS for Windows** dialog box superimposed on the **Data Editor** can be prevented from being shown on your own computer the next time you access SPSS if you select the **Don't show this dialog in the future** check box near the bottom of the dialog box. Select **Cancel** to remove the dialog box to enter data into the cells of the **Data Editor**.

Listed at the top of this window are the names of various procedures such as **File**, **Edit** and so on. To see what these procedures are, we simply move the cursor to a particular option and press the left button on the mouse once when a *drop-down* menu will appear as shown in Box 2.3 where the **Analyze** option has been chosen. To see the other options, simply move the cursor to that option. Note that, if you press the Alt key, one of the letters in these keywords will be underlined. So, for example, the **A** of **Analyze** will be underlined to indicate that this is the key to select this option. We will show these underlines in case you want to use keys rather than the mouse.

A right-facing arrowhead ▶ after an option term such as on the **Descriptive Statistics** option indicates that a further submenu will appear to

4. Select **SPSS 13.0 for Windows**.

3. Select **SPSS for Windows**.

2. Select **Program** for menu of programs.

1. Select **Start** to show menu.

BOX 2.1 Windows 2000 opening window

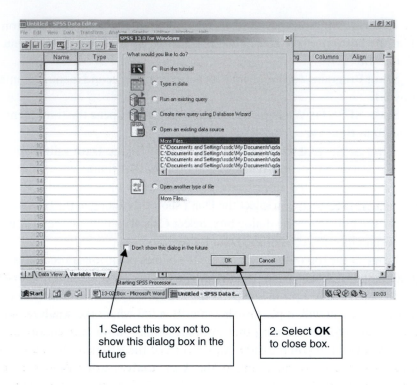

1. Select this box not to show this dialog box in the future

2. Select **OK** to close box.

BOX 2.2   SPSS Data Editor

the right of the drop-down as shown in Box 2.3. The ellipsis or three dots after an option term (**...**) on a drop-down menu, such as on the **Descriptives...** option, signifies a dialog box will appear when this option is chosen. If we select this option, for example, the **Descriptives** dialog box displayed in Box 2.12 will appear when data has already been entered into the **Data Editor**. To cancel a dialog box, select the **Cancel** button in the dialog box. An option with neither of these signs means that there are no further drop-down menus to select.

Below these options is a *toolbar* with *buttons* on it. These buttons enable you to carry out procedures directly without having to go to the options and selecting the appropriate procedure. The functions that the buttons carry out are displayed in a small yellow box near them and in the bottom line of the window. So, for example, the first button says **Open File**. You can add further buttons to the toolbar. The **Help** system described on pp. 41–3 gives instructions on how to do this.

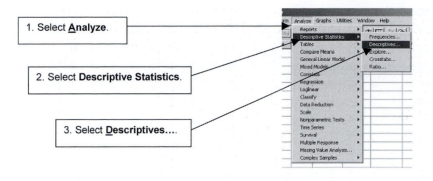

1. Select **Analyze**.

2. Select **Descriptive Statistics**.

3. Select **Descriptives**....

BOX 2.3 Analyze drop-down menu

The data file

Before you can analyse data, you need to create a file which holds them. To illustrate the way in which these files are produced, we will use an imaginary set of data from a questionnaire study which is referred to as the Job Survey. The data relating to this study derive from two sources: a questionnaire study of employees who answer questions about themselves and a questionnaire study of their supervisors who answer questions relating to each of the employees. The questions asked are shown in Appendix 2.1 at the end of this chapter, while the coding of the information or data collected is presented in Table 2.1. The cases consist of people, traditionally called *respondents* by sociologists and *subjects* by psychologists whose preferred term now is *participants*. Although questionnaire data have been used as an example, it should be recognised that SPSS and the data analysis procedures described in this book may be used with other forms of quantitative data, such as official statistics or observational measures.

As the data set is relatively large, it is more convenient to download the SPSS data file from the Psychology Press website on the Internet at the following address: http://www.psypress.co.uk/brymancramer.

If you have SPSS installed on the computer you are using to download the file and you download the file directly, SPSS will open showing the first part of the data file in the **Data View** window of the **Data Editor** as illustrated in Box 2.4. What is actually displayed on your screen will depend on its size, with smaller screens showing less information.

The **Data View** window consists of a matrix of columns and numbered rows. The columns represent the variables in the data file and the rows the

TABLE 2.1 The Job Survey data

01	1	1	16600	29	1	4	0	3	4	4	2	4	2	2	2	2	3	2	2	3	0	1	7
02	2	1	14600	26	5	2	0	0	2	3	2	2	1	2	3	4	4	4	1	3	4	4	8
03	3	1	17800	40	5	4	4	4	4	1	2	1	2	2	2	1	2	3	1	4	3	4	0
04	3	1	16400	46	15	2	2	5	2	4	1	2	2	2	3	2	2	3	2	3	3	4	4
05	2	2	18600	63	36	4	3	4	4	1	2	3	3	3	4	5	5	4	1	3	5	3	0
06	1	1	16000	54	31	2	2	5	3	3	2	1	1	2	4	4	4	4	1	1	3	4	1
07	1	1	16600	29	2	0	3	3	2	3	2	2	3	2	3	5	4	2	2	3	5	2	0
08	3	1	17600	35	2	5	2	2	4	2	3	4	3	2	3	3	3	2	2	3	4	4	2
09	2	2	17600	33	4	3	3	1	2	4	2	3	4	1	2	2	3	2	2	2	1	1	5
10	2	2	13800	27	6	4	3	2	3	3	2	1	3	2	3	4	3	5	1	2	2	4	4
11	1	1	14200	29	4	2	2	4	1	4	2	1	1	2	5	4	3	4	2	2	2	3	8
12	2	1	0	19	2	1	1	5	2	4	1	1	1	1	3	4	3	3	1	3	2	3	4
13	4	1	18000	55	35	3	3	3	4	2	2	2	3	2	5	5	5	4	1	4	3	5	1
14	1	2	17000	29	1	2	3	4	2	4	2	2	3	1	4	3	4	4	1	1	2	2	0
15	3	1	18200	48	8	3	3	2	2	1	3	2	4	4	2	3	3	3	2	4	5	5	1
16	2	1	15800	32	7	3	3	4	2	2	2	3	1	2	4	2	2	2	2	2	2	3	4
17	1	1	16600	48	14	3	3	3	2	4	1	2	2	2	4	5	4	4	1	2	5	3	1
18	1	2	13400	18	1	2	2	4	2	4	2	3	2	2	5	5	5	1	1	2	3	3	6
19	3	2	15000	28	2	4	4	2	3	2	3	4	3	3	3	2	3	2	2	3	4	4	3
20	3	2	17600	37	1	3	2	3	3	3	3	2	1	2	5	4	4	5	1	1	4	1	3
21	1	1	0	43	16	1	4	4	3	3	3	2	3	3	3	2	4	4	2	4	5	2	6
22	1	1	17400	39	6	3	2	3	2	3	3	2	2	3	4	3	5	3	2	1	1	5	5
23	1	1	18000	53	5	1	4	3	4	4	4	3	2	2	3	5	4	2	1	3	3	5	13
24	2	2	16000	34	9	1	3	4	1	5	1	2	1	1	3	4	4	3	2	1	3	3	9
25	3	2	17000	43	17	4	3	4	5	3	3	1	3	2	3	2	4	4	1	3	5	2	2
26	1	1	14000	21	1	4	4	2	2	3	4	3	3	4	2	3	2	2	1	2	5	5	3
27	1	1	16200	50	28	3	2	3	3	4	2	1	1	2	5	5	5	4	1	2	2	4	8
28	1	2	12400	31	9	1	2	5	1	4	2	2	1	2	4	4	5	4	2	3	5	5	0
29	1	1	13600	31	12	3	3	4	3	3	3	2	2	3	2	3	1	2	1	3	5	4	6
30	2	2	16400	52	21	2	3	2	3	2	3	3	3	3	2	2	2	2	2	4	4	3	10
31	1	1	14400	54	12	3	5	3	3	3	3	2	3	2	4	3	4	4	2	4	4	2	99
32	3	2	12400	28	10	2	2	4	1	5	1	2	2	2	3	3	3	2	1	2	4	4	9
33	2	2	16600	50	23	4	4	3	4	3	4	2	3	4	3	3	3	3	2	3	4	5	5
34	2	2	16000	52	21	5	4	3	3	3	3	4	3	3	2	3	3	3	2	1	3	2	5	4

35	1	2	15000	40	21	1	1	3	4	3	3	2	3	2	2	3	2	2	1	2	2	3	6
36	2	1	11800	19	1	2	2	5	2	4	2	1	2	2	5	5	5	5	2	2	3	2	3
37	2	1	17600	38	4	5	4	1	4	3	5	3	3	3	2	1	2	1	2	4	4	4	8
38	2	1	18000	61	41	5	3	2	4	1	3	2	2	2	2	2	1	2	2	3	5	4	3
39	1	2	15600	37	8	3	2	4	2	3	2	3	3	2	4	5	4	5	1	3	4	4	8
40	2	1	13400	31	5	2	2	5	2	5	2	2	2	1	5	5	5	4	2	1	1	2	5
41	2	2	15000	43	21	4	3	2	2	2	3	4	2	3	3	3	3	3	1	1	4	2	0
42	3	1	13600	23	3	1	2	5	3	5	1	1	2	1	4	4	4	5	1	3	2	2	8
43	2	2	14000	27	5	1	1	4	1	4	1	1	1	2	4	5	4	4	2	1	2	1	9
44	1	1	15000	28	7	3	3	1	3	3	3	5	3	3	1	2	2	1	1	2	4	3	9
45	1	1	13200	0	10	1	1	4	1	4	2	2	2	2	4	2	5	5	1	4	1	3	10
46	3	1	13400	18	1	4	2	3	4	2	2	3	3	2	4	3	5	4	1	4	3	4	3
47	1	2	20600	48	23	3	4	3	3	3	2	2	3	2	2	1	3	2	2	4	4	3	8
48	1	2	13600	29	10	2	3	5	4	4	2	2	2	1	3	4	2	2	1	3	4	4	11
49	1	2	14600	42	10	2	2	3	3	3	2	2	1	2	5	5	5	5	2	1	4	4	0
50	1	1	18200	53	12	4	5	2	5	1	4	5	3	4	2	2	2	2	4	4	4	1	
51	1	1	15200	32	12	3	2	4	1	4	3	2	2	3	3	3	4	2	1	2	3	2	1
52	1	2	13000	31	2	1	3	5	1	5	2	2	3	2	5	4	4	5	2	1	3	1	8
53	1	1	19000	55	19	5	4	3	5	3	5	4	3	3	3	4	3	3	1	3	4	3	0
54	3	2	14800	26	8	4	4	1	3	3	4	5	2	3	1	2	1	2	2	4	3	3	2
55	1	2	17200	53	22	3	4	2	3	1	3	4	4	3	2	1	2	2	1	3	5	5	0
56	1	1	15600	51	31	2	3	3	3	3	3	2	4	4	5	4	5	5	1	4	1	1	8
57	1	1	15400	48	23	3	1	4	3	4	2	2	2	2	5	5	4	5	1	1	3	2	6
58	1	2	13800	48	28	1	1	4	1	5	2	2	2	1	5	5	5	5	2	1	4	3	4
59	2	2	15800	62	40	1	2	3	2	5	2	2	3	2	5	4	4	5	2	1	1	5	7
60	2	1	17400	57	13	2	3	4	2	3	2	3	1	2	3	3	4	3	1	4	4	1	4
61	1	2	17800	42	20	5	4	2	2	2	3	3	3	3	2	1	2	4	2	3	3	3	2
62	1	1	14200	21	2	1	2	3	1	4	2	3	2	1	3	3	3	3	1	4	2	2	0
63	3	2	12800	26	8	3	1	3	2	4	1	2	1	1	2	3	3	2	1	4	1	1	4
64	1	2	13600	46	0	1	2	5	2	4	3	1	2	2	5	5	5	5	2	2	3	4	5
65	1	2	21000	59	21	4	3	2	4	2	2	2	3	3	2	3	2	2	2	4	5	1	4
66	4	2	14200	30	8	0	3	3	2	4	2	3	2	2	5	4	4	4	1	2	2	3	2
67	1	1	14600	29	8	3	2	2	3	3	2	3	2	1	5	3	4	3	2	1	4	5	10
68	3	1	13800	45	9	2	3	4	3	4	3	3	3	3	4	3	3	2	2	3	4	9	
69	3	1	16000	53	30	3	2	5	3	2	2	1	2	2	4	5	3	4	2	2	1	4	2
70	1	1	13800	47	22	2	3	4	2	5	2	3	4	2	4	3	5	4	1	2	4	4	11

Columns contain variables.

Toolbar

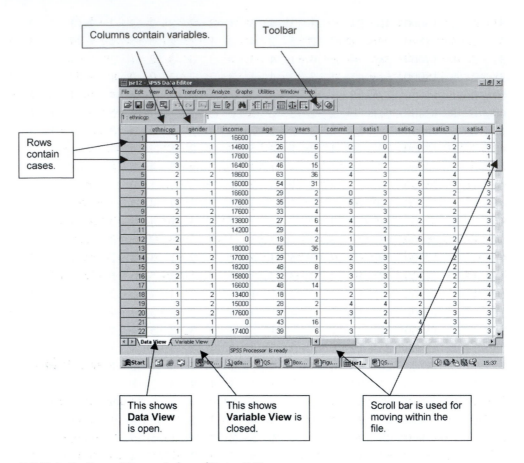

Rows contain cases.

This shows **Data View** is open.

This shows **Variable View** is closed.

Scroll bar is used for moving within the file.

BOX 2.4 **Data View** window of **Data Editor**

cases. For these data the cases are people but for other data the cases can be any unit of interest such as families, schools, hospitals, regions or nations. At the top of each column is the SPSS name or label we have given to the variables in this survey.

SPSS names

Variable and file names in SPSS have to meet certain specifications. Unlike earlier versions of SPSS, they can now be longer than eight characters and can begin with a capital letter. However, it is most probably preferable to keep the names short. Names must begin with an alphabetic character (A–Z).

The remaining characters can be any letter, number, period, @ (at), $ (dollar) or _ (underscore). Blank spaces are not allowed and they cannot end with a period and, preferably, not with an underscore. In addition certain words, known as *keywords*, cannot be used because they can only be interpreted as commands by SPSS. They include words such as **add**, **and**, **any**, **or**, and **to**, to give but a few examples. If you accidentally use a prohibited keyword as a name, you will be told this is invalid when you try to run this procedure by selecting the **OK** button. No keyword contains numbers so you can be certain that names which include numbers will always be recognised as such. It is important to remember that the same name cannot be used for different variables or files. Thus, for example, you could not use the name **satis** to refer to all four of the questions which measure job satisfaction. You would need to distinguish them in some way such as calling the answer to the first question **satis1**, the answer to the second one **satis2**, and so on. The SPSS names given to the variables in the Job Survey are presented in Table 2.2.

Moving within the **Data Editor**

There are two ways of seeing more of the SPSS names of the variables in the data file. The way to display more of the columns in the **Data View** window is to use the *scroll* box, bar or buttons at the bottom right-hand part of the **Data Editor** as shown in Box 2.4. To move the **Data View** window to the right one column at a time, move the arrow or *cursor* to the button with the right-pointing arrowhead on the extreme right of the scroll bar and press or click once the left button of the *mouse*. To move the **Data View** window to the right more quickly, either move the cursor to the right of the scroll bar and click the left button of the mouse or move the cursor onto the scroll box, pressing the left button of the mouse and holding the button down, and move the mouse to the right.

The alternative way to view the SPSS names is to move the cursor to **Variable View** in the box at the bottom left-hand corner of the **Data Editor** and click on the left button of the mouse. This opens up the **Variable View** window of the **Data Editor** as shown in Box 2.5. To scroll down this window use the scroll box, bar or buttons on the right of the window in the same ways as previously described.

TABLE 2.2   The SPSS names of the Job Survey variables

Variable name	SPSS name
Identification number	id
Ethnic group	ethnicgp
Gender	gender
Gross annual income	income
Age	age
Years worked	years
Organisational commitment	commit
Job-satisfaction scale	
Item 1	satis1
Item 2	satis2
Item 3	satis3
Item 4	satis4
Job-autonomy scale	
Item 1	autonom1
Item 2	autonom2
Item 3	autonom3
Item 4	autonom4
Job-routine scale	
Item 1	routine1
Item 2	routine2
Item 3	routine3
Item 4	routine4
Attendance at meeting	attend
Rated skill	skill
Rated productivity	prody
Rated quality	qual
Absenteeism	absence

Numerical coding of data

As it is easier to analyse data consisting of numbers rather than a mixture of numbers and other characters such as alphabetic letters, all of the variables or answers in the Job Survey have been coded as numbers. So, for instance, each of the five possible answers to the first question on racial or ethnic group has been given a number varying from 1 to 5. If the respondent has put a tick

Variable **Name**.

Number of **Decimal** places.

Value labels.

Missing values.

	Name	Type	Width	Decimals	Label	Values	Missing	Columns	Align	Measure
1	ethnicgp	Numeric	1	0		{1, White}...	0	8	Right	Ordinal
2	gender	Numeric	1	0		{1, Men}...	None	8	Right	Ordinal
3	income	Numeric	5	0		None	None	8	Right	Scale
4	age	Numeric	2	0		None	0	8	Right	Scale
5	years	Numeric	2	0		None	None	8	Right	Scale
6	commit	Numeric	1	0		None	None	8	Right	Ordinal
7	satis1	Numeric	1	0		None	0	8	Right	Ordinal
8	satis2	Numeric	1	0		None	0	8	Right	Ordinal
9	satis3	Numeric	1	0		None	None	8	Right	Ordinal
10	satis4	Numeric	1	0		None	None	8	Right	Ordinal
11	autonom1	Numeric	1	0		None	None	8	Right	Ordinal
12	autonom2	Numeric	1	0		None	None	8	Right	Ordinal
13	autonom3	Numeric	1	0		None	None	8	Right	Ordinal
14	autonom4	Numeric	1	0		None	None	8	Right	Ordinal
15	routine1	Numeric	1	0		None	None	8	Right	Ordinal
16	routine2	Numeric	1	0		None	None	8	Right	Ordinal
17	routine3	Numeric	1	0		None	None	8	Right	Ordinal
18	routine4	Numeric	1	0		None	None	8	Right	Ordinal
19	attend	Numeric	1	0		None	None	8	Right	Ordinal
20	skill	Numeric	1	0		None	None	8	Right	Ordinal
21	prody	Numeric	1	0		None	None	8	Right	Ordinal
22	qual	Numeric	1	0		None	None	8	Right	Ordinal
23	absence	Numeric	2	0		None	99	8	Right	Ordinal

This shows **Variable View** is open.

BOX 2.5   Variable View window of **Data Editor**

against White/European, then this response is coded as 1. (Although the use of these categories may be questioned, as may many of the concepts in the social sciences, this kind of information is sometimes collected in surveys and is used here as an example of a categorical (nominal) variable. We shall shorten the name of the first category to 'white' throughout the book to simplify matters.) It is preferable in designing questionnaires that, wherever possible, numbers should be clearly assigned to particular answers so that little else needs to be done to the data before they are typed in by someone else. Before multiple copies of the questionnaire are made, it is always worth checking with the person who types in this information that this has been adequately done.

It is also important to reserve a number for *missing data*, such as a failure to give a clear and unambiguous response, since we need to record this information. Numbers which represent real or non-missing data should not be used to code missing values. Thus, for example, since the answers to the first question on ethnic group in the Job Survey are coded 1 to 5, it is necessary to use some other number to identify a missing response. In this survey all missing data except that for absenteeism have been coded as zero since this value cannot be confused with the way that non-missing data are represented. Because some employees have not been absent from work (i.e. zero days), missing data for absenteeism could not be coded as '0'. Instead, it is indicated by '99' since no employee has been away that long. Sometimes it might be necessary to distinguish different kinds of missing data, such as a 'Don't know' response from a 'Does not apply' one, in which case these two answers would be represented by different numbers.

It is advisable to give each participant an identifying number to be able to refer to them if necessary. This number should be placed in the first column of each row or line.

Entering and editing data in Data Editor

The easiest way of entering data in SPSS yourself is to type it directly into the matrix of columns and numbered rows in the **Data Editor** window shown in Box 2.2. Initially the cursor will be in the *cell* in the first row of the first column. The *frame* of this cell will be shown in bold to denote that it is the *active* cell. To enter a value in any one cell, make that cell active by moving to it with either the cursor keys or the mouse, type in the value and then move to the next cell into which you want to put a value. Columns are consecutively numbered once you enter a value. So if you enter a value in the fifth column the first five columns will be labelled **var00001** to **var00005**. To change any value already entered, move to the cell containing that value, type in the new value and move to another cell. If you want to leave a cell empty delete the entry with the Backspace or Delete key and move to another cell, when a full stop (.) will be left denoting a missing value.

Naming variables in Data Editor

To name a variable in **Data Editor**, select **Variable View** near the bottom of the window. Select the appropriate row under the **Name** column and type in the name (e.g. **ethnicgp** in the first row as shown in Box 2.5).

Defining other aspects of variables in Data Editor

We can define nine other aspects of variables when naming them. These aspects are listed just above the data matrix and range from **Type** on the left to **Measure** on the right. You may not see all these nine aspects at once. You can change the width of each column by selecting the line next to the name of the column whose width you want to change and moving the column line to the desired position, as we have done in Box 2.5.

The pre-selected settings for these aspects are shown and are known as the default options. If we wish to change any of these settings, we select the appropriate row and column to make the desired change. In general and for our purposes the most important of these other aspects is **Missing** values

Defining missing values

In the Job Survey, we have missing values for **income** (cases 12 and 21), **age** (case 45), **satis1** (cases 1 and 2), **satis2** (case 2), **prody** (case 1) and **absence** (case 31). So we have to specify the appropriate missing values for these variables, which are **0** for the first five (**income**, **age**, **satis1**, **satis2** and **prody**) and **99** for the sixth variable called **absence**. We do this by selecting the appropriate row of the **Missing** column in the **Variable View** of the **Data Editor** and then selecting the ellipsis or three dots in that cell. This opens the **Missing Values** dialog box shown in Box 2.6. In our case we select **Discrete missing values**, type the appropriate value in the first box and then select **OK**. If we type in **0**, then **None** in that row of the **Missing** column of **Variable View** will be replaced with **0** as shown in Box 2.5.

If someone else is entering the data, we need to let them know how missing data for any of the variables are to be coded. We could enter this code here to remind us what it is. Thus, in this example, missing data for all variables other than **absence** has been defined as **0**.

Defining decimal places

The default number of decimal places is two. For most purposes it is easier to code all variables as numbers, which we have done for the Job Survey. Since all our values are whole numbers we could change **2** to **0** in the **Decimals** column of the **Variable View** window. To do this, we select each row in turn in this column, and select the downwards button to give **0**. Alternatively, we can

3. Select **OK** to close box.

1. Select **Discrete missing values**.

2. Enter number (e.g. **0**) for missing value.

Missing Values

- ○ No missing values
- ⊙ Discrete missing values
- ○ Range plus one optional discrete missing value
  - Low: _____ High: _____
  - Discrete value: _____

OK

Cancel

Help

BOX 2.6 Missing Values dialog box

copy **0**, highlight the consecutive column of cells we want to change and paste in the **0**.

Defining variable and value labels

SPSS variable names were restricted to eight characters in earlier versions of SPSS, which usually meant that they had to be abbreviated, making their meaning less clear. Using this option, variable labels can be created which will be displayed on the output. These variable labels can be very long, although most output will not present very long labels. For example, the SPSS variable name **ethnicgp** could be labelled **ethnic group**. To do this, we type in this name for the first row of the **Labels** column in the **Variable View** window. If we do this, then the extended variable name will be presented first in the section of dialog boxes where the variable names are listed followed by the abbreviated name in brackets. We have used abbreviated names as these are used in the other sections of the dialog boxes and are generally less cumbersome. As variables names can now be as long as we need them to be, this option no longer seems necessary.

We could also label the values of a variable by selecting the appropriate row in the **Values** column (e.g. **ethnicgp**) and then selecting the ellipsis or three dots in that cell. This opens the **Value Labels** dialog box shown in Box 2.7. Type in the value (e.g. **1**) in the box entitled **Value:**, the label (e.g. **white**) in the box entitled **Value Label:** and select **Add**. The value labels for the five ethnic

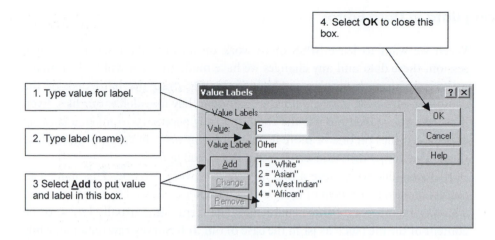

BOX 2.7 Value Labels dialog box

groups in the Job Survey are presented in Box 2.7. Value labels can be up to 60 characters long, although most output will not show labels this long. To remove a label we first select it and then **Remove**. To change a label, we first select it, make the desired changes and then select **Change**. When we have what we want, we select **OK** to close the **Value Labels** dialog box.

Defining column format and alignment

It is unlikely that you would wish to change the width of the column in **Data Editor**, but if you do, select the appropriate row in the **Columns** column and then select the upwards or downwards button to enter your desired value. If you wish to alter the alignment of data within a column, select the appropriate row in the **Align** column, select the downwards arrow and then select one of the other two options.

Defining consecutive variables simultaneously

If you want to define consecutive variables simultaneously with the same format (such as **sat1** to **routine4**), define the first variable (**satis1**), copy that row, highlight the subsequent rows to be defined (**9** to **19**), select **Paste** or **Paste Variables. . .** and re-name variables as appropriate.

Saving data in Data Editor

When we want to leave SPSS or to work on another data set in the same session, these data and any changes we have made to them will be lost unless we save them as a file. We could save this file onto the hard disk of the computer. However, if others use the computer, they may delete our files. Even if no one else is likely to use the computer, it is necessary to make a *back-up* copy of our files on one or more formatted *floppy disks* in case we should lose them. The floppy disk is inserted into a slot called a *drive*.

To be able to retrieve a file, we need to give it a name. This name can consist of a prefix or *stem* of up to eight characters followed by a full stop and a suffix or *extension* of three characters. The stem name usually refers to the content of the file (such as **jsr** in the case of our **J**ob **S**urvey **r**aw data file) while the extension name refers to the type of file. The default extension name for files in **Data Editor** is **sav**. Thus, we could call our data file **jsr.sav**. Extensions are now usually displayed as icons and not names (as shown in Box 2.10).

We will generally use a particular notation throughout this book as shorthand to describe the steps involved in any application. The selection of a step or option will be indicated with a right-facing arrow ➔ pointing to the term(s) on the menu or dialog box to be chosen. Any explanations will be placed in square parentheses after the option shown. Steps in a dialog box or a *subdialog* box (which is a box which can only be accessed after the initial dialog box has been opened) will begin on a new line. The sequence will be indented. Thus, the notation for saving this file on a floppy disk in Drive A is

➔**File** [shown in Box 2.8] ➔**Save As...** [opens **Save Data As** dialog box shown in Box 2.9]

type **jsr** in box beside **File name:** ➔**Save**

Retrieving a saved Data Editor file

To retrieve this file at a later stage when it is no longer the current file, use the following procedure

➔**File** [as shown in Box 2.11] ➔**Open** ➔**Data** [opens **Open File** dialog box shown in Box 2.10]

➔downward arrow in box next to **Look in:** ➔$3\frac{1}{2}$ **Floppy (A):**

➔**jsr** (to put in **File name:** box) ➔**Open**

type **jsr** in box beside **File name:** ➔**Open**

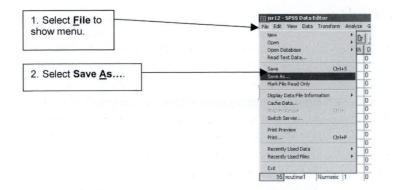

1. Select **File** to show menu.

2. Select **Save As....**

BOX 2.8 **File** drop-down menu

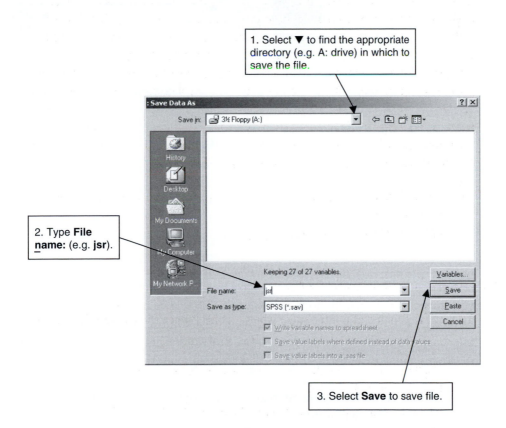

1. Select ▼ to find the appropriate directory (e.g. A: drive) in which to save the file.

2. Type **File name:** (e.g. **jsr**).

3. Select **Save** to save file.

BOX 2.9 **Save Data As** dialog box

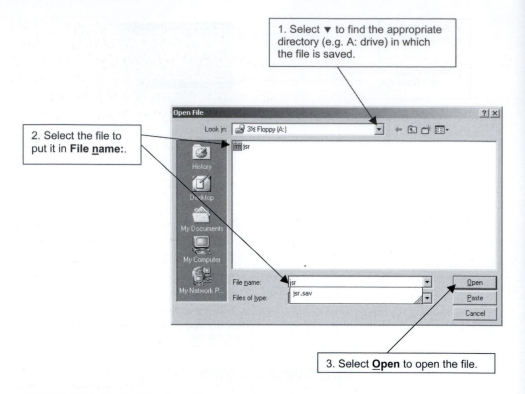

BOX 2.10   Open File dialog box

Statistical procedures

After entering the data set in **Data Editor**, we are now ready to analyse it. The rest of the book describes numerous ways in which you can do this. To show you how this is generally done, we will ask SPSS to calculate the average or *mean* age of the sample. This can be done with a number of SPSS commands, but we shall use the one called **Descriptive Statistics**. This works out a number of other descriptive statistics as well. The procedure for doing this is:

→**Analyze** →**Descriptive Statistics** →**Descriptives...** [opens **Descriptives** dialog box shown in Box 2.12]

→variable [e.g. **age**; note variables are listed in their order in **Data Editor**]
→►button [puts the selected variable in box under **Variable[s]:**] →**OK**

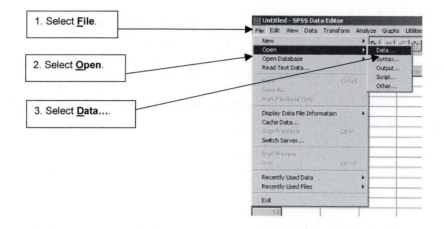

1. Select **File**.

2. Select **Open**.

3. Select **Data**....

BOX 2.11 **File** drop-down menu

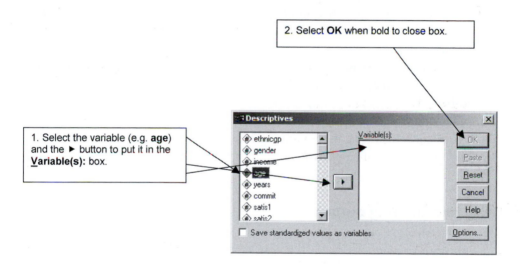

2. Select **OK** when bold to close box.

1. Select the variable (e.g. **age**) and the ▶ button to put it in the **Variable(s):** box.

BOX 2.12 **Descriptives** dialog box

The output for this procedure is displayed in the **Viewer** window as shown in Table 2.3. The mean age is **39.19**. The other descriptive statistics provided by default are the standard deviation (see Chapter 5), the minimum age, the maximum age, and the number of cases (**N**) on which this information is based. If we look at the ages in our Job Survey data, then we can confirm

TABLE 2.3 Default **Descriptives** output

Descriptives

Descriptive Statistics

	N	Minimum	Maximum	Mean	Std. Deviation
age	69	18	63	39.19	12.317
Valid N (listwise)	69				

that the minimum age is indeed 18 (for the first case) while the maximum is 63 (for case number 5). We should also notice that the age for one of our participants (case number 45) is missing, making the number of cases which provide valid data for this variable 69 and not 70.

As shown in Table 2.3 the output in the **Viewer** window will always be preceded by the name of the statistical procedure. In this case, it is **Descriptives**. These titles will be omitted from subsequent presentations of output to save space.

If we just wanted the mean age and not the other statistics, we could do this as follows. Select **Options...** in the **Descriptives** dialog box to open the **Descriptives: Options** subdialog box shown in Box 2.13. Then de-select **Std. deviation**, **Minimum** and **Maximum** by moving the cursor onto them and pressing the left button. The output for this procedure is presented in Table 2.4.

If an SPSS operation has been started but not completed (in that all dialog boxes concerned with that operation have not been closed), scrolling through the **Viewer** will not be possible.

Saving and printing output

To print the contents of any window, enter that window and then execute the following sequence:

→File →Print... →OK

TABLE 2.4 Mean Descriptive output

Descriptive Statistics

	N	Mean
age	69	39.19
Valid N (listwise)	69	

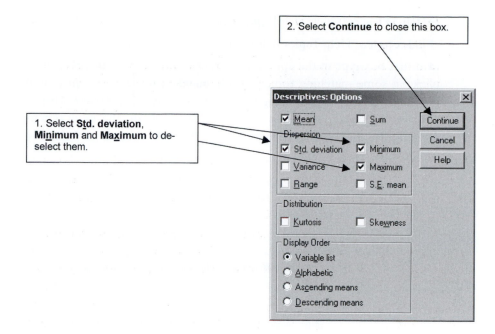

2. Select **Continue** to close this box.

1. Select **Std. deviation**, **Minimum** and **Maximum** to de-select them.

BOX 2.13   Descriptives: Options subdialog box

If you want to store the contents of any window on a floppy disk, then carry out the following steps

→**File** →**Save As** →window [opens **Save As** dialog box]

→type the drive and file name in the box beside **File name**: [e.g. **jsr.spo**]
→**Save**

The default extension name for output files is **spo** which is short for **sp**ss **o**utput file. You can edit output files before saving them. For example, you may wish to delete certain analyses or type in some further explanation.

Help system

SPSS has a **Help** system which you may like to use to avoid having to refer to a book like this one or to find out more about the program. As this system is meant to be self-explanatory you should be able to learn to use it yourself after a little experience. To find help on a topic such as **file**, carry out the following procedure:

➔**Help** ➔**Topics** [opens **Help Topics Contents** window shown in Box 2.14]

➔**Index** [opens **Help Topics Index** window shown in Box 2.15]

➔in first box type in the appropriate or closest term [e.g. **file**] ➔double-click on some matching topic [e.g. **file opening**] to narrow your search [opens the **Topics Found** dialog box shown in Box 2.16] ➔select a topic, then click **Display** [e.g. **Open file**] or double-click on the topic [opens **Help** information window shown in Box 2.17] ➔✕ button [to **Minimize** or **Close** the **Help** system]

BOX 2.14   Help Topics Contents window

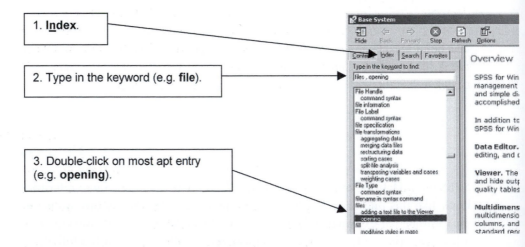

BOX 2.15   Help Topics Index window

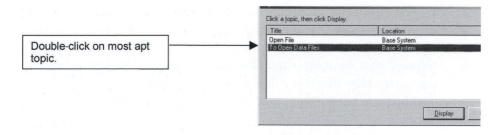

Double-click on most apt topic.

BOX 2.16 Topics Found dialog box

Information on opening data files.

BOX 2.17 Help information box

If you want help while in a dialog box, select the **Help** option in the dialog box.

Leaving SPSS

To leave SPSS, select **File** and then **Exit**. If you have edited or analysed data in a session, you will be asked if you wish to save the contents in the **data editor** or **output viewer**. If you don't, select **No**. If you do, select **Yes** and name the file if you have not already done so. Note that if you exit without saving any changes that you may need to keep, those changes will be lost.

Exercises

1   You need to collect information on the religious affiliation of your respondents. You have thought of the following options: Agnostic, Atheist, Buddhist, Catholic, Jewish, Hindu, Muslim, Protestant and Taoist. Which further category has to be included?

2   You want to record this information in a data file to be stored in a computer. How would you code this information?

3   Looking through your completed questionnaires, you notice that on one of them no answer has been given to this question. What are you going to put in your data file for this person?

4   Suppose that on another questionnaire the respondent had ticked two categories. How would you deal with this situation?

5   The first two of your sample of fifty participants describe themselves as agnostic and the second two as atheists. The ages of these four participants are 25, 47, 33, and 18. How would you arrange this information in your data file?

6   How does SPSS know to what the numbers in the data file refer?

Appendix 2.1: The Job Survey questions

Employee questionnaire

This questionnaire is designed to find out a few things about yourself and your job. Please answer the questions truthfully. There are no right or wrong answers.

                                                                    Code
1   To which one of the following racial or ethnic groups do you belong? (Tick one)

       ____ White/European   1
       ____ Asian   2
       ____ West Indian   3
       ____ African   4
       ____ Other   5

2   Are you male or female

       Male   1
       Female   2

3   What is your current annual income before tax and other deductions?   £_____

4   What was your age last birthday (in years)?   ____ years

5   How many years have you worked for this firm?   ____ years

6   Please indicate whether you (1) strongly disagree, (2) disagree, (3) are undecided, (4) agree, or (5) strongly agree with each of the the following statements. Circle one answer only for each statement.

	SD	D	U	A	SA
(a) I would not leave this firm even if another employer could offer me a little more money	1	2	3	4	5
(b) My job is like a hobby to me	1	2	3	4	5
(c) Most of the time I have to force myself to go to work	1	2	3	4	5
(d) Most days I am enthusiastic about my work	1	2	3	4	5
(e) My job is pretty uninteresting	1	2	3	4	5
(f) I am allowed to do my job as I choose	1	2	3	4	5
(g) I am able to make my own decisions about how I do my job	1	2	3	4	5
(h) People in my section of the firm are left to do their work as they please	1	2	3	4	5
(i) I do not have to consult my supervisor if I want to perform my work slightly differently	1	2	3	4	5
(j) I do my job in much the same way every day	1	2	3	4	5
(k) There is little variety in my work	1	2	3	4	5
(l) My job is repetitious	1	2	3	4	5
(m) Very few aspects of my job change from day to day	1	2	3	4	5

7   Did you attend the firm's meeting this month?

_____ Yes   1

_____ No   2

Supervisor questionnaire

I would be grateful if you could answer the following questions about one of the people for whom you act as supervisor – [Name of employee]

1   Please describe the skill level of work that this person performs.
Which one of the following descriptions best fits her/his work?
(Tick one)

_____ Unskilled   1

_____ Semi-skilled   2

_____ Fairly skilled   3

_____ Highly skilled   4

45

2   How would you rate her/his productivity? (Tick one)

                                      ____ Very poor   1
                                        ____ Poor   2
                                        ____ Average   3
                                        ____ Good   4
                                        ____ Very good   5

3   How would you rate the quality of her/his work? (Tick one)

                                        ____ Very poor   1
                                        ____ Poor   2
                                        ____ Average   3
                                        ____ Good   4
                                        ____ Very good   5

4   How many days has s/he been absent in the last twelve months?   ____ days

Chapter 3

Analysing data with computers: further steps with SPSS 12 and 13

N OW THAT WE have described how you generally set up and analyse a data
file, we can introduce you to some further procedures which you may find
very useful. These procedures will enable you to do the following: select certain
cases (such as all white men under the age of 40) for separate analyses; and
create new variables (such as scoring an attitude or personality scale) and new
data files to store them. SPSS can also carry out other operations which are not
described in this book such as combining files in various ways. If you want to do
things which are not mentioned here, then consult the Help system or SPSS
Guide.

Selecting cases

To select cases with certain characteristics, you select **Data** and **Select Cases...**
which opens the **Select Cases** dialog box shown in Box 3.1. If, for example,
you wanted to find out the average age of only the men in the Job Survey
sample, select **If condition is satisfied** and then **If...** which opens the **Select
Cases: If** subdialog box presented in Box 3.2. In the empty box you enter the
condition(s) cases must satisfy if they are to be selected. In this instance, we
select in sequence **gender = 1** since men are coded **1**. We then select **Continue**
to close the **Select Cases: If** subdialog box and **OK** to close the **Select Cases**
dialog box.

To calculate just the mean age of men we carry out the following
sequence:

→**Analyze** →**Descriptive Statistics** →**Descriptives...** [opens **Descriptives**
dialog box shown in Box 2.12]

→**age** →▶button →**Options...** [opens the **Descriptives: Options** subdialog
box shown in Box 2.13]

→**Std. deviation** [to de-select] →**Minimum** →**Maximum**

→**Continue**

→**OK**

The output for this procedure is presented in Table 3.1.

1. Select **If condition is satisfied**.

2. Select **If....**

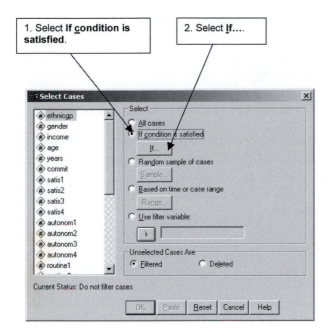

BOX 3.1 **Select Cases** dialog box

1. Either select or type in variable used for selection (e.g. **gender**), the relational operator (e.g. **=**) and the value (e.g. **1**).

2. Select **Continue** to close this box.

BOX 3.2 **Select Cases: If** subdialog box

TABLE 3.1 Mean age of the men in the Job Survey

Descriptive Statistics

	N	Mean
age	38	39.21
Valid N (listwise)	38	

This selection will remain in force until you change it. If you want to carry out statistical analyses on the whole sample or on females, you need to alter the selection. For analyses on the whole sample you would need to select **All cases** while for those on women you would have to enter the conditional expression **gender** = 2.

Relational operators

A relational operator such as **=** compares the value on its left (for example, **gender**) with that on its right (for example, **1**). There are six such operators, which are represented by the following symbols:

    =   equal to
    ~=   not equal to
    <   less than
    <=   less than or equal to
    >   greater than
    >=   greater than or equal to

The question of which is the most appropriate operator to use in selecting cases will depend on the selection criteria. To select cases under 40 years of age, we could use less than (**<**):

    age < 40

It would also, of course, have been possible to use less than or equal to (**<=**) 39 in this instance since we are dealing with whole numbers:

    age <= 39

To select non-whites, we could use not equal to (**~=**) **1** since whites are coded **1**:

    ethnicgp ~= 1

Combining logical relations

We can combine logical expressions with the logical operators **&** (**and**) and **|** (**or**). For example, we can select white men under 40 with the following conditional expression:

ethnicgp = 1 & gender = 1 & age < 40

To select people of only West Indian and African origin, we would have to use the **|** (**or**) logical operator:

ethnicgp = 3 | ethnicgp = 4

Note that it is necessary to repeat the full logical relation. It is *not* permissible to abbreviate this command as:

ethnicgp = 3 | 4

An alternative way of doing the same thing is to use the **any** logical function where any case with a value of either **3** or **4** for the variable **ethnicgp** is selected:

any(ethnicgp,3,4)

The variable and the values to be selected are placed in parentheses.

To select people between the ages of 30 and 40 inclusively, we can use the expression:

age >= 30 & age <= 40

Here, we have to use the **&** (**and**) logical operator. If we used **|** (**or**), we would in effect be selecting the whole sample since everybody is either above 30 or below 40 years of age.

Another way of selecting people aged 30 to 40 inclusively is to use the **range** logical function where any case with a value in the range of 30 to 40 for the variable **age** is selected:

range(age,30,40)

Recoding the values of variables

Sometimes it is necessary to change or to recode the values of some variables. For example, it is recommended that the wording of questions which go to make up a scale or index should be varied in such a way that people who say yes to everything (*yeasayers*) or no (*naysayers*) do not end up with an extreme score. To illustrate this, we have worded two of the four questions assessing job satisfaction in the Job Survey ('6c. Most of the time I have to force myself to go to work.' and '6e. My job is pretty uninteresting.') in the opposite direction from the other two ('6b. My job is like a hobby to me.' and '6d. Most days I am enthusiastic about my work.'). These questions are answered in terms of a five-point scale ranging from 1 ('strongly disagree') to 5 ('strongly agree'). While we could reverse the numbers for the two negatively worded items (6c and 6e) on the questionnaire, this would draw the attention of our respondents to what we were trying to accomplish. It is simpler to reverse the coding when we come to analyse the data. Since we want to indicate greater job satisfaction with a higher number, we will recode the answers to the two negatively worded questions, so that 1 becomes 5, 2 becomes 4, 4 becomes 2, and 5 becomes 1. We can do this with the **Recode** procedure which is on the **Transform** menu. We can recode values using either the same (**Into Same Variables...**) or different (**Into Different Variables...**) variable names.

If we want to compare the original values with the recoded ones or if we want to retain the original values, we use the **Into Different Variables...** option which opens the **Recode Into Different Variables** dialog box presented in Box 3.3. For instance, if we wish to recode **satis2** and **satis4** into the respective two new variables of **rsatis2** and **rsatis4**, we select **satis2** which puts it in the box entitled **Numeric Variable −> Output Variable:**, type the new variable name of **rsatis2** in the box entitled **Name:**, select **Change** and repeat the procedure for **satis4**, renaming it **rsatis4**.

Then we select **Old and New Values...** which opens the **Recode into Different Variables: Old and New Values** subdialog box displayed in Box 3.4. In the box entitled **Value:** (in the **Old Value** section where the **V** of **Value:** is underlined to distinguish it from **Value:** in the **New Value** section where the **l** of **Value:** is underscored) we type the first value to be changed (e.g. **1**) while in the box called **Value:** (in the **New Value** section) we type the new value (e.g. **5**) and select **Add**. We do this consecutively for the three other old values of **2**, **4** and **5**. For the values which remain the same (e.g. **3**) we can type the old value in the box called **Value:**, and select **Copy old value[s]** and **Add**. The values for each case are recoded from left to right and are only changed once so that when 1 is initially recoded as 5 (**1 −> 5**) in the above example, it is not subsequently

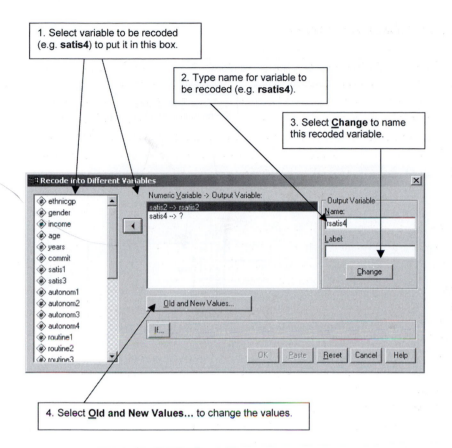

1. Select variable to be recoded (e.g. **satis4**) to put it in this box.

2. Type name for variable to be recoded (e.g. **rsatis4**).

3. Select **Change** to name this recoded variable.

4. Select **Old and New Values...** to change the values.

BOX 3.3 **Recode into Different Variables** dialog box

reconverted to 1 (**5 −> 1**). If there are missing values, as in this case, select **System- or user-missing** (in **Old Value** section) and **System-missing** (in **New Value** section).

After doing this we select **Continue** to close the **Recode into Different Variables: Old and New Values** subdialog box and **OK** to close the **Recode into Different Variables** dialog box. We can then check the recoded values in the appropriate columns (**satis2**, **rsatis2**, **satis4** and **rsatis4**) in the **Data Editor**.

Alternatively, we can check the recoded values of **rsatis2** and **rsatis4** by selecting **Summarize Cases** and listing the values of **satis2**, **rsatis2**, **satis4** and **rsatis4** for, say, the first ten cases as shown in Table 3.2.

→**Analyze** →**Reports** →**Case Summaries...** [opens **Summarize Cases** dialog box shown in Box 3.5]

1. Type old value (e.g. **1**) in this box.

2. Type new value (e.g. **5**) in this box.

3. Select **Add** to enter the change in this box.

4. Select **Continue** to close this box.

BOX 3.4   Recode into Different Variables: Old and New Values subdialog box

→select variables [e.g. **satis2**] →►button →**Limit cases to first** and type number [e.g. **10**]

→**OK**

For each variable there can only be one new value, whereas there can be any number of old values. For example, if we wished to form a three-point scale with only one 'agree', one 'disagree', and one 'undecided' answer, we could do this by recoding **1** and **2** into **1**, **3** into **2**, and **4** and **5** into **3**. Since only one value can be entered at a time into the box entitled **Value** we would have to do this sequentially.

We can specify a range of old values by selecting the **Range:** option (which is distinguished by having the **n** of **Range:** underlined) and typing the lowest value in the first box and the highest value in the second box. For

TABLE 3.2 **Case Summaries** output showing recoded values of **rsatis2** and **rsatis4**

Case Summaries[a]

	satis2	rsatis2	satis4	rsatis4
1	3	3.00	4	2.00
2	0	.	3	3.00
3	4	2.00	1	5.00
4	5	1.00	4	2.00
5	4	2.00	1	5.00
6	5	1.00	3	3.00
7	3	3.00	3	3.00
8	2	4.00	2	4.00
9	1	5.00	4	2.00
10	2	4.00	3	3.00
Total N	9	9	10	10

a. Limited to first 10 cases.

example, we could recode ethnic group into whites and non-whites by putting **3** into the first box and **5** into the second box and recoding **3** through **5** as **2**.

If we do not wish to find out what the lowest value is, we can specify it by selecting **Range:**. If we want to specify the highest value without determining what it is, we select **Range:**. For example, we could use these options to categorise our sample into those 40 years old or above and those below by recoding the **Lowest through 39** as **1** and the **40 through highest** as **2**.

If we had ages which were not whole numbers and which fell between 39 and 40, such as 39.9, they would not be recoded. To avoid this problem, we would use overlapping end-points so that **Lowest through 40** is recoded as **1** and **40 through highest** as **2**. In this example all people aged 40 and less would be coded as 1. Since values are recoded consecutively and once only, age 40 will not also be recoded as 2.

Computing a new variable

Sometimes we want to create a new variable. For example, we have used four items to assess what may be slightly different aspects of job satisfaction. Rather than treat these items as separate measures, it may be preferable and reasonable to combine them into one index. To do this, we select the **Com-pute...** procedure on the **Transform** menu which displays the **Compute Variable** dialog box shown in Box 3.6. We can use this procedure to create a new variable called **satis** by adding together **satis1**, the recoded **rsatis2**, **satis3** and

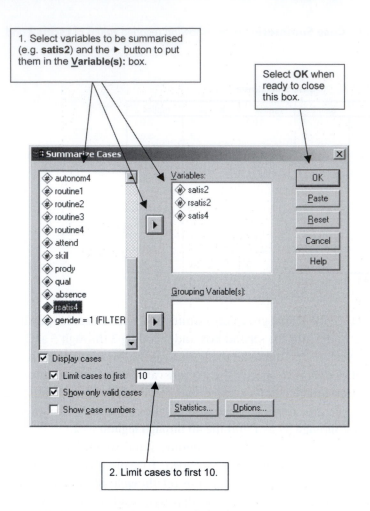

1. Select variables to be summarised (e.g. **satis2**) and the ▶ button to put them in the **Variable(s):** box.

Select **OK** when ready to close this box.

2. Limit cases to first 10.

BOX 3.5 Summarize Cases dialog box

the recoded **rsatis4**. We do this by first typing the name of the new variable **satis** in the box entitled **Target Variable:**. We select **All** under **Function group:**, **Sum** scrolling through **Functions and Special Variables:**, and then the upward point-ing button which puts **SUM(?,?)** into the box entitled **Numeric Expression:**. In this box we replace the **?,?** with **satis1,rsatis2,satis3,rsatis4** and then select **OK**. If the items had the same stem of **satis** and were listed sequentially, we need list only the first item (**satis1**) followed by **to** and the last item (**satis4**).

If we look at the value of **satis** in the **Data Editor** we see that it is missing for the first two cases as if they have one or more missing values for the first two items. It is **15.00** for the third case (**4 + 2.00 + 4 + 5.00 = 15.00**) and **7.00** for the fourth case (**2 + 1.00 + 2 + 2.00 = 7.00**). Once again, we could list the

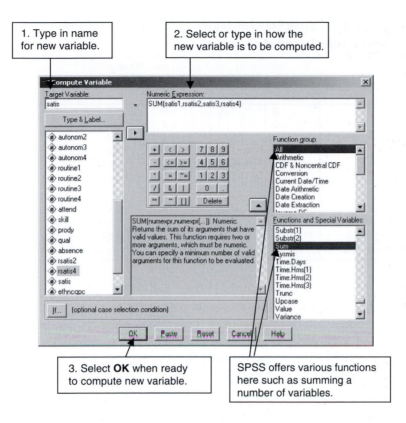

1. Type in name for new variable.

2. Select or type in how the new variable is to be computed.

3. Select **OK** when ready to compute new variable.

SPSS offers various functions here such as summing a number of variables.

BOX 3.6   Compute Variable dialog box

appropriate values for a selection of cases by using the **Case Summaries...** procedure. Table 3.3 shows the output for the first ten cases.

Missing data and computing scores to form new measures

As we have seen, the **satis1** score for the first participant and the **satis1** and **satis2** scores for the second participant are missing. In research, it is quite common for some scores to be missing. Participants may omit to answer questions, they may circle two different answers to the same question, the experimenter may forget to record a response, and so on. It is important to consider carefully how you are going to deal with missing data. If many of the data for one particular variable are missing, this suggests that there are problems with its measurement which need to be sorted out. Thus, for example, it may be a question which does not apply to most people, in which

TABLE 3.3 Case Summaries output showing values of **satis1**, **rsatis2**, **satis3**, **rsatis4** and **satis**

Case Summaries[a]

	satis1	rsatis2	satis3	rsatis4	satis
1	0	3.00	4	2.00	.
2	0	.	2	3.00	.
3	4	2.00	4	5.00	15.00
4	2	1.00	2	2.00	7.00
5	3	2.00	4	5.00	14.00
6	2	1.00	3	3.00	9.00
7	3	3.00	2	3.00	11.00
8	2	4.00	4	4.00	14.00
9	3	5.00	2	2.00	12.00
10	3	4.00	3	3.00	13.00
Total　N	8	9	10	10	8

a. Limited to first 10 cases.

case it is best omitted. If many scores for an individual are missing, it is most probably best to omit this person from the sample since there may be problems with the way in which these data were collected. Thus, for example, it could be that the participant was not paying attention to the task at hand.

Where data for an index such as job routine are missing for some individuals, it is not appropriate to use the sum of the responses as an index since the total score will not reflect the same number of responses. For example, someone who answers 'strongly agree' (coded 5) to all four job routine items will have a total score of 20 whereas someone who strongly agrees with all items but who, for some reason, did not give an answer to one of them will have a total score of only 15. In other words, when we have missing data for items that constitute an index we need to take account of the missing data. In this situation a more appropriate index is the mean score of the non-missing values which would be 5 for the first (20/4 = 5) and the second (15/3 = 5) individual. Another advantage of using the mean score for a scale such as job routine is that the mean score now corresponds to the answers to the individual items, so that an average score of 4.17 indicates that that person generally answers 'agree' to those items.

However, we would not generally want to derive an average score for someone who has a relatively large amount of data missing. A criterion sometimes applied to what constitutes too much missing data is if more than 10 per cent of the data are missing for an index, then the index itself is defined as missing for that participant. If we applied this principle to the two participants in the Job Survey, no score for job satisfaction would be computed for them, although they would have scores for job routine and autonomy.

To compute a mean score we use the **Mean** function in the **Compute Variable** dialog box. If we want to specify a minimum number of values that must be non-missing for the mean to be produced we type a full stop after **MEAN** followed by the minimum number. We will use the four **satis** items to illustrate how this is done. With only four items, we cannot use a cut-off point of more than 10 per cent for exclusion as missing. Therefore, we will adopt a more lenient criterion of more than 50 per cent. If more than 50 per cent (i.e. two or more) of the scores for the job-satisfaction items are missing, we will code that variable for participants as missing. In other words, the minimum number of values that must be non-missing for the mean to be computed is 3. As before, the new variable is called **satis** but the numeric expression in the **Numeric Expression:** is **MEAN.3(satis1,rsatis2,satis3,rsatis4)**. If we examine the new values of **satis** in the **Data Editor** we see that it is **3.00** for the first case (**9.00/3 = 3.00**), . for the second case (since there are only two valid values) and **3.75** for the third case (**15.00/4 = 3.75**).

To display the mean value as a zero when it is missing, we use the **Recode into Same Variables** procedure in which we select **System-missing** in the box called **Old Value** and enter **0** in the box called **Value:** (in the **New Value** section) and select **Add**.

To convert this mean score back into a total score (which takes into account numbers of valid scores that might vary between three and four), we simply multiply this mean by the maximum number of items which is 4. To do this we use the **Compute Variable** procedure where the new variable is still called **satis** and where the numeric expression is **satis*4**.

Since we wish to form three new variables (job satisfaction, job autonomy and job routine), we have to repeat this **Compute Variable** procedure for the job routine and job autonomy items. Although we know there are no missing values for these two sets of variables, it does no harm to be cautious and assume there may be some as we have done. To determine if there are any rogue or missing values in data sets with which we are unfamiliar, we use the **Frequencies** procedure (see Chapter 5).

Aggregate measures of job satisfaction, job autonomy and job routine used in subsequent chapters have been based on summing the four items within each scale and assigning the summed score as missing where more than 10 per cent of the items were missing. Since two of the seventy cases in the Job Survey had one or two of the answers to the individual job satisfaction items missing, the number of cases for whom a summed job satisfaction score could be computed is 68. The summed scores for job satisfaction, job autonomy and job routine have been called **satis**, **autonom** and **routine** respectively. To do this for **satis**, for example, we first compute the mean score with the numeric expression **MEAN.4(satis1 to satis4)** and then convert this to a total score with the numeric expression **satis*4**.

When we have a data set which has a large number of variables which we may not need for a particular set of analyses, we may find it more convenient to create a new file which only contains those variables that we are going to examine. For example, if we intend to analyse the aggregate variables of **satis**, **routine** and **autonom** and not the individual items that constitute them, then we can create a new file which holds these new variables (together with any of the other variables we need) but which does not contain the individual items. We delete the individual items by selecting the variable names **satis1** to **routine4** in the **Data Editor** and selecting **Edit** and **Cut**. We then save the data in the **Data Editor** in a new file which we will call **'jssd.sav'** (for **j**ob **s**cored **s**urvey **d**ata) and which we will use in subsequent analyses. The data in this file are presented in Table 3.4.

Exercises

1   What is the SPSS procedure for selecting men and women of African origin in the Job Survey data?

2   Write the conditional expression for SPSS to select women of Asian or West Indian origin who are 25 years old or younger in the Job Survey data.

3   What is the conditional expression for selecting participants who had no missing job satisfaction scores in the Job Survey data?

4   What is the SPSS procedure for recoding the Job Survey variable **skill** into the same variable but with only two categories (unskilled/semi-skilled vs fairly/highly skilled)?

5   What is the SPSS procedure for recoding the variable **income** into the new variable of **incomec** comprising three groups of those earning less than £5,000, between £5,000 and under £10,000, and £10,000 and over, and where missing values are assigned as zero?

6   Using the arithmetic operator *, express the variable **weeks** as **days**. In other words, convert the number of weeks into the number of days.

TABLE 3.4 The scored Job Survey data

id	ethnicgp	gender	income	age	years	commit	satis	autonom	routine	attend	skill	prody	qual	absence
1	1	1	16600	29	1	4	0	10	9	2	3	0	1	7
2	2	1	14600	26	5	2	0	7	15	1	3	4	4	8
3	3	1	17800	40	5	4	15	7	8	1	4	3	4	0
4	3	1	16400	46	15	2	7	7	10	2	3	3	4	4
5	2	2	18600	63	36	4	14	11	18	1	3	5	3	0
6	1	1	16000	54	31	2	9	6	16	1	1	3	4	1
7	1	1	16600	29	2	0	11	9	14	2	3	5	2	0
8	3	1	17600	35	2	5	14	12	11	2	3	4	4	2
9	2	2	17600	33	4	3	12	10	9	2	2	1	1	5
10	2	2	13800	27	6	4	13	8	15	1	2	2	4	4
11	1	1	14200	29	4	2	7	6	16	2	2	2	3	8
12	2	1	0	19	2	1	6	4	13	1	3	2	3	4
13	4	1	18000	55	35	3	14	9	19	1	4	3	5	1
14	1	2	17000	29	1	2	9	8	15	1	1	2	2	0
15	3	1	18200	48	8	3	14	13	11	2	4	5	5	1
16	2	1	15800	32	7	3	11	8	10	2	2	2	3	4
17	1	1	16600	48	14	3	10	7	17	1	2	5	3	1
18	1	2	13400	18	1	2	8	9	16	1	2	3	3	6
19	3	2	15000	28	2	4	15	13	10	2	3	4	4	3
20	3	2	17600	37	1	3	11	8	18	1	1	4	1	3
21	1	1	0	43	16	1	12	11	13	2	4	5	2	6
22	1	1	17400	39	6	3	10	10	15	2	1	1	5	5

TABLE 3.4 — *continued*

id	ethnicgp	gender	income	age	years	commit	satis	autonom	routine	attend	skill	prody	qual	absence
23	1	1	18000	53	5	1	13	11	14	1	3	3	5	13
24	2	2	16000	34	9	1	7	5	14	2	1	3	3	9
25	3	2	17000	43	17	4	13	9	13	1	3	5	2	2
26	1	1	14000	21	1	4	13	14	9	1	2	5	5	3
27	1	1	16200	50	28	3	10	6	19	1	2	2	4	8
28	1	2	12400	31	9	1	6	7	17	2	3	5	5	0
29	1	1	13600	31	12	3	11	10	8	1	3	5	4	6
30	2	2	16400	52	21	2	14	12	8	2	4	4	3	10
31	1	1	14400	54	12	3	14	10	15	2	4	4	2	99
32	3	2	12400	28	10	2	6	7	11	1	2	4	4	9
33	2	2	16600	50	23	4	14	13	12	2	3	4	5	5
34	2	2	16000	52	21	5	13	13	10	1	3	2	5	4
35	1	2	15000	40	21	1	11	10	9	1	2	2	3	6
36	2	1	11800	19	1	2	7	7	20	2	2	3	2	3
37	2	1	17600	38	4	5	16	14	6	2	4	4	4	8
38	2	1	18000	61	41	5	16	9	7	2	3	5	4	3
39	1	2	15600	37	8	3	9	10	18	1	3	4	4	8
40	2	1	13400	31	5	2	6	7	19	2	1	1	2	5
41	2	2	15000	43	21	4	13	12	12	1	1	4	2	0
42	3	1	13600	23	3	1	7	5	17	1	3	2	2	8
43	2	2	14000	27	5	1	6	5	17	2	1	2	1	9
44	1	1	15000	28	7	3	14	14	6	1	2	4	3	9

45	1	1	13200	0	10	1	6	8	16	1	4	1	3	10
46	3	1	13400	18	1	4	13	10	16	1	4	3	4	3
47	1	2	20600	48	23	3	13	9	8	2	4	4	3	8
48	1	2	13600	29	10	2	10	7	11	1	3	4	4	11
49	1	2	14600	42	10	2	11	7	20	2	1	4	4	0
50	1	1	18200	53	12	4	19	16	8	2	4	4	4	1
51	1	1	15200	32	12	3	7	10	12	1	2	3	2	1
52	2	2	13000	31	2	1	6	9	18	2	1	3	1	8
53	1	1	19000	55	19	5	15	15	13	1	3	4	3	0
54	3	2	14800	26	8	4	15	14	6	2	4	3	3	2
55	1	2	17200	53	22	3	16	14	7	1	3	5	5	0
56	1	1	15600	51	31	2	12	13	19	1	4	1	1	8
57	1	1	15400	48	23	3	8	8	19	1	1	3	2	6
58	1	2	13800	48	28	1	5	7	20	2	1	4	3	4
59	2	2	15800	62	40	1	8	9	18	2	1	1	5	7
60	2	1	17400	57	13	2	10	8	13	1	4	4	1	4
61	1	2	17800	42	20	5	14	12	9	2	3	3	3	2
62	1	1	14200	21	2	1	8	8	12	1	4	2	2	0
63	3	2	12800	26	8	3	8	5	10	1	4	1	1	4
64	1	2	13600	46	0	1	7	8	20	2	2	3	4	5
65	1	2	21000	59	21	4	15	10	9	2	4	5	1	4
66	4	2	14200	30	8	0	10	9	17	1	2	2	3	2
67	1	1	14600	29	8	3	12	8	15	2	1	4	5	10
68	3	1	13800	45	9	2	10	12	13	2	2	3	4	9
69	3	1	16000	53	30	3	10	7	16	2	2	1	4	2
70	1	1	13800	47	22	2	8	11	16	1	2	4	4	11

Chapter 4

Concepts and their measurement

CONCEPTS FORM A linchpin in the process of social research. Hypotheses contain concepts which are the products of our reflections on the world. Concepts express common elements in the world to which we give a name. We may notice that some people have an orientation in which they dislike people of a different race from their own, often attributing to other races derogatory characteristics. Still others are highly supportive of racial groups, perhaps seeing them as enhancing the 'host' culture through instilling new elements into it and hence enriching it. Yet others are merely tolerant, having no strong views one way or the other about people of other racial groups. In other words, we get a sense that people exhibit a variety of positions in regard to racial groups. We may want to suggest that there is a common theme to these attitudes, even though the attitudes themselves may be mutually antagonistic. What seems to bind these dispositions together is that they reflect different positions in regard to 'racial prejudice'. In giving the various dispositions that may be held regarding persons of another race a name, we are treating it as a concept, an entity over and above the observations about racial hostility and supportiveness that prompted the formulation of a name for those observations. Racial prejudice has acquired a certain abstractness, so that it transcends the reflections that prompted its formulation. Accordingly, the concept of racial prejudice becomes something that others can use to inform their own reflections about the social world. In this way, hypotheses can be formulated which postulate connections between racial prejudice and other concepts, such as that it will be related to social class or to authoritarianism.

Once formulated, a concept and the concepts with which it is purportedly associated, such as social class and authoritarianism, will need to be *operationally defined*, in order for systematic research to be conducted in relation to it. An operational definition specifies the procedures (operations) that will permit differences between individuals in respect of the concept(s) concerned to be precisely specified. What we are in reality talking about here is *measurement*, that is, the assignment of numbers to the units of analysis – be they people, organisations, or nations – to which a concept refers. Measurement allows small differences between units to be specified. We can say that someone who actively speaks out against members of other races is racially prejudiced, while someone who actively supports them is the obverse of this, but it is difficult to specify precisely the different positions that people may hold in between these extremes. Measurement assists in the specification of such differences by allowing systematic differences between people to be stipulated.

In order to provide operational definitions of concepts, *indicators* are required which will stand for those concepts. It may be that a single indicator will suffice in the measurement of a concept, but in many instances it will not. For example, would it be sufficient to measure 'religious commitment' by conducting a survey in which people are asked how often they attend church services? Clearly it would not, since church attendance is but one way in which an individual's commitment to his or her religion may be expressed. It does not cover personal devotions, behaving as a religious person should in secular activities, being knowledgeable about one's faith, or how far they adhere to central tenets of faith (Glock and Stark, 1965). These reflections strongly imply that more than one indicator is likely to be required to measure many concepts; otherwise our findings may be open to the argument that we have only tapped one facet of the concept in question.

If more than one indicator of a concept can be envisaged, it may be necessary to test hypotheses with each of the indicators. Imagine a hypothesis in which 'organisational size' was a concept. We might measure (i.e. operationally define) this concept by the number of employees in a firm, its turnover or its net assets. While these three prospective indicators are likely to be interconnected, they will not be perfectly related (Child, 1973), so that hypotheses about organisational size may need to be tested for each of the indicators. Similarly, if religious commitment is to be measured, it may be necessary to employ indicators which reflect all of the facets of such commitment in addition to church attendance. For example, individuals may be asked how far they endorse central aspects of their faith in order to establish how far they adhere to the beliefs associated with their faith.

When questionnaires are employed to measure concepts, as in the case of religious commitment, researchers often favour multiple-item measures. In the Job Survey data, **satis** is an example of a multiple-item measure. It entails asking individuals their positions in relation to a number of indicators, which stand for one concept. Similarly, there are four indicators of both **autonom** and **routine**. One could test a hypothesis with each of the indicators. However, if one wanted to use the Job Survey data to examine a hypothesis relating to **satis** and **autonom**, each of which contains four questions, sixteen separate tests would be required. The procedure for analysing such multiple-item measures is to aggregate each individual's response in relation to each question and to treat the overall measure as a scale in relation to which each unit of analysis has a score. In the case of **satis**, **autonom** and **routine**, the scaling procedure is *Likert scaling*, which is a popular approach to the creation of multiple-item measures. With Likert scaling, individuals are presented with a number of statements which appear to relate to a common theme; they then indicate their degree of agreement or disagreement on a five- or seven-point range. The answer to each constituent question (often called an *item*) is scored, for example from 1 for Strongly Disagree to 5 for Strongly Agree if the range of answers is in terms of five points. The individual scores are added up to form an overall score for each respondent. Multiple-item scales can be very long; the four **satis** questions are taken from an often-used scale developed by Brayfield and Rothe (1951) which comprised eighteen questions.

These multiple-item scales are popular for various reasons. First, a number of items are more likely to capture the totality of a broad concept like job satisfaction than a single question. Second, we can draw finer distinctions between people. The **satis** measure comprises four questions which are scored from 1 to 5, so that respondents' overall scores can vary between 4 and 20. If only one question was asked, the variation would be between 1 and 5 – a considerably narrower range of potential variation. Third, if a question is misunderstood by a respondent, when only one question is asked that respondent will not be appropriately classified; if a few questions are asked, a misunderstood question can be offset by those which are properly understood.

It is common to speak of measures as *variables*, to denote the fact that units of analysis differ in respect to the concept in question. If there is no variation in a measure, it is a *constant*. It is fairly unusual to find concepts whose measures are constants. On the whole, the social sciences are concerned with variables and with expressing and analysing the variation that variables exhibit. When *univariate analysis* is carried out, we want to know how individuals are distributed in relation to a single variable. For example, we may want to know how many cases can be found in each of the categories or levels of the measure in question, or we may be interested in what the average response is, and so on. With *bivariate analysis* we are interested in the connections between two variables at a time. For example, we may want to know whether the variation in **satis** is associated with variation in another variable like **autonom** or whether men and women differ in regard to **satis**. In each case, it is variation that is of interest.

Types of variable

One of the most important features of an understanding of statistical operations is an appreciation of when it is permissible to employ particular tests. Central to this appreciation is an ability to recognise the different forms that variables take, because statistical tests presume certain kinds of variable, a point that will be returned to again and again in later chapters.

The majority of writers on statistics draw upon a distinction developed by Stevens (1946) between nominal, ordinal and interval/ratio scales or levels of measurement. First, *nominal* (sometimes called *categorical*) scales entail the classification of individuals in terms of a concept. In the Job Survey data, the variable **ethnicgp**, which classifies respondents in terms of five categories – White, Asian, West Indian, African and Other – is an example of a nominal variable. Individuals can be allocated to each category, but the measure does no more than this and there is not a great deal more that we can say about it as a measure. We cannot order the categories in any way, for example.

This inability contrasts with *ordinal* variables, in which individuals are categorised but the categories can be ordered in terms of 'more' and 'less' of the concept in question. In the Job Survey data, **skill**, **prody** and **qual** are all ordinal variables. If we take the first of these, **skill**, we can see that people are not merely categorised into each of four categories – highly skilled, fairly skilled, semi-skilled and unskilled – since we can see that someone who is fairly skilled is at a higher point on the scale than someone who is semi-skilled. We cannot make the same inference with **ethnicgp** since we cannot order the categories that it comprises. Although we can order the categories comprising **skill**, we are still limited in the things that we can say about it. For example, we cannot say that the skill difference between being highly skilled and fairly skilled is the same as the skill difference between being fairly skilled and semi-skilled. All we can say is that those rated as highly skilled have more skill than those rated as fairly skilled, who in turn have greater skill than the semi-skilled, and so on. Moreover, in coding semi-skilled as 2 and highly skilled as 4, we cannot say that people rated as highly skilled are twice as skilled as those rated as semi-skilled. In other words, care should be taken in attributing to the categories of an ordinal scale an arithmetic quality that the scoring seems to imply.

With *interval/ratio variables*, we can say quite a lot more about the arithmetic qualities. In fact, this category subsumes two types of variable – interval and ratio. Both types exhibit the quality that differences between categories are identical. For example, someone aged 20 is one year older than someone aged 19, and someone aged 50 is one year older than someone aged 49. In each case, the difference between the categories is identical – one year. A scale is called an interval scale because the intervals between categories are identical. Ratio measures have a fixed zero point. Thus age, absence and income have logical zero points. This quality means that one can say that

somebody who is aged 40 is twice as old as someone aged 20. Similarly, someone who has been absent from work six times in a year has been absent three
times as often as someone who has been absent twice. However, the distinction
between interval and ratio scales is often not examined by writers because, in
the social sciences, true interval variables frequently are also ratio variables
(e.g. income, age). In this book, the term *interval variable* will sometimes be
employed to embrace ratio variables as well.

Interval/ratio variables are recognised to be the highest level of measurement because there is more that can be said about them than about the other
two types. Moreover, a wider variety of statistical tests and procedures are
available to interval/ratio variables. It should be noted that if an interval/ratio
variable like age is grouped into categories – such as 20–29, 30–39, 40–49,
50–59 and so on – it becomes an ordinal variable. We cannot really say that the
difference between someone in the 40–49 group and someone in the 50–59 is
the same as the difference between someone in the 20–29 group and someone
in the 30–39 group, since we no longer know the points within the groupings at
which people are located. On the other hand, such groupings of individuals
are sometimes useful for the presentation and easy assimilation of information. It should be noted too, that the position of *dichotomous* variables within
the threefold classification of types of variable is somewhat ambiguous. With
such variables, there are only two categories, such as male and female for
the variable gender. A dichotomy is usually thought of as a nominal variable,
but sometimes it can be considered an ordinal variable. For example, when
there is an inherent ordering to the dichotomy, such as passing and failing, the
characteristics of an ordinal variable seem to be present.

Strictly speaking, measures like **satis**, **autonom** and **routine**, which derive
from multiple-item scales, are ordinal variables. For example, we do not know
whether the difference between a score of 20 on the **satis** scale and a score of
18 is the same as the difference between 10 and 8. This poses a problem for
researchers since the inability to treat such variables as interval means that
methods of analysis like correlation and regression (see Chapter 8), which are
both powerful and popular, could not be used in their connection since these
techniques presume the employment of interval variables. On the other hand,
most of the multiple-item measures created by researchers are treated by them
as though they are interval variables because these measures permit a large
number of categories to be stipulated. When a variable allows only a small
number of ordered categories, as in the case of **commit**, **prody**, **skill** and **qual**
in the Job Survey data, each of which comprises only either four or five
categories, it would be unreasonable in most analysts' eyes to treat them as
interval variables. When the number of categories is considerably greater, as in

the case of **satis**, **autonom** and **routine**, each of which can assume sixteen categories from 5 to 20, the case for treating them as interval variables is more compelling.

Certainly, there seems to be a trend in the direction of this more liberal treatment of multiple-item scales as having the qualities of an interval variable. On the other hand, many purists would demur from this position. Moreover, there does not appear to be a rule of thumb which allows the analyst to specify when a variable is definitely ordinal and when interval. None the less, in this book it is proposed to reflect much of current practice and to treat multiple-item measures such as **satis**, **autonom** and **routine** as though they were interval scales. Labovitz (1970) goes further in suggesting that almost all ordinal variables can and should be treated as interval variables. He argues that the amount of error that can occur is minimal, especially in relation to the considerable advantages that can accrue to the analyst as a result of using techniques of analysis like correlation and regression which are both powerful and relatively easy to interpret. However, this view is controversial (Labovitz, 1971) and, whereas many researchers would accept the treatment of variables like **satis** as interval, they would cavil about variables like **commit**, **skill**, **prody** and **qual**. Table 4.1 summarises the main characteristics of the types of scale discussed in this section, along with examples from the Job Survey data.

In order to help with the identification of whether variables should be classified as nominal, ordinal, dichotomous, or interval/ratio, the steps articulated in Figure 4.1 can be followed. We can take some of the job survey variables to illustrate how this table can be used. First, we can take **skill**. This variable has more than two categories; the distances between the categories are not equal; the categories *can* be rank ordered; therefore the variable is ordinal. Now **income**. This variable has more than two categories; the distances between them are equal; therefore the variable is interval/ratio. Now **gender**. This variable does not have more than two categories; therefore it is dichotomous. Finally, we can take **ethnicgp**. This variable has more than two categories; the distances between the categories are not equal; the categories cannot be rank ordered; therefore, the variable is nominal.

Dimensions of concepts

When a concept is very broad, serious consideration needs to be given to the possibility that it comprises underlying dimensions which reflect different aspects of the concept in question. Very often it is possible to specify those dimensions on *a priori* grounds, so that possible dimensions are established in

TABLE 4.1 Types of variable

Type	Description	Example in Job Survey data
Nominal (categorical)	A classification of objects (people, firms, nations, etc.) into discrete categories that cannot be rank ordered.	**ethnicgp**
Ordinal	The categories associated with an ordinal variable can be rank ordered. Objects can be ordered in terms of a criterion from highest to lowest.	**commit** **skill** **prody** **qual**
Interval (a)	With 'true' interval variables, categories associated with a variable can be rank ordered, as with an ordinal variable, but the distances between the categories are equal.	**income** **age** **years** **absence**
Interval (b)	Variables which strictly speaking are ordinal, but which have a large number of categories, such as multiple-item questionnaire measures. These variables are assumed to have similar properties to 'true' interval variables.	**satis** **routine** **autonom**
Dichotomous	A variable that comprises only two categories	**gender** **attend**

advance of the formation of indicators of the concept. There is much to recommend deliberation about the possibility of such underlying dimensions, since it encourages systematic reflection on the nature of the concept that is to be measured.

Lazarsfeld's (1958) approach to the measurement of concepts viewed the search for underlying dimensions as an important ingredient. Figure 4.2 illustrates the steps that he envisaged. Initially, the researcher forms an image from a theoretical domain. This image reflects a number of common characteristics, as in the previous example of job satisfaction which denotes the tendency for people to have a distinctive range of experiences in relation to their jobs. Similarly, Hall (1968) developed the idea of 'professionalism'

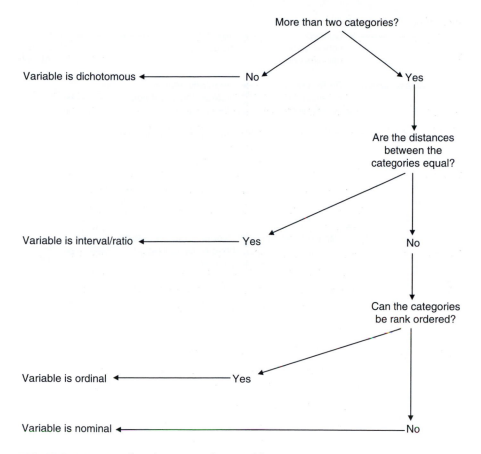

FIGURE 4.1 Deciding the nature of a variable

as a consequence of his view that members of professions have a distinctive constellation of attitudes to the nature of their work. In each case, out of this *imagery* stage, we see a concept starting to form. At the next stage, *concept specification* takes place, whereby the concept is developed to show whether it comprises different aspects or dimensions. This stage allows the complexity of the concept to be recognised. In Hall's case, five dimensions of professionalism were proposed:

1   *The use of the professional organisation as a major reference.* This means that the professional organisation and other members of the profession are the chief source of ideas and judgements for the professional in the context of his or her work.

2   *A belief in service to the public.* According to this aspect, the profession is regarded as indispensable to society.

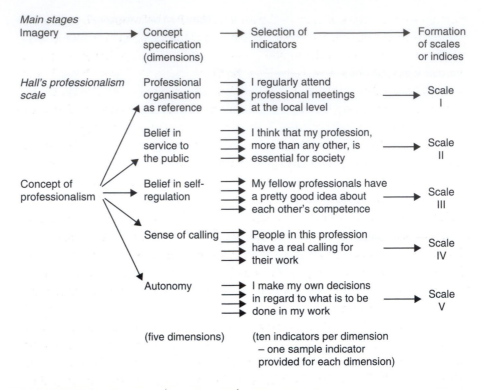

FIGURE 4.2 Concepts, dimensions and measurements
Sources: Lazarsfeld (1958); Hall (1968); Snizek (1972)

3   *Belief in self-regulation.* This notion implies that the work of a professional can and should only be judged by other members of the profession, because only they are qualified to make appropriate judgements.

4   *A sense of calling to the field.* The professional is someone who is dedicated to his or her work and would probably want to be a member of the profession even if material rewards were less.

5   *Autonomy.* This final dimension suggests that professionals ought to be able to make decisions and judgements without pressures from either clients, the organisations in which they work, or any other non-members of the profession.

Not only is the concept specification stage useful in order to reflect and to capture the full complexity of concepts, but it also serves as a means of bridging the general formulation of concepts and their measurement, since the establishment of dimensions reduces the abstractness of concepts.

The next stage is the *selection of indicators*, in which the researcher searches for indicators of each of the dimensions. In Hall's case, ten indicators of each dimension were selected. Each indicator entailed a statement in relation to which respondents had to answer whether they believed that it agreed Very Well, Well, Poorly, or Very Poorly in the light of how they felt and behaved as members of their profession. A neutral category was also provided. Figure 4.2 provides both the five dimensions of professionalism and one of the ten indicators for each dimension. Finally, Lazarsfeld proposed that the indicators need to be brought together through the *formation of indices* or *scales*. This stage can entail either of two possibilities. An overall scale could be formed which comprised all indicators relating to all dimensions. However, more frequently, separate scales are formulated for each dimension. Thus, in Hall's research, the indicators relating to each dimension were combined to form scales, so that we end up with five separate scales of professionalism. As Hall shows, different professions exhibit different 'profiles' in respect of these dimensions – one may emerge as having high scores for dimensions 2, 3, and 5, moderate for 1, and low for 4, whereas other professions will emerge with different combinations.

In order to check whether the indicators bunch in the ways proposed by an *a priori* specification of dimensions, *factor analysis*, a technique that will be examined in Chapter 11, is often employed. Factor analysis allows the researcher to check whether, for example, all of the ten indicators developed to measure 'autonomy' are really related to each other and not to indicators that are supposed to measure other dimensions. We might find that an indicator that is supposed to measure autonomy seems to be associated with many of the various indicators of 'belief in service to the public', while one or two of the latter might be related to indicators which are supposed to denote 'belief in self-regulation', and so on. In fact, when such factor analysis has been conducted in relation to Hall's professionalism scale, the correspondence between the five-dimensions and their putative indicators has been shown to be poor (Snizek, 1972; Bryman, 1985). However, the chief point that should be recognised in the foregoing discussion is that the specification of dimensions for concepts is often an important step in the development of an operational definition.

Some measurement is carried out in psychology and sociology with little (if any) attention to the quest for dimensions of concepts. For example, the eighteen-item measure of job satisfaction developed by Brayfield and Rothe (1951), which was mentioned above, does not specify dimensions, though it is possible to employ factor analysis to search for *de facto* ones. The chief point that can be gleaned from this section is that the search for dimensions can provide an important aid to understanding the nature of concepts and that when established on the basis of *a priori* reasoning can be an important step in moving from the complexity and abstractness of many concepts to possible measures of them.

Validity and reliability of measures

It is generally accepted that when a concept has been operationally defined, in that a measure of it has been proposed, the ensuing measurement device should be both reliable and valid.

Reliability

The reliability of a measure refers to its consistency. This notion is often taken to entail two separate aspects – external and internal reliability. External reliability is the more common of the two meanings and refers to the degree of consistency of a measure over time. If you have kitchen scales which register different weights every time the same bag of sugar is weighed, you would have an externally unreliable measure of weight, since the amount fluctuates over time in spite of the fact that there should be no differences between the occasions that the item is weighed. Similarly, if you administered a personality test to a group of people, re-administered it shortly afterwards and found a poor correspondence between the two *waves* of measurement, the personality test would probably be regarded as externally unreliable because it seems to fluctuate. When assessing external reliability in this manner, that is by administering a test on two occasions to the same group of subjects, *test–retest reliability* is being examined. We would anticipate that people who scored high on the test initially will also do so when retested; in other words, we would expect the relative position of each person's score to remain comparatively constant. The problem with such a procedure is that intervening events between the test and the retest may account for any discrepancy between the two sets of results. For example, if the job satisfaction of a group of workers is gauged and three months later is reassessed, it might be found that in general respondents exhibit higher levels of satisfaction than previously. It may be that in the intervening period they have received a pay increase or a change to their working practices, or some grievance that had been simmering before has been resolved by the time job satisfaction is retested. Also, if the test and retest are too close in time, subjects may recollect earlier answers, so that an artificial consistency between the two tests is created. However, test–retest reliability is one of the main ways of checking external reliability.

Internal reliability is particularly important in connection with multiple-item scales. It raises the question of whether each scale is measuring a single idea and hence whether the items that make up the scale are internally consistent. A number of procedures for estimating internal reliability exist, two of which can be readily computed in SPSS. First, with *split-half reliability* the items in a scale are divided into two groups (either randomly or on an odd–even basis) and the relationship between respondents' scores for the two halves is computed. Thus, the Brayfield–Rothe job satisfaction measure, which contains eighteen items, would be divided into two groups of nine, and the relationship between respondents' scores for the two halves would be estimated. A correlation coefficient is then generated (see Chapter 8), which varies between 0 and 1 and the nearer the result is to 1 – and preferably at or over 0.8 – the more internally reliable is the scale. Second, the currently widely used *Cronbach's alpha* essentially calculates the average of all possible split-half reliability coefficients. Again, the rule of thumb is that the result should be 0.8 or above. This rule of thumb is also generally used in relation to test–retest reliability. When a concept and its associated measure are deemed to comprise underlying dimensions, it is normal to calculate reliability estimates for each of the constituent dimensions rather than for the measure as a whole. Indeed, if a factor analysis confirms that a measure comprises a number of dimensions the overall scale will probably exhibit a low level of internal reliability, since the split-half reliability estimates may be lower as a result.

Both split-half and alpha estimates of reliability can be easily calculated with SPSS. It is necessary to ensure that all items are coded in the same direction. Thus, in the case of **satis** it is necessary to ensure that the reverse items (**satis2** and **satis4**) have been recoded (using **Recode**) so that agreement is indicative of job satisfaction. These two items have been recoded in the following illustration as **rsatis2** and **rsatis4**. In order to generate a reliability test of the four items that make up **satis**, the following sequence would be used:

→**Analyze** →**Sc**a**le** →**R**eliability **Analysis...** [opens **Reliability Analysis** dialog box shown in Box 4.1]

→**satis1**, **rsatis2**, **satis3** and **rsatis4** while holding down the Ctrl button [all four of the variables should be highlighted] →►button [puts **satis1**, **rsatis2**, **satis3** and **rsatis4** in the **Items:** box]

→**M**odel: →**Alpha** in the drop-down menu that appears

→**OK**

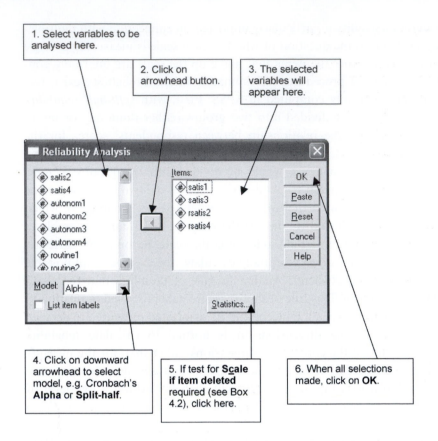

BOX 4.1   Reliability Analysis dialog box

If split-half reliability testing is preferred, click on **Split-half** in the **Model:** pull-down menu rather than **Alpha**. The output for alpha (Table 4.2) suggests that **satis** is in fact internally reliable since the coefficient is 0.76. This is only just short of the 0.8 criterion and would be regarded as internally reliable for most purposes. If a scale turns out to have low internal reliability, a strategy for dealing with this eventuality is to drop one item or more from the scale in order to establish whether reliability can be boosted. To do this, select the **Statistics...** button in the **Reliability Analysis** dialog box. This brings up the **Reliability Analysis: Statistics** subdialog box (shown in Box 4.2). Then **Scale if item deleted**. The output shows the alpha reliability levels when each constituent item is deleted. Of course, in the case of **satis**, this exercise would not be necessary.

Two other aspects of reliability, that is in addition to internal and external reliability, ought to be mentioned. First, when material is being

TABLE 4.2   Reliability Analysis output for **satis** (Job Survey data)

Case Processing Summary

		N	%
Cases	Valid	68	97.1
	Excluded[a]	2	2.9
	Total	70	100.0

a. Listwise deletion based on all
   variables in the procedure.

Reliability Statistics

Cronbach's Alpha	N of Items
.762	4

coded for themes, the reliability of the coding scheme should be tested. This problem can occur when a researcher needs to code people's answers to interview questions that have not been pre-coded, in order to search for

1. Select this option to assess the impact on the scale if an item is deleted from it.

2. Click on **Continue**, which returns you to Box 4.1.

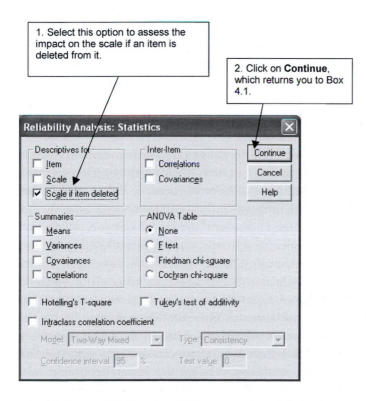

BOX 4.2   Reliability Analysis: Statistics subdialog box

general underlying themes to answers or when a content analysis of newspaper articles is conducted to elucidate ways in which news topics tend to be handled. When such exercises are carried out, more than one coder should be used and an estimate of *inter-coder reliability* should be provided to ensure that the coding scheme is being consistently interpreted by coders. This exercise would entail gauging the degree to which coders agree on the coding of themes deriving from the material being examined. Second, when the researcher is classifying behaviour an estimate of *inter-observer reliability* should be provided. For example, if aggressive behaviour is being observed, an estimate of inter-observer reliability should be presented to ensure that the criteria of aggressiveness are being consistently interpreted. Methods of bivariate analysis (see Chapter 8) can be used to measure inter-coder and inter-observer reliability. A discussion of some methods which have been devised specifically for the assessment of inter-coder or inter-observer reliability can be found in Cramer (1998).

Validity

The question of validity draws attention to how far a measure really measures the concept that it purports to measure. How do we know that our measure of job satisfaction is really getting at job satisfaction and not at something else? At the very minimum, a researcher who develops a new measure should establish that it has *face validity*, that is, that the measure apparently reflects the content of the concept in question.

The researcher might seek also to gauge the *concurrent validity* of the concept. Here the researcher employs a criterion on which people are known to differ and which is relevant to the concept in question. For example, some people are more often absent from work (other than through illness) than others. In order to establish the concurrent validity of our job satisfaction measure we may see how far people who are satisfied with their jobs are less likely than those who are not satisfied to be absent from work. If a lack of correspondence was found, such as frequent absentees being just as likely to be satisfied as not satisfied, we might be tempted to question whether our measure is really addressing job satisfaction. Another possible test for the validity of a new measure is *predictive validity*, whereby the researcher uses a future criterion measure, rather than a contemporaneous one as in the case of concurrent validity. With predictive validity, the researcher would take later levels of absenteeism as the criterion against which the validity of job satisfaction would be examined.

Some writers advocate that the researcher should also estimate the *construct validity* of a measure (Cronbach and Meehl, 1955). Here, the researcher is encouraged to deduce hypotheses from a theory that is relevant to the concept. For example, drawing upon ideas about the impact of technology on the experience of work (e.g. Blauner, 1964), the researcher might anticipate that people who are satisfied with their jobs are less likely to work on routine jobs; those who are not satisfied are more likely to work on routine jobs. Accordingly, we could investigate this theoretical deduction by examining the relationship between job satisfaction and job routine. On the other hand, some caution is required in interpreting the absence of a relationship between job satisfaction and job routine in this example. First, the theory or the deduction that is made from it may be faulty. Second, the measure of job routine could be an invalid measure of the concept.

All of the approaches to the investigation of validity that have been discussed up to now are designed to establish what Campbell and Fiske (1959) refer to as *convergent validity*. In each case, the researcher is concerned to demonstrate that the measure harmonises with another measure. Campbell and Fiske argue that this process usually does not go far enough in that the researcher should really be using different measures of the same concept to see how far there is convergence. For example, in addition to devising a questionnaire-based measure of job routine, a researcher could use observers to rate the characteristics of jobs in order to distinguish between degrees of routineness in jobs in the firm (e.g. Jenkins *et al.*, 1975). Convergent validity would entail demonstrating a convergence between the two measures, although it is difficult to interpret a lack of convergence since either of the two measures could be faulty. Many of the examples of convergent validation that have appeared since Campbell and Fiske's (1959) article have not involved different methods, but have employed different questionnaire research instruments (Bryman, 1989). For example, two questionnaire-based measures of job routine might be used, rather than two different methods. Campbell and Fiske went even further in suggesting that a measure should also exhibit *discriminant validity*. The investigation of discriminant validity implies that one should also search for *low* levels of correspondence between a measure and other measures which are supposed to represent other concepts. Although discriminant validity is an important facet of the validity of a measure, it is probably more important for the student to focus upon the various aspects of convergent validation that have been discussed. In order to investigate both the various types of convergent validity and discriminant validity, the various techniques covered in Chapter 8, which are concerned with relationships between pairs of variables, can be employed.

Exercises

1   Which of the following answers is true? A Likert scale is (a) a test for validity; (b) an approach to generating multiple-item measures; (c) a test for reliability; or (d) a method for generating dimensions of concepts?

2   When operationalising a concept, why might it be useful to consider the possibility that it comprises a number of dimensions?

3   Consider the following questions which might be used in a social survey about people's drinking habits and decide whether the variable is nominal, ordinal, interval/ratio or dichotomous:

(a) Do you ever consume alcoholic drinks?

   Yes _____

   No _____   (go to question 5)

(b) If you have ticked **Yes** to the previous question, which of the following alcoholic drinks do you consume most frequently (tick one category only)?

   Beer _____
   Spirits _____
   Wine _____
   Liquors _____
   Other _____

(c) How frequently do you consume alcoholic drinks? Tick the answer that comes closest to your current practice.

   Daily _____
   Most days _____
   Once or twice week _____
   Once or twice a month _____
   A few times a year _____
   Once or twice a year _____

(d) How many units of alcohol did you consume last week? [We can assume that the interviewer would help respondents to translate into units of alcohol.]

   Number of units _____

4   In the Job Survey data, is **absence** a nominal, an ordinal, an interval/ratio, or a dichotomous variable?

5   Is test–retest reliability a test of internal or external reliability?

6   What would be the SPSS procedure for computing Cronbach's alpha for **autonom**?

7   Following on from question 6, would this be a test of internal or external reliability?

8   A researcher develops a new multiple-item measure of 'political conservatism'. He/she administers the measure to a sample of individuals and also asks them how they voted at the last general election in order to validate the new measure. The researcher relates respondents' scores to how they voted. Which of the following is the researcher assessing: (a) the measure's concurrent validity; (b) the measure's predictive validity; or (c) the measure's discriminant validity?

Summarising data

W HEN RESEARCHERS ARE confronted with a bulk of data relating to each of a number of variables, they are faced with the task of summarising the information that has been amassed. If large amounts of data can be summarised, it becomes possible to detect patterns and tendencies that would otherwise be obscured. It is fairly easy to detect a pattern in a variable when, say, we have data on ten cases. But once we go beyond about twenty, it becomes difficult for the eye to catch patterns and trends unless the data are treated in some way. Moreover, when we want to present our collected data to an audience, it would be extremely difficult for readers to take in the relevant information. This chapter is concerned with the various procedures that may be employed to summarise a variable.

Frequency distributions

Imagine that we have data on fifty-six students regarding which faculty they belong to at a university (see Table 5.1). The university has only four faculties: engineering, pure sciences, arts, and social sciences. Even though fifty-six is not a large number on which to have data, it is not particularly easy to see how students are distributed across the faculties. A first step that might be considered when summarising data relating to a nominal variable such as this (since each faculty constitutes a discrete category) is the construction of a *frequency distribution* or *frequency table*. The idea of a frequency distribution is to tell us the number of cases in each category. By 'frequency' is simply meant the number of times that something occurs. Very often we also need to compute percentages, which tell us the proportion of cases contained within each frequency, that is, *relative frequency*. In Table 5.2, the number 11 is the frequency relating to the arts category, that is, there are eleven arts students in the sample, which is 20 per cent of the total number of students.

The procedure for generating a frequency distribution with SPSS will be addressed in a later section, but in the meantime it should be realised that all that is happening in the construction of a frequency table is that the number of cases in each category is added up. Additional information in the form of the percentage that the number of cases in each category constitutes is usually provided. This provides information about the relative frequency of

TABLE 5.1 The faculty membership of fifty-six students (imaginary data)

Case number	Faculty	Case number	Faculty
1	Arts	29	Eng
2	PS	30	SS
3	SS	31	PS
4	Eng	32	SS
5	Eng	33	Arts
6	SS	34	SS
7	Arts	35	Eng
8	PS	36	PS
9	Eng	37	Eng
10	SS	38	SS
11	SS	39	Arts
12	PS	40	SS
13	Eng	41	Eng
14	Arts	42	PS
15	Eng	43	SS
16	PS	44	PS
17	SS	45	Eng
18	Eng	46	Arts
19	PS	47	Eng
20	Arts	48	PS
21	Eng	49	Eng
22	Eng	50	Arts
23	PS	51	SS
24	Arts	52	Eng
25	Eng	53	Arts
26	PS	54	Eng
27	Arts	55	SS
28	PS	56	SS

Eng = Engineering; PS = Pure Sciences; SS = Social Sciences

the occurrence of each category of a variable. It gives a good indication of the relative preponderance of each category in the sample. Table 5.2 provides the frequency table for the data in Table 5.1. Percentages have been rounded up or down to a whole number (using the simple rule that 0.5 and above are rounded up and below 0.5 are rounded down) to make the table easier to read. The

TABLE 5.2 Frequency table showing faculty membership

Faculty	n	Per cent
Engineering	18	32
Pure Sciences	13	23
Arts	11	20
Social Sciences	14	25
Total	56	100

letter *n* is often employed to refer to the number of cases in each category (i.e. the frequency). An alternative way of presenting a frequency table for the data summarised in Table 5.2 is to omit the frequencies for each category and to present only the relative percentages. This approach reduces the amount of information that the reader must absorb. When this option is taken, it is necessary to provide the total number of cases (i.e. $n = 56$) beneath the column of percentages.

Table 5.2 can readily be adapted to provide a diagrammatic version of the data. Such diagrams are usually called *bar charts* or *bar diagrams* and are often preferred to tables because they are more easily assimilated. A bar chart presents a column for the number or percentage of cases relating to each category. Figure 5.1 presents a bar chart for the data in Table 5.1 in terms of the number of cases. On the horizontal axis the name of each category is presented. There is no need to order them in any way (e.g. short to long bars).

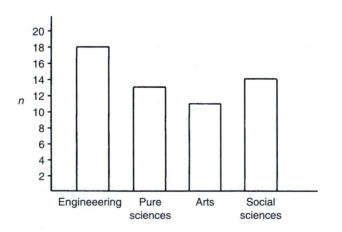

FIGURE 5.1 Bar chart of data on number of students per faculty

The bars should not touch each other but should be kept clearly separate. It should be realised that the bar chart does not provide more information than Table 5.2; indeed, some information is lost – the percentages. Its main advantage is the ease with which it can be interpreted, a characteristic that may be especially useful when data are being presented to people who may be unfamiliar with statistical material.

When a variable is at the interval/ratio level, the data will have to be grouped in order to be presented in a frequency table. The number of cases in each grouping must then be calculated. As an example, the Job Survey data on **income** may be examined. We have data on sixty-eight individuals (two are missing), but if the data are not grouped there are thirty-three categories, which is far too many for a frequency table. Moreover, the frequencies in each category would be far too small. In Table 5.3, a frequency table is presented of the data on **income**. Six categories are employed. In constructing categories such as these a number of points should be borne in mind. First, it is sometimes suggested that the number of categories should be between six and twenty, since too few or too many categories can distort the shape of the distribution of the underlying variable (e.g. Bohrnstedt and Knoke, 1982). However, it is not necessarily the case that the number of categories will affect the shape of the distribution. Also, when there are relatively few cases the number of categories will have to fall below six in order for there to be a reasonable number of cases in each category. On the other hand, a large number of categories will not be easy for the reader to assimilate and in this regard Bohrnstedt and Knoke's rule of thumb that the upper limit should be twenty categories seems slightly high. Second, the categories must be discrete. You should never group so that you have categories such as: 12,000 or less;

TABLE 5.3 Frequency table for **income** (Job Survey data)

£	n	Per cent
Below 12,000	1	1.5
12,000–13,999	16	23.5
14,000–15,999	20	29.4
16,000–17,999	22	32.4
18,000–19,999	7	10.3
20,000 and over	2	2.9
Total	68	100.0

12,000–14000; 14,000–16,000; and so on. Which categories would incomes of £12,000 and £14,000 belong to? Categories must be discrete, as in Table 5.3, so that there can be no uncertainty about which one a case should be allocated to. Note that in Table 5.3, the reader's attention is drawn to the fact that there are two missing cases. The presence of two missing cases raises the question of whether percentages should be calculated in terms of all seventy cases in the Job Survey sample or the sixty-eight on whom we have income data. Most writers prefer the latter since the inclusion of all cases in the base for the calculation of the percentage can result in misleading interpretations, especially when there might be a large number of missing cases in connection with a particular variable.

The information in Table 5.3 can be usefully presented diagrammatically as a *histogram*. A histogram is similar to a bar chart, except that the bars are in contact with each other to reflect the continuous nature of the categories of the variable in question. Figure 5.2 presents a histogram produced by SPSS for the **income** data. Its advantages are the same as those for the bar chart.

If an ordinal variable is being analysed, grouping of categories is rarely

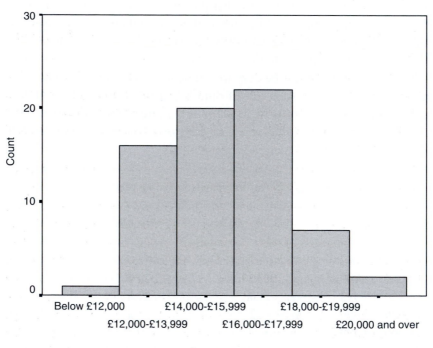

FIGURE 5.2 Histogram for **income** data (Job Survey data)

necessary. In the case of the Job Survey data, a variable like **skill**, which can assume only four categories, will not need to be grouped. The number of cases in each of the four categories can simply be added up and the percentages computed. A histogram can be used to display such data since the categories of the variable are ordered.

Using SPSS to produce frequency tables and histograms

In order to generate a frequency table for **income**, we will need to group the data; otherwise we will get a frequency count and percentage for every single income in the sample. We would have separate bars for each income within the sample. In a large sample, that could represent a lot of bars. To group the data, we will need to use the **Recode** procedure. In doing this, we will be creating a new variable which will be called **incomegp** (i.e. **income** **group**s). The aim is to group people into six income groups: below £12,000; £12,000–13,999; £14,000–15,999; £16,000–17,999; £18,000–19,999; and £20,000 and above. The following sequence will accomplish this:

→**Transform** →**Recode** →**Into Different Variables...** [opens **Recode into Different Variables** dialog box shown in Box 5.1]

→**income** →▶button [puts **income** in **Numeric Variable->Output Variable:** box] →box beneath **Output Variable Name:** and type **incomegp** →**Change** [puts **incomegp** in **Numeric Variable->Output Variable:** box] →**Old and New Values...** [opens **Recode into Different Variables: Old and New Values** subdialog box shown in Box 5.2]

→circle by **System- or user-missing** and in the box to the right of **Value** type **0** [this specifies that 0 will be recognised as a missing value] →**Add** [MISSING --> appears in the **Old --> New:** box] → circle by **Range: Lowest through** and type **11999** in box after **through** →box by **Value:** below **New Value** and type **1** → **Add** [the new value will appear in the **Old --> New:** box] → circle by **Range:** and in box below type **12000** and in box after **through** type **13999** → box by **Value** below **New Value** and type **2** → first box below **Range:** and type **14000** and in box after **through** type **15999** → box by **Value** below **New Value** and type **3** → box below **Range:** and type **16000** and in box after **through** type **17999** → box by **Value** below **New Value** and type **4** → box below **Range:** and type **18000** and in box after **through** type **19999** → box by **Value** below **New Value** and type **5** → circle by **Range: through highest** and type **20000** in box →box by

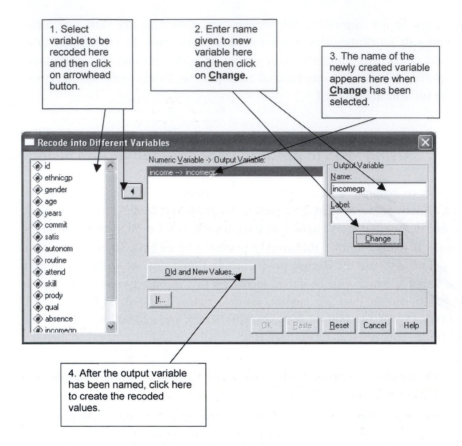

1. Select variable to be recoded here and then click on arrowhead button.

2. Enter name given to new variable here and then click on **Change**.

3. The name of the newly created variable appears here when **Change** has been selected.

4. After the output variable has been named, click here to create the recoded values.

BOX 5.1   Recoding **income** into **incomegp**

Value below **New Value** and type **6 → Add → Continue** [closes **Recode into Different Variables: Old and New Values** subdialog box]
→OK

It would then be necessary to define the **value labels** for the six categories of **incomegp** (see Chapter 2 for a description of how this is done).

The following sequence will generate the frequency table output in Table 5.4:

→Analyze →Descriptive Statistics →Frequencies... [opens **Frequencies** dialog box shown in Box 5.3]
→income groups [incomegp] → ▶button [puts **incomegp** in **Variable[s]:** box]
→OK

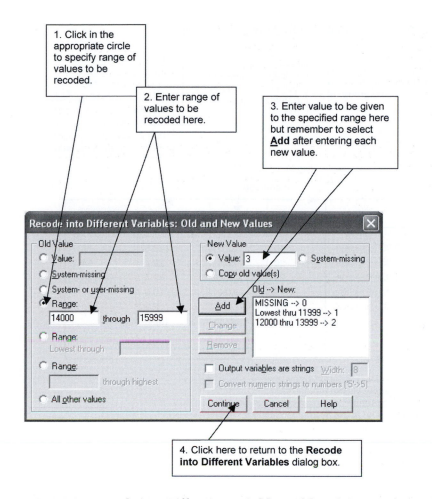

1. Click in the appropriate circle to specify range of values to be recoded.

2. Enter range of values to be recoded here.

3. Enter value to be given to the specified range here but remember to select **Add** after entering each new value.

4. Click here to return to the **Recode into Different Variables** dialog box.

BOX 5.2   Recode into Different Variables: Old and New Values subdialog box

Table 5.4 provides the number of people in each category (**Frequency**) and three percentages: the frequency associated with each category as a percentage of all cases (**Percent**); the frequency associated with each category as a percentage of all cases on which data exist and which therefore excludes the two cases for whom data are missing (**Valid Percent**); and the cumulative percentage (**Cum Percent**).

For a histogram of **income**, the following sequence should be followed:

→**Graphs** →**Hi̲stogram ...** [opens **Histogram** dialog box]

→**income** →▶button [puts **income** in **V̲ariable:** box] →**OK**

TABLE 5.4 Frequency table for **incomegp** (SPSS output)

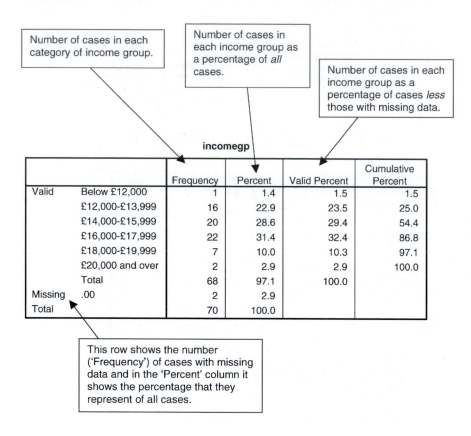

Number of cases in each category of income group.

Number of cases in each income group as a percentage of *all* cases.

Number of cases in each income group as a percentage of cases *less* those with missing data.

incomegp

		Frequency	Percent	Valid Percent	Cumulative Percent
Valid	Below £12,000	1	1.4	1.5	1.5
	£12,000-£13,999	16	22.9	23.5	25.0
	£14,000-£15,999	20	28.6	29.4	54.4
	£16,000-£17,999	22	31.4	32.4	86.8
	£18,000-£19,999	7	10.0	10.3	97.1
	£20,000 and over	2	2.9	2.9	100.0
	Total	68	97.1	100.0	
Missing	.00	2	2.9		
Total		70	100.0		

This row shows the number ('Frequency') of cases with missing data and in the 'Percent' column it shows the percentage that they represent of all cases.

The resulting histogram will employ income bands defined by the SPSS default criteria.

To produce a bar chart for a nominal variable like **ethnicgp**, the following sequence can be followed:

→**Graphs** →**Bar. . .** [opens **Bar Charts** dialog box shown in Box 5.4]

→**Simple** →**Summaries for groups of cases** →**Define** [opens **Define Simple Bar: Summaries for Groups of Cases** subdialog box shown in Box 5.5]

→**ethnicgp** →▶button by **Category Axis** [puts **ethnicgp** in box] →**N of cases** beneath **Bars Represent** [if this has not already been selected, otherwise continue without doing this] →**OK**

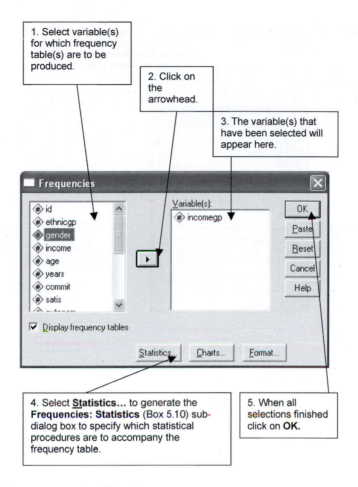

1. Select variable(s) for which frequency table(s) are to be produced.

2. Click on the arrowhead.

3. The variable(s) that have been selected will appear here.

4. Select **Statistics...** to generate the **Frequencies: Statistics** (Box 5.10) sub-dialog box to specify which statistical procedures are to accompany the frequency table.

5. When all selections finished click on **OK**.

BOX 5.3 **Frequencies** dialog box

An alternative way of presenting data relating to a nominal variable is a *pie chart*, which displays the number of cases in each category in terms of slices of a circle. This can be a useful means of presenting data when the object is to emphasise the relative size of each slice in relation to the sample as a whole. Figure 5.3 presents a basic pie chart for **ethnicgp** generated by SPSS. Initially, the following sequence should be followed:

→**G**raphs →**Pie**. . . [opens **Pie Charts** dialog box shown in Box 5.6]
→**Summaries for groups of **c**ases** →**Define** [opens **Define Pie: Summaries for Groups of Cases** subdialog box shown in Box 5.7]

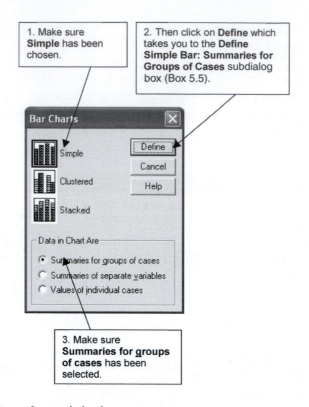

1. Make sure **Simple** has been chosen.

2. Then click on **Define** which takes you to the **Define Simple Bar: Summaries for Groups of Cases** subdialog box (Box 5.5).

3. Make sure **Summaries for groups of cases** has been selected.

BOX 5.4 **Bar Charts** dialog box

→**ethnicgp** →►button by **Define slices by** [puts **ethnicgp** in the box] →**N of cases** beneath **Slices Represent:** [if this has *not* already been selected, otherwise continue without doing this] →**OK**

A pie chart will be produced with each slice in a different colour. If you are not able to print this out with a colour printer, you will need to edit the chart so that each slice is distinguishable. The chart in Figure 5.3 was drawn using two separate steps: white was applied to all of the slices and separate patterns were applied to each slice. The following steps will achieve this:

Double-click anywhere in the chart. This will bring up the **Chart Editor**. The chart will appear in the **Chart Editor** and the main figure will appear shaded.

To fill each slice with white and to apply a pattern to each slice:

→the first slice you want to fill with white and a pattern and then →**Edit** →**Properties** (**Properties** box will appear) →the **Fill & Border** tab [a palette of colours will appear] (the **Fill & Border** tab is visible in Box 5.8) →white and make sure that the **Fill** box now has white in it →the downward pointing arrow by **Pattern** →your chosen pattern and then →**Apply**

The slice relating to the colour you had chosen will appear in white with a pattern. You then need to do the same for each of the other colours in the legend, though it may be useful to have one slice in a very dark colour.

Note that **value labels** will need to have been previously assigned to produce the labels found in Figure 5.3. The percentage of cases in each category of the variable can also be shown (as in Figure 5.3). To insert the

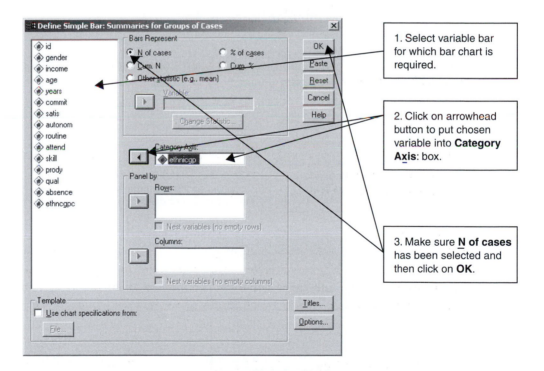

BOX 5.5 Define Simple Bar: Summaries for Groups of Cases subdialog box

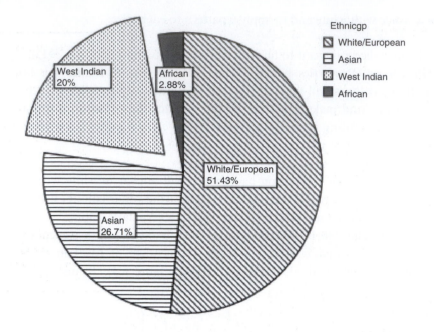

FIGURE 5.3 Pie chart for **ethnicgp** (Job Survey data)

value labels and the percentages, when in the **Chart Editor** ➔ **Elements** ➔ **Show Data Labels** (to open **Properties** dialog box) ➔ **Count** and the red × not to display count ➔ **ethnicgp** and the curved upward arrow to display it ➔ **Percent** to do the same, ➔ **Apply** ➔ **Close**.

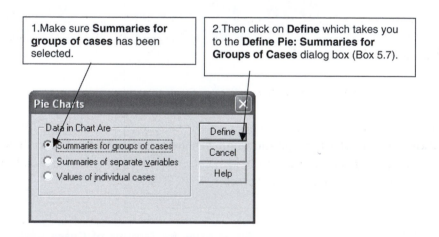

BOX 5.6   Pie Charts dialog box

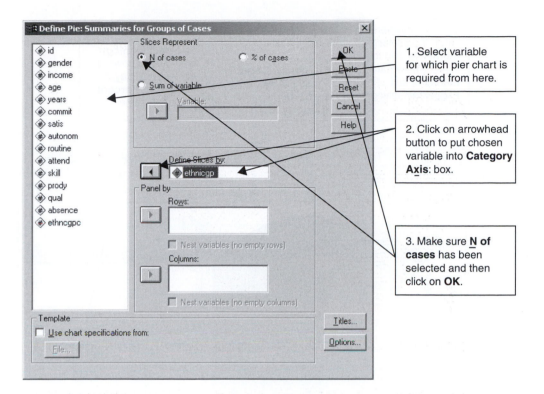

BOX 5.7   Define Pie: Summaries for Groups of Cases subdialog box

You can also create an 'exploded' pie effect (as in Figure 5.3), whereby one slice becomes detached from the pie so that it can be emphasised. To do this, while in the **Chart Editor**

→**Chart Elements** →**Explode Slice**

Similar changes can be made to all SPSS figures (e.g. bar charts), by double-clicking on the chart in question and bringing up the **Chart Editor**. This allows you to change colours, introduce patterns, provide figure titles, and to provide various items of additional information.

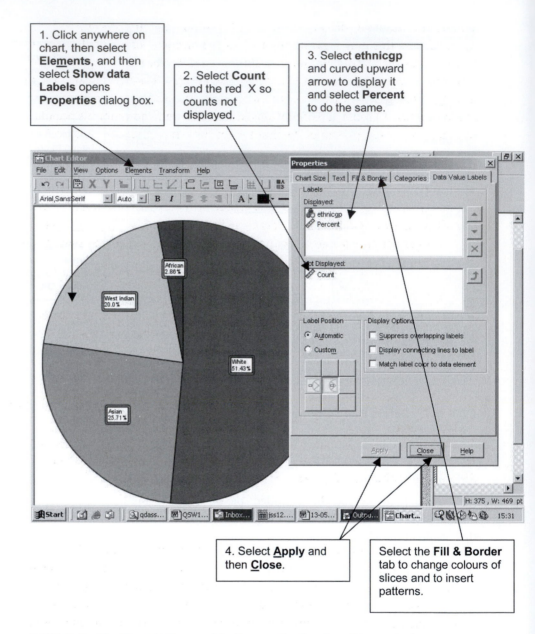

BOX 5.8 The **Chart Editor** and the **Properties** box for editing a pie chart

Measuring central tendency

One of the most important ways of summarising a distribution of values for a variable is to establish its *central tendency* – the typical value in a distribution.

Where, for example, do values in a distribution tend to concentrate? To many readers this may mean trying to find the 'average' of a distribution of values. However, statisticians mean a number of different measures when they talk about averages. Three measures of average (i.e. central tendency) are usually discussed in textbooks: the arithmetic mean, the median and the mode. Stephen J. Gould, a palaeontologist who was well known for his popular writings on science, illustrates the first two of these measures of average when he wrote:

> A politician in power might say with pride, 'The mean income of our citizens is $15,000 per year.' The leader of the opposition might retort, 'But half our citizens make less than $10,000 per year.' Both are right, but neither cites a statistic with impassive objectivity. The first invokes a mean, the second a median.
>
> (Gould, 1991: 473)

While this comment does little to reassure us about the possible misuse of statistics, it does illustrate well the different ways in which average can be construed.

The arithmetic mean

The arithmetic mean is a method for measuring the average of a distribution which conforms to most people's notion of what an average is. Consider the following distribution of values:

12   10   7   9   8   15   2   19   7   10   8   16

The arithmetic mean consists of adding up all of the values (i.e. 123) and dividing by the number of values (i.e. 12), which results in an arithmetic mean of 10.25. It is this kind of calculation which results in such seemingly bizarre statements as 'the average number of children is 2.37'. However, the arithmetic mean, which is often symbolised as x, is by far the most commonly used method of gauging central tendency. Many of the statistical tests encountered later in this book are directly concerned with comparing means deriving from different samples or groups of cases (e.g. analysis of variance – see Chapter 7). The arithmetic mean is easy to understand and to interpret, which heightens its appeal. Its chief limitation is that it is vulnerable to extreme values, in that it may be unduly affected by very high or very low values which can respectively increase or decrease its magnitude. This is particularly likely to occur when there are relatively few values; when there are many values, it would take a very extreme value to distort the arithmetic mean. For example, if the number 59 is substituted for 19 in the previous distribution of twelve values, the mean would be 13.58, rather than 10.25, which constitutes a substantial difference and could be taken to be a poor representation of the distribution as a whole. Similarly, in Table 8.10 in Chapter 8, the variable 'size of firm' contains an outlier (case number 20) which is a firm of 2,700 employees whereas the next largest has 640 employees. The mean for this variable is 499, but if we exclude the outlier it is 382.6. Again, we see that an outlier can have a very large impact on the arithmetic mean, especially when the number of cases in the sample is quite small.

The median

The median is the mid-point in a distribution of values. It splits a distribution of values in half. Imagine that the values in a distribution are arrayed from low to high, e.g. 2, 4, 7, 9, 10, the median is the middle value, that is, 7. When there is an even number of values, the average of the two middle values is taken. Thus, in the former group of twelve values, to calculate the median we need to array them as follows

2   7   7   8   8   <u>9   10</u>   10   12   15   16   19

Thus in this array of twelve values, we take the two underlined values – the sixth and seventh – and divide their sum by 2, that is, (9 + 10)/2 = 9.5. This is slightly lower than the arithmetic mean of 10.25, which is almost certainly due to the presence of three fairly large values at the upper end – 15, 16, 19. If we had the value 59 instead of 19, although we know that the mean would be higher at 13.58 the median would be unaffected, because it emphasises the middle of the distribution and ignores the ends. For this reason, many writers suggest that when there is an outlying value which may distort the mean, the median should be considered because it will engender a more representative indication of the central tendency of a group of values. On the other hand, the median is less intuitively easy to understand and it does not use all of the values in a distribution in order for it to be calculated. Moreover, the mean's vulnerability to distortion as a consequence of extreme values is less pronounced when there is a large number of cases.

SUMMARISING DATA

The mode

This final indicator of central tendency is rarely used in research reports, but is often mentioned in textbooks. The mode is simply the value that occurs most frequently in a distribution. In the foregoing array of twelve values, there are three modes – 7, 8, and 10. Unlike the mean, which strictly speaking should only be used in relation to interval variables, the mode can be employed at any measurement level. The median can be employed in relation to interval and ordinal, but not nominal, variables. Thus, although the mode appears more flexible, it is infrequently used, in part because it does not use all of the values of a distribution and is not easy to interpret when there is a number of modes.

Measuring dispersion

In addition to being interested in the typical or representative score for a distribution of values, researchers are usually interested in the amount of variation shown by that distribution. This is what is meant by *dispersion* – how widely spread a distribution is. Dispersion can provide us with important information. For example, we may find two roughly comparable firms in which the mean income of manual workers is identical. However, in one firm the salaries of these workers are more widely spread, with both considerably lower and higher salaries than in the other firm. Thus, although the mean income is the same, one firm exhibits much greater dispersion in incomes than the other. This is important information that can usefully be employed to add to measures of central tendency.

The most obvious measure of dispersion is to take the highest and lowest value in a distribution and to subtract the latter from the former. This is known as the *range*. While easy to understand, it suffers from the disadvantage of being susceptible to distortion from extreme values. This point can be illustrated by the imaginary data in Table 5.5, which shows the marks out of a hundred achieved on a mathematics test by two classes of twenty students, each of which was taught by a different teacher. The two classes exhibit similar means, but the patterns of the two distributions of values are highly dissimilar. Teacher A's class has a fairly bunched distribution, whereas that of Teacher B's class is much more dispersed. Whereas the lowest mark attained in Teacher A's class is 57, the lowest for Teacher B is 45. Indeed, there are eight marks in Teacher B's class that are below 57. However, whereas the highest mark in Teacher A's class is 74, three of Teacher B's class exceed this figure – one with a very high 95. Although the latter distribution is more dispersed, the

103

TABLE 5.5 Results of a test of mathematical ability for the students of two teachers (imaginary data)

	Teacher A	Teacher B
	65	57
	70	49
	66	46
	59	79
	57	72
	62	54
	66	66
	71	65
	58	63
	67	76
	61	45
	68	95
	63	62
	65	68
	71	50
	69	53
	67	58
	74	65
	72	69
	60	72
Arithmetic mean	65.55	63.2
Standard deviation	4.91	12.37
Median	66	64

calculation of the range seems to exaggerate its dispersion. The range for Teacher A is 74–57, i.e. a range of 17. For Teacher B, the range is 95–45, that is, 50. This exaggerates the amount of dispersion since all but three of the values are between 72 and 45, implying a range of 27 for the majority of the values.

One solution to this problem is to eliminate the extreme values. The *inter-quartile range*, for example, is sometimes recommended in this connection (see Figure 5.4). This entails arraying a range of values in ascending order. The array is divided into four equal portions, so that the lowest 25 per cent are in the first portion and the highest 25 per cent are in the last portion.

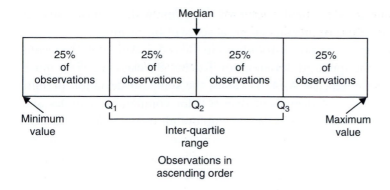

FIGURE 5.4 The inter-quartile range

These portions are used to generate quartiles. Take the earlier array from which the median was calculated.

$$2 \quad 7 \quad 7 \quad 8 \quad 8 \quad 9 \quad 10 \quad 10 \quad 12 \quad 15 \quad 16 \quad 19$$

⇧   ⇧

1st   3rd

quartile   quartile

The first quartile (Q1), often called the 'lower quartile' will be between 7 and 8. SPSS calculates it as 7.25. The third quartile (Q3), often called the 'upper quartile', is 14.25. Therefore the inter-quartile range is the difference between the third and first quartiles, that is, 14.25 – 7.25 = 7. As Figure 5.4 indicates, the median is the second quartile, but is not a component of the calculation of the inter-quartile range. The main advantage of this measure of dispersion is that it eliminates extreme values, but its chief limitation is that in ignoring 50 per cent of the values in a distribution, it loses a lot of information. A compromise is the *decile range*, which divides a distribution into ten portions (deciles) and, in a similar manner to the inter-quartile range, eliminates the highest and lowest portions. In this case, only 20 per cent of the distribution is lost.

By far the most commonly used method of summarising dispersion is the *standard deviation*. In essence, the standard deviation calculates the average amount of deviation from the mean. Its calculation is somewhat more complicated than this definition implies. A further description of the standard deviation can be found in Chapter 7. The standard deviation reflects the degree to which the values in a distribution differ from the arithmetic mean.

The standard deviation is usually presented in tandem with the mean, since it is difficult to determine its meaning in the absence of the mean.

We can compare the two distributions in Table 5.5. Although the means are very similar, the standard deviation for Teacher B's class (12.37) is much larger than that for Teacher A (4.91). Thus, the standard deviation permits the direct comparison of degrees of dispersal for comparable samples and measures. A further advantage is that it employs all of the values in a distribution. It summarises in a single value the amount of dispersion in a distribution, which, when used in conjunction with the mean, is easy to interpret. The standard deviation can be affected by extreme values, but since its calculation is affected by the number of cases, the distortion is less pronounced than with the range. On the other hand, the possibility of distortion from extreme values must be borne in mind. None the less, unless there are very good reasons for not wanting to use the standard deviation, it should be used whenever a measure of dispersion is required. It is routinely reported in research reports and widely recognised as the main measure of dispersion.

This consideration of dispersion has tended to emphasise interval variables. The standard deviation can only be employed in relation to such variables. The range and inter-quartile range can be used in relation to ordinal variables, but this does not normally happen, while tests for dispersion in nominal variables would be inappropriate. Probably the best ways of examining dispersion for nominal and ordinal variables is through bar charts, histograms and frequency tables.

Measuring central tendency and dispersion with SPSS

All of these statistics can be generated in SPSS. Taking **income** as an illustration, the following sequence should be followed:

→**Analyze** →**Descriptive Statistics** →**Explore...** [opens **Explore** dialog box shown in Box 5.9]

→**income** →▶button by **Dependent List:** [puts **income** in **Dependent List:** box] →**OK**

The resulting output is in Table 5.6. The following items that have been covered above will be produced: arithmetic mean (**Mean**), median, range, minimum and maximum values, standard deviation (**Std. Deviation**), and the inter-quartile range.

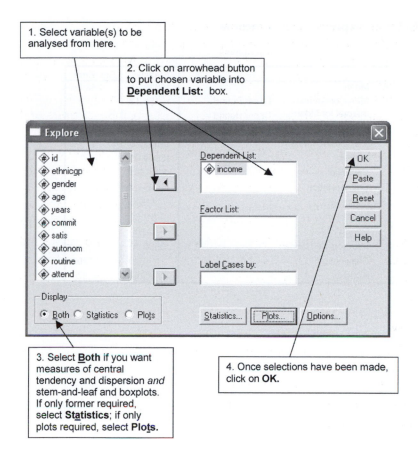

1. Select variable(s) to be analysed from here.

2. Click on arrowhead button to put chosen variable into **Dependent List:** box.

3. Select **Both** if you want measures of central tendency and dispersion *and* stem-and-leaf and boxplots. If only former required, select **Statistics**; if only plots required, select **Plots.**

4. Once selections have been made, click on **OK.**

BOX 5.9 Explore dialog box

Stems and leaves, boxes and whiskers

In 1977, John Tukey published a highly influential book entitled *Exploratory Data Analysis*, which sought to introduce readers to a variety of techniques he had developed which emphasise simple arithmetic computation and diagrammatic displays of data. Although the approach he advocates is anti-thetical to many of the techniques conventionally employed by data analysts, including the bulk of techniques examined in this book, some of Tukey's displays can be usefully appended to more orthodox procedures. Two dia-grammatic presentations of data are very relevant to the present discussion – the *stem and leaf display* and the *boxplot* (sometimes called the *box and whisker plot*).

TABLE 5.6 Explore output for **income**

Descriptives

			Statistic	Std. Error
INCOME	Mean		15638.24	242.04
	95% Confidence Interval for Mean	Lower Bound	15155.13	
		Upper Bound	16121.34	
	5% Trimmed Mean		15582.35	
	Median		15600.00	
	Variance		3983591	
	Std. Deviation		1995.89	
	Minimum		11800	
	Maximum		21000	
	Range		9200	
	Interquartile Range		3500.00	
	Skewness		.370	.291
	Kurtosis		-.294	.574

```
INCOME Stem-and-Leaf Plot

Frequency    Stem &  Leaf

    1.00       11 .  8
    3.00       12 .  448
   13.00       13 .  0244466668888
   10.00       14 .  0022246668
   10.00       15 .  0000246688
   11.00       16 .  00002446666
   11.00       17 .  00244666688
    6.00       18 .  000226
    1.00       19 .  0
    1.00       20 .  6
    1.00       21 .  0

Stem width:    1000
Each leaf:       1 case(s)
```

The stem and leaf display

The stem and leaf display is an extremely simple means of presenting data on an interval variable in a manner similar to a histogram, but without the loss of information that a histogram necessarily entails. It can be easily constructed by hand, although this would be more difficult with very large amounts of data. In order to illustrate the stem and leaf display, data on one indicator of local authority performance are taken. For a number of years, the British government has given the Audit Commission the task of collecting data on the performance of local authorities, so that their performance can be compared. One of the criteria of performance relates to the percentage of special needs reports issued within six months. A good deal of variation could be discerned with respect to this criterion, as the author of an article in *The Times* noted:

> If a child in Sunderland needs a report drawn up on its special educational needs, it has no chance of receiving this within six months. If the child moved a mile or two down the road into Durham, there would be an 80 per cent chance that the report would be issued in that time.
>
> (Murray, 1995: 32)

Whether such data really measure efficiency is, of course, a matter of whether the measure is *valid* (see Chapter 4), but there is no doubt that there is a great deal of variation with respect to the percentage of reports issued within six months. As Table 5.7 shows, the percentage varies between 0 and 95 per cent.

Figure 5.5 provides a stem and leaf display for this variable which we call 'needs'. The display has two main components. First, the digits in the middle column make up the stem. These constitute the starting parts for presenting each value in a distribution. Each of the digits that form the stem represents the percentage of special needs reports issued in tens, that is, 0 refers to single digit numbers; 1 to tens; 2 to twenties; 3 to thirties; and so on. To the right of the stem are the leaves, each of which represents an item of data which is linked to the stem. Thus, the 0 to the right of the 0 refers to the lowest value in the distribution, namely the percentage figure of 0. We can see that three authorities failed to issue any reports within six months and four issued only 1 per cent of reports within six months. When we come to the row starting with 1, we can see that five managed to issue 10 per cent of reports within six months. It is important to ensure that all of the leaves – the digits to the right of the stem – are vertically aligned. It is not necessary for the leaves to be ordered in magnitude, that is, from 0 to 9, but it is easier to read. We can see that the distribution is very bunched in the middle of the distribution. The appearance of the diagram has been controlled by requesting that incremental jumps are in tens, that is, first tens, then twenties, then thirties, and so on. The output can also be controlled by requesting that any outliers are separately positioned. Practitioners of exploratory data analysis use a specific criterion for the identification of outliers. Outliers at the low end of the range are identified by the formula

first quartile – (1.5 × the inter-quartile range)

TABLE 5.7 Percentage of special needs reports issued within six months in local authorities in England and Wales, 1993–4

London boroughs		English counties		Metropolitan authorities		Welsh counties	
Inner London		Avon	11	**Greater**		Clwyd	30
City of London	*	Bedfordshire	25	**Manchester**		Dyfed	67
Camden	48	Berkshire	16	Bolton	9	Gwent	17
Greenwich	14	Buckinghamshire	69	Bury	16	Gwynedd	88
Hackney	36	Cambridgeshire	7	Manchester	35	Mid	
Ham & Fulham	6	Cheshire	25	Oldham	50	Glamorgan	48
Islington	44	Cleveland	32	Rochdale	0	Powys	80
Ken & Chelsea	8	Cornwall	3	Salford	10	South	
Lambeth	4	Cumbria	35	Stockport	16	Glamorgan	45
Lewisham	12	Derbyshire	17	Tameside	16	West	
Southwark	10	Devon	55	Trafford	11	Glamorgan	4
Tower Hamlets	37	Dorset	33	Wigan	21		
Wandsworth	4	Durham	72	**Merseyside**			
Westminster	63	East Sussex	8	Knowsley	8		
Outer London		Essex	29	Liverpool	95		
Barking &		Gloucestershire	45	St Helens	21		
Dagenham	22	Hampshire	12	Sefton	37		
Barnet	40	Hereford & Worcs	3	Wirral	13		
Bexley	37	Hertfordshire	61	**South Yorkshire**			
Brent	23	Humberside	14	Barnsley	15		
Bromley	24	Isle of Wight	60	Doncaster	1		
Croydon	27	Kent	15	Rotherham	10		
Ealing	3	Lancashire	14	Sheffield	4		
Enfield	2	Leicestershire	*	**Tyne & Wear**			
Haringey	10	Lincolnshire	36	Gateshead	4		
Harrow	1	Norfolk	1	Newcastle upon			
Havering	0	Northamptonshire	48	Tyne	30		
Hillingdon	7	Northumberland	79	North Tyneside	48		
Hounslow	20	North Yorkshire	34	South Tyneside	5		
Kingston upon		Nottinghamshire	10	Sunderland	0		
Thames	27	Oxfordshire	22	**West Midlands**			
Merton	16	Shropshire	15	Birmingham	5		
Newham	3	Somerset	50	Coventry	20		
Redbridge	34	Staffordshire	20	Dudley	41		
Richmond		Suffolk	27	Sandwell	1		
upon Thames	27	Surrey	55	Solihull	31		
Sutton	6	Warwickshire	26	Walsall	3		
Walthan Forest	24	West Sussex	14	Wolverhampton	3		
		Wiltshire	30	**West Yorkshire**			
				Bradford	25		
				Calderdale	2		
				Kriklees.	38		
				Leeds	17		
				Wakefield	15		

Note: * = missing or doubtful information.
Source: Adapted from *The Times*, 30 March 1995: 32.

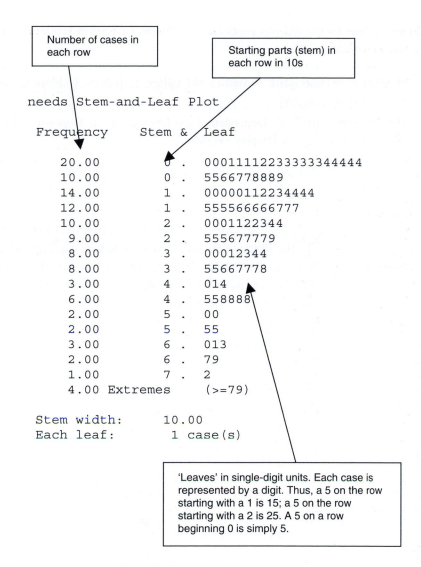

Number of cases in each row

Starting parts (stem) in each row in 10s

```
needs Stem-and-Leaf Plot

 Frequency      Stem &  Leaf

     20.00        0 .  00011112233333344444
     10.00        0 .  5566778889
     14.00        1 .  00000112234444
     12.00        1 .  555566666777
     10.00        2 .  0001122344
      9.00        2 .  555677779
      8.00        3 .  00012344
      8.00        3 .  55667778
      3.00        4 .  014
      6.00        4 .  558888
      2.00        5 .  00
      2.00        5 .  55
      3.00        6 .  013
      2.00        6 .  79
      1.00        7 .  2
      4.00   Extremes    (>=79)

 Stem width:      10.00
 Each leaf:        1 case(s)
```

'Leaves' in single-digit units. Each case is represented by a digit. Thus, a 5 on the row starting with a 1 is 15; a 5 on the row starting with a 2 is 25. A 5 on a row beginning 0 is simply 5.

FIGURE 5.5 Stem and leaf display for **needs**

and at the high end of the range by the formula

third quartile − (1.5 × the inter-quartile range)

The first quartile for 'needs' is 8.0 and the third quartile is 36.0. Substituting in these two simple equations means that outliers will need to be below −36.0 or above 78.0. Using this criterion, four outliers (**Extremes**) are identified (see Figure 5.5). To produce a stem and leaf display, we follow almost exactly the same procedure as we did for producing measures of central tendency and dispersion (see Box 5.9):

> →**Analyze** →**Descriptive Statistics** →**Explore. . .** [opens **Explore** dialog box shown in Box 5.9]
>
> →**needs** →▶ button by **Dependent List:** [puts **needs** in **Dependent List:** box] →**Plots** in box by **Display** →**OK**

The output is in Figure 5.5. The figures in the column to the left of the starting parts represent the frequency for each. We can also see that there are missing data for two authorities.

The stem and leaf display provides a similar presentation to a histogram, in that it gives a sense of the shape of the distribution (such as whether values tend to be bunched at one end), the degree of dispersion, and whether there are outlying values. However, unlike the histogram it retains all the information, so that values can be directly examined to see whether particular ones tend to predominate.

The boxplot

Figure 5.6 provides the skeletal outline of a basic boxplot. The box comprises the middle 50 per cent of observations. Thus the lower end of the box, in terms of the measure to which it refers, is the first quartile and the upper end is the third quartile. In other words, the box comprises the inter-quartile range. The line in the box is the median. The broken lines (the whiskers) extend downwards to the lowest value in the distribution and upwards to the largest value *excluding outliers*, that is, extreme values, which are separately indicated. It has a number of advantages. Like the stem and leaf display, the boxplot provides information about the shape and dispersion of a distribution. For example, is the box closer to one end or is it near the middle? The former would denote that values tend to bunch at one end. In this case, the bulk of the observations are at the lower end of the distribution, as is the median. This provides further information about the shape of the distribution, since it raises the question of whether the median is closer to one end of the box, as it is in this case. On the other hand, the boxplot does not retain information like the stem and leaf display. Figure 5.7 provides a boxplot of the data from Table 5.6. The four outliers are signalled, using the previously discussed criterion. It is clear that in half the authorities (all those below the line representing the median) 20 per cent or fewer reports are issued within six months.

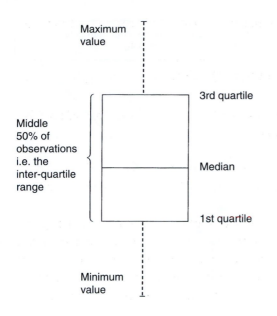

FIGURE 5.6 Boxplot

When a stem and leaf display is requested as above, a boxplot will also be produced and will appear in the SPSS Output Viewer. In other words, following the sequence stipulated on page 112 will generate both a stem and leaf display *and* a boxplot.

Both of these exploratory data analysis techniques can be recommended as providing useful first steps in gaining a feel for data when you first start to analyse them. Should they be used as alternatives to histograms and other more common diagrammatic approaches? Here they suffer from the disadvantage of not being well known. The stem and leaf diagram is probably the easier of the two to assimilate, since the boxplot diagram requires an understanding of quartiles and the median. If used in relation to audiences who are likely to be unfamiliar with these techniques, they may generate some discomfort even if a full explanation is provided. On the other hand, for audiences who are (or should be) familiar with these ideas, they have much to recommend them.

The shape of a distribution

On a number of occasions, reference has been made to the shape of a distribution. For example, values in a distribution may tend to cluster at one end of

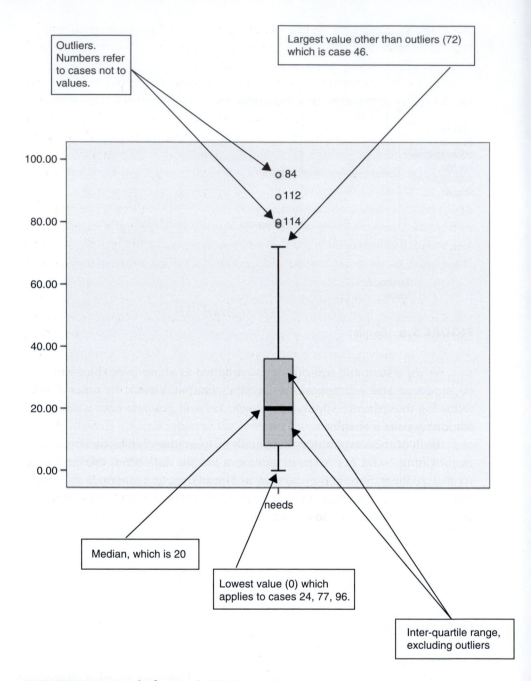

Outliers. Numbers refer to cases not to values.

Largest value other than outliers (72) which is case 46.

o 84

o 112

o 114

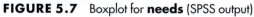
needs

Median, which is 20

Lowest value (0) which applies to cases 24, 77, 96.

Inter-quartile range, excluding outliers

FIGURE 5.7 Boxplot for **needs** (SPSS output)

the distribution or in the middle. In this section, we will be more specific about the idea of shape and introduce some ideas that are central to some aspects of data analysis to be encountered in later chapters.

Statisticians recognise a host of different possible distribution curves. By far the most important is the normal distribution. The *normal distribution* is a bell-shaped curve. It can take a number of different forms depending upon the degree to which the data are dispersed. Two examples of normal distribution curves are presented in Figure 5.8. The term 'normal' is potentially very misleading, because perfectly normal distributions are very rarely found in reality. However, the values of a variable may approximate to a normal distribution and when they do, we tend to think of them as having the properties of a normal distribution. Many of the most common statistical techniques used by social scientists presume that the variables being analysed are nearly normally distributed (see the discussion of parametric and non-parametric tests in Chapter 7).

The normal distribution should be thought of as subsuming all of the cases which it describes beneath its curve: 50 per cent will lie on one side of the arithmetic mean; the other 50 per cent on the other side (see Figure 5.9). The median value will be identical to the mean. As the curve implies, most values will be close to the mean. This is why the curve peaks at the mean. But the tapering off at either side indicates that as we move in either direction away from the mean, fewer and fewer cases are found. Only a small proportion will be found at its outer reaches. People's heights illustrate this fairly well. The mean height for an adult woman in the UK is 5 ft 3 in (160.9 cm). If women's heights are normally distributed, we would expect that most women would cluster around this mean. Very few will be very short or very tall. We know that women's heights have these properties, though whether they are perfectly normally distributed is another matter.

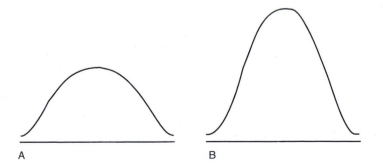

A   B

FIGURE 5.8   Two normal distributions

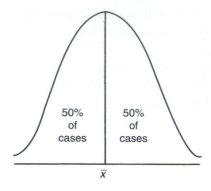

FIGURE 5.9 The normal distribution and the mean

The normal distribution displays some interesting properties that have been determined by statisticians. These properties are illustrated in Figure 5.10. In a perfectly normal distribution:

68.26 per cent of cases will be within one standard deviation of the mean
95.44 per cent of cases will be within two standard deviations of the mean
99.7 per cent of cases will be within three standard deviations of the mean.

These features of a normal distribution become very significant when we explore the ways in which social scientists seek to infer features of populations from samples, which is the focus of Chapter 6.

It is important to realise that some variables will not follow the shape of the normal distribution curve. In some cases, they may depart very strikingly from it. This tendency is most clearly evident when the values in a distribution are *skewed* – that is, they tend to cluster at either end. When this occurs, the mean and median no longer coincide. These ideas are illustrated in Figure 5.11. The left-hand diagram shows a curve that is *positively skewed* in that cases tend to cluster to the left and there is a long 'tail' to the right. The variable 'needs' is an illustration of a positively skewed distribution, as the boxplot in Figure 5.7 suggests (the mean is 24.75 and the median is 20.00). In the right-hand diagram, the curve is *negatively skewed*. Another kind of distribution is one which possesses more than one peak.

Although there is a recognition that some variables in the social sciences do not exhibit the characteristics of a normal curve and that therefore we often have to treat variables as though they were normally distributed, when

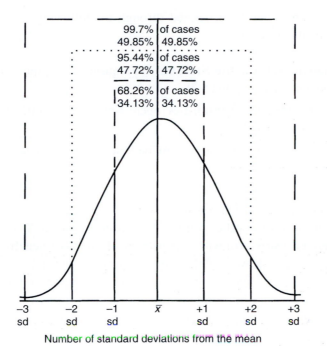

FIGURE 5.10 Properties of the normal distribution

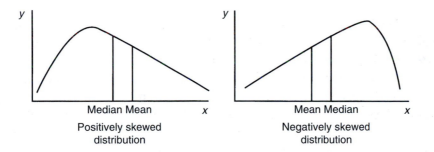

FIGURE 5.11 Positively and negatively skewed distributions

there is a very marked discrepancy from a normal distribution, such as in the two cases in Figure 5.11, some caution is required. For example, many writers would argue that it would not be appropriate to apply certain kinds of statistical test to variables which are profoundly skewed when that test presumes normally distributed data. Very often, skewness or other pronounced departures from a normal distribution can be established from the examination of a frequency table or of a histogram. SPSS provides a measure of skewness, which can be generated through the following sequence (using **income** as an illustration):

→**Analyze** →**Descriptive Statistics** →**Frequencies. . .** [opens **Frequencies** dialog box shown in Box 5.3]

→**income** →►button →**Statistics** [opens **Frequencies: Statistics** subdialog box shown in Box 5.10]

→**Skewness** below **Distribution** →**Continue** [closes **Frequencies: Statistics** subdialog box]

→**OK**

If there is no skew, or in other words if the variable is normally distributed, a value of zero or nearly zero will be registered. If there is a negative value, the data are negatively skewed; if the value is positive, the data are positively skewed. On the other hand, this test is not easy to interpret and there is much to be said for a visual interpretation of the data to discern excessive skew. This can be done through a frequency table, or through a diagrammatic presentation, such as a histogram or a stem and leaf display.

1. Click here to generate a measure of skewness.

2. Click on **Continue** to return to the **Frequencies** dialog box (Box 5.3).

BOX 5.10 Frequencies: Statistics subdialog box

Exercises

1   What is the appropriate SPSS procedure for producing a frequency table for **prody** (Job Survey data), along with percentages and median?

2   Implement the procedure from Question 1. What is the percentage of respondents in the 'poor' category?

3   What problem would you anticipate if you used the mean and the range as measures of central tendency and dispersion respectively for the variable 'size of firm' in Table 8.10?

4   Which of the following should *not* be used to represent an interval variable: (a) a boxplot; (b) a stem and leaf display; (c) a bar chart; or (d) a histogram?

5   What is the appropriate SPSS procedure for calculating the inter-quartile range for **income** (Job Survey data)?

6   What is the inter-quartile range for **satis**?

7   Why might the standard deviation be a superior measure of dispersion to the inter-quartile range?

Sampling and statistical significance

I N T H I S C H A P T E R, we will be encountering some issues which are fundamental to an appreciation of how people (or whatever is the unit of analysis)
should be selected for inclusion in a study and of how it is possible to generalise
to the population from which people are selected. These two related issues are
concerned with sampling and the statistical significance of results. In examining
sampling we will be examining the procedures for selecting people so that they
are representative of the population from which they are selected. The topic of
statistical significance raises the issue of how confident we can be that findings
relating to a sample of individuals will also be found in the population from
which the sample was selected.

Sampling

The issue of sampling is important because it is rarely the case that we have
sufficient time and resources to conduct research on all of those individuals
who could potentially be included in a study. Two points of clarification are
relevant at this early stage. We talk about sampling from a population in the
introduction to this chapter. It should be recognised that when we sample, it is
not necessarily people who are being sampled. We can just as legitimately
sample other units of analysis such as organisations, schools, local authorities,
and so on. Second, by a 'population' is meant a discrete group of units of
analysis and not just populations in the conventional sense, such as the population of England and Wales. Populations can be populations of towns, of
particular groups (e.g. all accountants in the UK), of individuals in a firm, or
of firms themselves. When we sample, we are selecting units of analysis from a
clearly defined population.

Clearly, some populations can be very large and it is unlikely that all of
the units in a population can be included because of the considerable time and
cost that such an exercise would entail. Sometimes, they can be sufficiently
small for all units to be contacted; or if they are not too large, it may be
possible to carry out postal questionnaire or telephone interview surveys on a
whole population. On the other hand, researchers are very often faced with the
need to sample. By and large, researchers will want to form a representative
sample, that is, a sample that can be treated as though it were the population.

It is rare that perfectly representative samples can be created, but the chances of forming a representative sample can be considerably enhanced by probability sampling. The distinction between probability and non-probability sampling is a basic distinction in discussions of sampling. With probability sampling, each unit of a population has a specifiable probability of inclusion in a sample. In the basic forms of probability sampling, such as simple random samples (see below), each unit will have an equal probability of inclusion.

As an example of a non-probability sampling procedure, consider the following scenario. An interviewer is asked to obtain answers to interview questions for fifty people – twenty-five of each gender. She positions herself in a shopping area in a town at 9.00 a.m. on a Monday and starts interviewing people one by one. Will a representative sample be acquired? While it is not impossible that the sample is representative, there are too many doubts about its representativeness. For example, most people who work will not be shopping; she may have chosen people to be interviewed who were well-dressed; and some people may be more likely than others to use the shops by which she positions herself. In other words, there is a strong chance that the sample is not representative of the people of the town. If the sample is unrepresentative, then our ability to generalise our findings to the population from which it was selected is sharply curtailed. If we do generalise, our inferences may be incorrect. If the sample is heavily biased towards people who do not work, who appeal to the interviewer because of their appearance and who only shop in certain retail outlets, it is likely to be a poor representation of the wider population.

By contrast, probability sampling permits the selection of a sample that should be representative. The following is a discussion of the main types of probability sample that are likely to be encountered.

Simple random sample

The simple random sample is the most basic type of probability sample. Each unit in the population has an equal probability of inclusion in the sample. Like all forms of probability sample, it requires a sampling frame, which provides a complete listing of all the units in a population. Let us say that we want a representative sample of 200 non-manual employees from a firm which has 600 non-manual employees. The sample is often denoted as n and the population as N. A sampling frame is constructed which lists the 600 non-manual employees. Each employee is allocated a number between 1 and N (i.e. 600). Each employee has a probability of n/N of being included in the sample, that is,

1 in 3. Individuals will be selected for inclusion on a random basis to ensure that human choice is eliminated from decisions about who should be included and who excluded.

Each individual in the sampling frame is allocated a number 1 to N. The idea is to select n from this list. To ensure that the process is random, a table of random numbers should be consulted. These tables are usually in columns of five-digit numbers. For example, the figures might be

26938
37025
00352

Since we need to select a number of individuals which is in three digits (i.e. 200), only three digits in each five-digit random number should be considered. Let us say that we take the last three digits in each random number, that is we exclude the first two from consideration. The first case for inclusion would be that numbered 938. However, since the population is only 600, we cannot have a case numbered 938, so this figure is ignored and we proceed to the next random number. The figure 37025 implies that the case numbered 025 will be the first case for inclusion. The person numbered 025 will be the first sampled case. The next will be the person numbered 352, and so on. The process continues until n (i.e. 200) units have been selected.

By relying on a random process for the selection of individuals, the possibility of bias in the selection procedure is largely eliminated and the chance of generating a representative sample is enhanced. Sometimes, a systematic sample is selected rather than a simple random sample. With a systematic sample, the selection of individuals is undertaken directly from the sampling frame and without the need to connect random numbers and cases. In the previous example, a random start between 1 and 3 would be made. Let us say that the number is 1. The first case on the sampling frame would be included. Then, every third case would be selected, since 1 in 3 must be sampled. Thus, the fourth, seventh, tenth, thirteenth and so on would be selected. The chief advantage of the systematic sample over the simple random sample is that it obviates the need to plough through a table of random numbers and to tie in each number with a corresponding case. This procedure can be particularly time-consuming when a large sample must be selected. However, in order to select a systematic sample, the researcher must ensure that there is no inherent ordering to the list of cases in the sampling frame, since this would distort the ensuing sample and would probably mean that it was not representative.

Stratified sampling

Stratified sampling is commonly used by social scientists because it can lend an extra ingredient of precision to a simple random or systematic sample. When selecting a stratified sample, the researcher divides the population into strata. The strata must be categories of a criterion. For example, the population may be stratified according to the criterion of gender, in which case two strata – male and female – will be generated. Alternatively, the criterion may be department in the firm, resulting in possibly five strata: production, marketing, personnel, accounting, and research and development. Provided that the information is readily available, people are grouped into the strata. A simple random or systematic sample is then taken from the listing in each stratum. It is important for the stratifying criterion to be relevant to the issues in which the researcher is interested; it should not be undertaken for its own sake. The researcher may be interested in how the attitudes of non-manual employees are affected by the department to which they are attached in the firm. The advantage of stratified sampling is that it offers the possibility of greater accuracy, by ensuring that the groups that are created by a stratifying criterion are represented in the same proportions as in the population.

Table 6.1 provides an illustration of the idea of a stratified sample. The table provides the numbers of non-manual personnel in each department in the first column and the number of each department (i.e. stratum) that would be selected on a 1 in 3 basis. The important point to note is that the proportions of personnel from each department in the sample are the same as in the population. The largest department – production – has 35 per cent of all

TABLE 6.1 Devising a stratified random sample: non-manual employees in a firm

Department	Population N	Sample n
Production	210	70
Marketing	120	40
Personnel	63	21
Accounting	162	54
Research and Development	45	15
Total	600	200

non-manual employees in the firm and 35 per cent of non-manual employees in the sample. A simple random or systematic sample without stratification might have achieved the same result, but a stratified sample greatly enhances the likelihood of the proper representation of strata in the sample. Two or more stratifying criteria can be employed in tandem. For example, if the researcher were interested in the effects of gender on job attitudes, as well as belonging to different departments, we would then have ten strata (five departments × two sexes), that is, men and women in production, men and women in marketing, and so on. A 1 in 3 sample would then be taken from each of the ten strata.

If the numbers in some strata are likely to be small, it may be necessary to sample disproportionately. For example, we may sample 2 in 3 of those in Research and Development. This would mean that thirty, rather than fifteen, would be sampled from this department. However, to compensate for the extra fifteen individuals sampled in Research and Development, slightly less than 1 in 3 for Production and Accounting may need to be sampled. When this occurs, it has to be recognised that the sample is differentially weighted relative to the population, so that estimates of the sample mean will have to be corrected to reflect this weighting.

Multistage cluster sampling

One disadvantage of the probability samples covered so far is that they do not deal very well with geographically dispersed populations. If we took a simple random sample of all chartered accountants in the UK or indeed of the population of the UK itself, the resulting sample would be highly scattered. If the aim was to conduct an interview survey, interviewers would spend a great deal of time and money travelling to their respondents. A multistage cluster sample is a probability sampling procedure that allows such geographically dispersed populations to be adequately covered, while simultaneously saving interviewer time and travel costs.

Initially, the researcher samples clusters, that is, areas of the geographical region being covered. The case of seeking to sample households in a very large city can be taken as an example of the procedure. At the first stage, all of the electoral wards in the city would be ascribed a number from 1 to N and a simple random sample of wards selected. At the second stage, a simple random sample of streets in each ward might be taken. At the third stage, a simple random sample of households in the sampled streets would be selected from the list of addresses in the electoral rolls for the relevant wards. By concentrating interviewers in small regions of the city, much time and travel cost can be saved. Very often, stratification accompanies the sampling of clusters. For example, wards might be categorised in terms of an indicator of economic prosperity (e.g. high, medium and low) such as the percentage of heads of household in professional and managerial jobs. Stratification will ensure that clusters are properly represented in terms of this criterion.

Sampling problems

One of the most frequently asked questions in the context of sampling is 'How large should a sample be?' In reality, there can only be a few guidelines to answering this question, rather than a single definitive response.

First, the researcher almost always works within time and resource constraints, so that decisions about sample size must always recognise these boundaries. There is no point in working out an ideal sample size for a project if you have nowhere near the amount of resources required to bring it into effect. Second, the larger the sample the greater the accuracy. Contrary to expectations, the size of the sample relative to the size of the population (in other words n/N) is rarely relevant to the issue of a sample's accuracy. This means that sampling error – differences between the sample and the population which are due to sampling – can be reduced by increasing sampling size. However, after a certain level, increases in accuracy tend to tail off as sample size increases, so that greater accuracy becomes economically unacceptable.

Third, the problem of non-response should be borne in mind. Most sample surveys attract a certain amount of non-response. Thus, it is likely that only some of the 200 non-manual employees we sample will agree to participate in the research. If it is our aim to ensure as far as possible that 200 employees are interviewed and if we think that there may be a 20 per cent rate of non-response, it may be advisable to select 250 individuals, on the grounds that approximately 50 will be non-respondents. Finally, the researcher should bear in mind the kind of analysis he or she intends to undertake. For example, if the researcher intends to examine the relationship between department in the firm and attitudes to white-collar unions, a table in which department is crosstabulated against attitude can be envisaged. If 'attitude to white-collar unions' comprises four answers, since 'department' comprises five categories, a table of twenty 'cells' would be engendered (see discussion of contingency tables and crosstabulation in Chapter 8). In order for there to be an adequate number of cases in each cell a fairly large sample will be required.

Consequently, considerations of sample size should be sensitive to the kinds of analysis that will subsequently be required.

The issue of non-response draws attention to the fact that a well-crafted sample can be jeopardised by the failure of individuals to participate. The problem is that respondents and non-respondents may differ from each other in certain respects, so that respondents may not be representative of the population. Sometimes, researchers try to discern whether respondents are disproportionately drawn from particular groups, such as whether men are clearly more inclined not to participate than women. However, such tests can only be conducted in relation to fairly superficial characteristics like gender; deeper differences, such as attitudinal ones, cannot be readily tested. In addition, some members of a sample may not be contactable, because they have moved or are on holiday. Moreover, even when a questionnaire is answered, there may still be questions which, by design or error, are not answered. Each of these three elements – non-response, inability to contact and missing information for certain variables – may be a source of bias, since we do not know how representative those who do respond to each variable are of the population.

Finally, although social scientists are well aware of the advantages of probability sampling procedures, a great deal of research does not derive from probability samples. In a review of 126 articles in the field of organisation studies which were based on correlational research, Mitchell (1985) found that only twenty-one were based on probability samples. The rest used convenience samples, that is, samples which are either 'chosen' by the investigator or which choose themselves (e.g. volunteers). However, when it is borne in mind that response rates to sample surveys are often quite low and are declining (Goyder, 1988), the difference between research based on random samples and convenience samples in terms of their relative representativeness is not always as great as is sometimes implied. None the less, many of the statistical tests and procedures to be encountered later in this book assume that the data derive from a random sample. The point being made here is that this require-ment is often not fulfilled and that, even when a random sample has been used, factors like non-response may adversely affect its random qualities.

Statistical significance

How do we know if a sample is typical or representative of the population from which it has been drawn? To find this out we need to be able to describe the nature of the sample and the population. This is done in terms of the distributions of their values. Thus, for example, if we wanted to find out whether the proportion of men to women in our sample was similar to that in some specified population, we would compare the two proportions. The main tests for tackling such problems are described in Chapters 7 and 9. It should be noted that the same principle lies behind all statistical tests, including those concerned with describing the relationship between two or more variables. Here, the basic idea underlying them will be outlined.

To do this we will take the simple case of wanting to discover whether a coin was unbiased in the sense that it lands heads and tails an equal number of times. The number of times we tossed the coin would constitute the sample while the population would be the outcomes we would theoretically expect if the coin was unbiased. If we flipped the coin just once, then the probability of it turning up heads is once every two throws or 0.5. In other words, we would have to toss it at least twice to determine if both possibilities occur. If we were to do this, however, there would be four possible theoretical outcomes as shown in Table 6.2: (1) a tail followed by a head; (2) a head followed by a tail; (3) two tails; and (4) two heads. What happens on each throw is *independent* of, or not affected, by the outcome of any other throw. If the coin was unbiased, then each of the four outcomes would be equally probable. In other words, the probability of obtaining either two tails or two heads (but not both possibilities) is one in four, or 0.25, while that of obtaining a head and a tail is two in four, or 0.5. The probability of obtaining a head and a tail (0.5) is greater than that of two tails (0.25) or two heads (0.25) but is the same as that for two tails and two heads combined (0.25 + 0.25). From this it should be clear that it is not possible to draw conclusions about a coin being unbiased from so few throws or such a small sample. This is because the frequency of improbable events is much greater with smaller samples. Consequently, it is much more difficult with such samples to determine whether they come from a certain population.

TABLE 6.2   Four possible outcomes of tossing a coin twice

Possible outcomes			Probability (p)
1	Head	Tail	0.25 ⎱ = 0.5
2	Tail	Head	0.25 ⎰
3	Head	Head	0.25
4	Tail	Tail	0.25

If we plot or draw the distribution of the probability of obtaining the same proportion of heads to tails as shown in Figure 6.1, then it will take the shape of an inverted 'V'. This shape will contain all the possible outcomes which will add up to 1 (0.25 + 0.25 + 0.25 + 0.25 = 1).

Theoretically, the more often we throw the coin, the more similar the distribution of the possible outcomes will be to an inverted 'U' or normal distribution. Suppose, for example, we threw the same coin six times (or, what amounts to the same thing, six coins once). If we did this, there would be sixty-four possible outcomes. These are shown in Table 6.3. The total number of outcomes can be calculated by multiplying the number of possible outcomes on each occasion (2) by those of the other occasions ($2 \times 2 \times 2 \times 2 \times 2 \times 2 = 64$). The probability of obtaining six heads or six tails in a row (but not both) would be one in sixty-four or about 0.016. Since there are six possible ways in which one head and five tails can be had, the probability of achieving this is six out of sixty-four or about 0.10 (i.e. 0.016×6). The distribution of the probability of obtaining different sequences of the same number of tails and heads grouped together (for example, the six sequences of finding five tails and a head) is presented in Figure 6.2.

It should be clear from this discussion that we can never be 100 per cent certain that the coin is unbiased, because even if we threw it 1,000 times, there is a very small chance that it would turn up all heads or all tails on every one of those throws. So what we do is to set a criterion or cut-off point at or beyond which we assume the coin will be judged to be biased. This point is arbitrary and is referred to as the *significance level*. It is usually set at a probability or p level of 0.05 or five times out of a hundred. Since the coin can be biased in one of two ways, that is, in favour of either heads or tails, this 5 per cent is

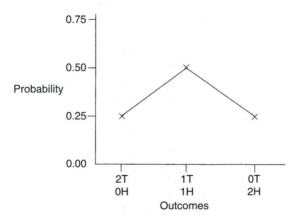

FIGURE 6.1 The distribution of similar theoretical outcomes of tossing a coin twice

TABLE 6.3 Theoretical outcomes of tossing a coin six times and the probabilities of similar outcomes

	Theoretical outcomes	Probability		Theoretical outcomes	Probability
1	TTTTTT	0.016	64	HHHHHH	0.016
2	TTTTTH		63	HHHHHT	
3	TTTTHT		62	HHHHTH	
4	TTTHTT	0.094	61	HHHTHH	0.094
5	TTHTTT		60	HHTHHH	
6	THTTTT		59	HTHHHH	
7	HTTTTT		58	THHHHH	
8	TTTTHH		57	HHHHTT	
9	TTTHHT		56	HHHTTH	
10	TTHHTT		55	HHTTHH	
11	TTTHTH		54	HHHTHT	
12	TTHTHT		53	HHTHTH	
13	TTHTTH		52	HHTHHT	
14	THTHTT		51	HTHTHH	
15	THHTTT	0.234	50	HTTHHH	0.234
16	THTTTH		49	HTHHHT	
17	THTTHT		48	HTHHTH	
18	HTTHTT		47	THHTHH	
19	HTTTHT		46	THHHTH	
20	HTHTTT		45	THTHHH	
21	HTTTTH		44	THHHHT	
22	HHTTTT		43	TTHHHH	
23	TTTHHH		42	HHHTTT	
24	TTHHHT		41	HHTTTH	
25	TTHHTH		40	HHTTHT	
26	TTHTHH		39	HHTHTT	
27	THTHTH		38	HTHTHT	
28	THTHHT		37	HTHTTH	0.312
29	THHTTH		36	HTTHHT	
30	THHTHT		35	HTTHTH	
31	THTTHH		34	HTHHTT	
32	THHHTT		33	HTTTHH	

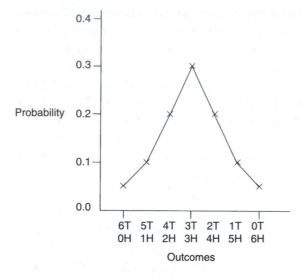

FIGURE 6.2   The distribution of similar theoretical outcomes of tossing a coin six times

shared equally between these two possibilities. This means, in effect, that the probability of the coin being biased towards heads will be 0.025 and that the probability of its being biased towards tails will also be 0.025. In other words, if it turns up heads or tails six times in a row, then the probability of both these outcomes occurring would be about 0.032 (i.e. 0.016 + 0.016), which is below the probability of 0.05. If either of these two events happened we would accept that the coin was biased. If, however, it landed tails once and heads five times, or heads once and tails five times, there are six ways in which either of these two outcomes could happen. Consequently, the probability of either one happening is six out of sixty-four or about 0.10. The probability of both outcomes occurring is about 0.2 (i.e. 0.10 + 0.10). In this case, we would have to accept that the coin was unbiased since this probability level is above the criterion of 0.05.

Because we can never be 100 per cent certain that the coin is either biased or unbiased, we can make one of two kinds of error. The first kind is to decide that the coin is biased when it is not. This is known as a *Type I error* and is sometimes referred to as α (alpha). For example, as we have seen, an unbiased coin may land heads six times in a row. The second kind of error is to judge the coin to be unbiased when it is biased. This is called a *Type II error* and is represented by β (beta). It is possible, for instance, for a biased coin to come up tails once and heads five times. We can reduce the possibility of making a Type I error by accepting a lower level of significance, say 0.01 instead of 0.05.

But doing this increases the probability of making a Type II error. In other words, the probability of a Type I error is inversely related to that of a Type II one. The more likely we are to make a Type I error, the less likely we are to commit a Type II error.

At this stage, it is useful to discuss briefly three kinds of probability distribution. The first is known as a *binomial* distribution and is based on the idea that if only either of two outcomes can occur on any one occasion (for example, heads or tails if a coin is thrown), then we can work out the theoretical distribution of the different combinations of outcomes which could occur if we knew the number of occasions that had taken place. One characteristic of this distribution is that it consists of a limited or finite number of events. If, however, we threw an infinite number of coins an infinite number of times, then we would have a distribution which would consist of an infinite possibility of events. This distribution is known variously as a DeMoivre's, Gaussian, standard normal or z curve distribution. If random samples of these probabilities are taken and plotted, then the shape of those distributions will depend on the size of the samples. Smaller samples will produce flatter distributions with thicker tails than the normal distribution, while larger ones will be very similar to it. These distributions are known as t distributions. What this means is that when we want to know the likelihood that a particular series of events could have occurred by chance, we need to take into account the size of the sample on which those events are based.

So far, in order to convey the idea that certain events may occur just by chance, we have used the example of tossing a coin. Although this may seem a bit remote from the kinds of data we collect in the social sciences, we use this underlying principle to determine issues such as whether a sample is representative of its population and whether two or more samples or treatments differ from each other. Suppose we drew a small sample of six people and wanted to determine if the proportion of males to females in it was similar to that of the population in which the number of men and women are equal. Each person can only be male or female. Since there are six people, there are sixty-four possible outcomes (i.e. $2 \times 2 \times 2 \times 2 \times 2 \times 2$). These, of course, are the same as those displayed in Table 6.3 except that we now substitute males for tails and females for heads. The joint probability of all six people being either male or female would be about 0.03 (i.e. 0.016 + 0.016), so that if this were the result we would reject the notion that the sample was representative of the population. However, if one was male and the other five female, or there was one female and five males, then the probability of this occurring by chance would be about 0.2 (i.e. 0.096 + 0.096). This would mean that at the 0.05

significance level we would accept either of these two outcomes or samples as being typical of the population because the probability of obtaining these outcomes is greater than the 0.05 level. This shows that sample values can diverge quite widely from those of their populations and still be drawn from them, although it should be emphasised that this outcome would be less frequent the larger the sample. Statistical tests which compare a sample with a population are known as *one-sample tests* and can be found in the next chapter.

The same principle underlies tests which have been developed to find out if two or more samples or treatments come from the same population or different ones, although this is a little more difficult to grasp. For example, we may be interested in finding out whether women are more perceptive than men, or whether alcohol impairs performance. In the first case, the two samples are women and men while in the second they are alcohol and no alcohol. Once again, in order to explain the idea that underlies these tests, it may be useful to think about it initially in terms of throwing a coin, except that this time we throw two coins. The two coins represent the two samples. We want to know whether the two coins differ in their tendency to be unbiased. If the two coins were unbiased and if we were to throw them six times each, then we should expect the two sets of theoretical outcomes obtained to be the same as that in Table 6.3. In other words, the two distributions should overlap each other exactly.

Now if we threw the two coins six times each, it is unlikely that the empirical outcomes would be precisely the same, even if the coins were unbiased. In fact, we can work out the theoretical probability of the two distributions being different in the same way as we did earlier for the coin turning up heads or tails. If we do this, there are four possible outcomes: (1) two tails; (2) two heads; (3) one tail and one head; and (4) one head and one tail. If we look at these outcomes in terms of whether they are the same or different, then two of them are the same (two tails and two heads) while two of them are different (one tail and one head, and vice versa). In other words, the probability of finding a difference is two out of four or 0.5, which is the same as that for discovering no difference. We stand an equal chance of finding no difference as we do of a difference if we throw two unbiased coins once.

Applying this idea to the kind of question that may be asked in the social sciences, we may wish to find out if women and men differ in their perceptiveness. There are three possible answers to this question: (1) women may be more perceptive than men; (2) they may be no different from them; or (3) they may be less perceptive than them. In other words, we can have three different expectations or hypotheses about what the answer might be. Not expecting any difference is known as the *null hypothesis*. Anticipating a difference but not being able to predict what it is likely to be is called a *non-directional hypothesis*. However, it is unlikely that we would ask this sort of question if we did not expect a difference of a particular nature, since there are an infinite number of such questions which can be posed. In carrying out research we are often concerned with showing that a particular relationship either holds or does not hold between two or more variables. In other words, we are examining the direction as well as the existence of a relationship. In this case, we may be testing the idea that women are more perceptive than men. This would be an example of a *directional hypothesis*. As we shall see, specifying the direction of the hypothesis means that we can adopt a slightly higher and more lenient level of significance.

Since there are three possible outcomes (i.e. a probability of 0.33 for any one outcome) for each paired comparison, if we tested this hypothesis on a small sample of five men and five women, then the probability of all five women being more perceptive than men just by chance would be about 0.004 (i.e. $0.33 \times 0.33 \times 0.33 \times 0.33 \times 0.33$). If we obtained this result, and if we adopted the usual 0.05 or 5 per cent as the significance level at or below which this finding is unlikely to be due to chance, then we would accept the hypothesis since 0.004 is less than 0.05. In other words, we would state that women were significantly more perceptive than men below the 5 per cent level – see Figure 6.3(a). As we shall see, SPSS usually provides the exact level of significance for each test. It has been customary in the social sciences to provide the significance level only for results which fall at or below the 0.05 level and to do so for certain cut-off points below that such as 0.01, 0.001, and 0.0001. However, with the advent of computer programs such as SPSS which give exact significance levels, it could be argued that this tradition does not maximise the information that could be supplied without any obvious disadvantages.

If, however, we found that only four of the women were more perceptive than the men, then the probability of this happening by chance would be about 0.04, since there are ten ways or sequences in which this result could occur ($0.004 \times 10 = 0.04$). This finding is still significant. However, if we had adopted a non-directional hypothesis and had simply expected a difference between men and women without specifying its direction, then this result would not be significant at the 0.05 level since this 0.05 would have to be shared between both tails of the distribution of possible outcomes as in Figure 6.3(b). In other words, it would become 0.025 at either end of the distribution. This result would require a probability level of 0.025 or less to be

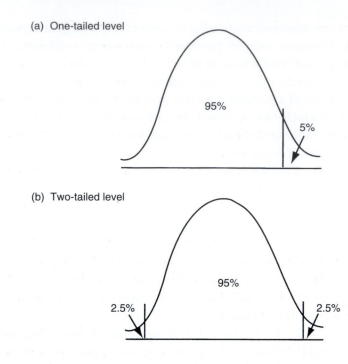

(a) One-tailed level

95%

5%

(b) Two-tailed level

95%

2.5%

2.5%

FIGURE 6.3 One-tailed and two-tailed 0.05 levels of significance

significant when stated as a non-directional hypothesis. As it is, the probability of either four women being more perceptive than men or four men being more perceptive than women is the sum of these two probabilities, namely 0.08, which is above the 0.05 level. The important point to note is that non-directional hypotheses require *two-tailed* significance levels while directional hypotheses only need *one-tailed* ones. If we find a difference between two samples or treatments we did not expect, then to test the significance of this result we need to use a two-tailed test.

It may be worth reiterating at this stage that a finding of four out of the five women being more perceptive than the five men may still be obtained by chance even at the 0.04 one-tailed level. In other words, this means that there remains a four in a hundred possibility that this result could be due to chance. In accepting this level of significance for rejecting the null hypothesis that there is no difference between men and women, we may be committing a Type I error, namely thinking that there is a difference between them when in fact there is no such difference. In other words, a Type I error is rejecting the null hypothesis when it is true, as shown in Table 6.4. We may reduce the probability of making this kind of error by lowering the significance level from 0.05 to 0.01, but this increases the probability of committing a Type II

TABLE 6.4 Type I and Type II errors

		Reality	
		No difference	*A difference*
Interpretation of reality	Accept no difference	Correct	Type II error β
	Accept a difference	Type I error α	Correct

error, which is accepting that there is no difference when there is one. A Type II error is accepting the null hypothesis when it is false. Setting the significance level at 0.01 means that the finding that four out of the five women were more perceptive than the men is assuming that this result is due to chance when it may be indicating a real difference.

The probability of correctly assuming that there is a difference when there actually is one is known as the *power* of a test. A powerful test is one that is more likely to indicate a significant difference when such a difference exists. Statistical power is inversely related to the probability of making a Type II error and is calculated by subtracting beta from one (i.e. $1 - \beta$).

Finally, it is important to realise that the level of significance has nothing to do with the size or importance of a difference. It is simply concerned with the probability of that difference arising by chance. In other words, a difference between two samples or two treatments which is significant at the 0.05 level is not necessarily bigger than one which is significant at the 0.0001 level. The latter difference is only less probable than the former one.

Inferring from samples to populations

The section so far has raised the prospect of being able to generalise from a sample to a population. We can never know for sure whether a characteristic we find in a sample applies to the population from which the sample was randomly selected. As the discussion so far suggests, what we can do is to estimate the degree of confidence we can have in the characteristic we find. If we find, as we did in Chapter 5, that the mean income in the Job Survey is £15,638.24, how confident can we be that this is the mean income for the population of workers in the firm as a whole?

A crucial consideration in determining the degree of confidence that we can have in a mean based on a sample of the population is the *standard error of the mean*, which is the standard deviation of the sample means. This notion is based on the following considerations. The sample that we select is only one of an incredibly large number of random samples that could have been selected. Some of these samples would find a mean that is the same as the population mean, some will be very close to it (either above or below) and some will be further away from it (again, either above or below the population mean). If we have a population that is normally distributed, the distribution of all possible sample means will also be normally distributed. This suggests that most sample means will be the same as or close to the population mean, but that some will deviate from it by quite a large amount. The standard error of the mean expresses the degree of dispersion of these means. We know from the discussion in Chapter 5 concerning the attributes of a normal distribution that 95.44 per cent of all cases lie within two standard deviations of the population mean. More precisely, we know that 95 per cent of cases will lie within a range that is plus or minus 1.96 standard deviations of the mean. Since the distribution of sample means is normally distributed around the population mean, we can deduce that 95 per cent of all samples will lie within a range that is plus or minus 1.96 standard errors from the population mean. Needless to say, the corollary of this is that 5 per cent of samples will lie outside that range. This is likely to occur when there is a high level of sampling error.

This reasoning becomes important in research because we can infer the upper and lower levels of range within which the population mean will fall. This range is known as the *confidence interval*. We can infer that there is a 95 per cent chance that the population mean will lie between the sample mean plus or minus 1.96 standard errors of the mean. In fact, we can see from Table 5.6 that not only does SPSS provide the standard error of the mean (242.04), it also gives us the 95% confidence intervals. We can be 95 per cent confident that the population mean will lie between £15,155.13 and £16,121.34. It is always possible that the mean that you find in your research is based on a highly unrepresentative sample and is therefore one of the 5 per cent of sample means falling outside the range of plus or minus 1.96 standard errors of the population mean. Essentially, we are taking a gamble that our sample mean is one of the 95 per cent that lies within the range.

The standard error of the mean is calculated by dividing the standard deviation (which in this case is 1995.89) by the square root of the sample size (68). As this calculation implies, the more dispersed the sample is around the mean (i.e. the larger the standard deviation), the larger the sample error of the mean will be. This in turn means that the confidence interval range will be larger.

A further consideration is that there may be research issues where you need to be more than 95 per cent confident that the population mean lies within the confidence interval. For the bulk of social issues, the 95 per cent level of confidence is adequate, but there may be occasions when you need to be more confident. If, for example, you wanted to be 99 per cent confident that the population mean fell within the confidence interval, a wider range of upper and lower values would need to be specified. This is calculated as the sample mean plus or minus 2.58 standard errors of the mean. When you use **Explore** to provide confidence interval information, it uses the 95 per cent confidence level as a default selection. To change the default confidence level, while in the **Explore** dialog box (Box 5.9):

→**Statistics...** [opens **Explore: Statistics** subdialog box] change **Confidence Interval for Mean:** from **95** to **99** %

→**Continue** [closes **Explore: Statistics** subdialog box]

→**OK**

The confidence interval is then £14996.54 to £16279.93. It means that you can be 99 per cent confident that the population mean lies within that range. Figure 6.4 attempts to capture these ideas.

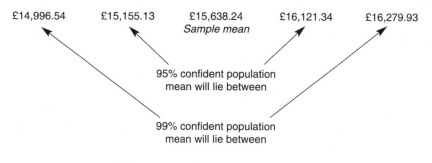

£14,996.54   £15,155.13   £15,638.24   £16,121.34   £16,279.93
                                    Sample mean

95% confident population
mean will lie between

99% confident population
mean will lie between

FIGURE 6.4 Confidence intervals

Exercises

1   What is the difference between a random sample and a representative sample?

2   Why might a stratified sample be superior to a simple random sample?

3   In what context might multistage cluster sampling be particularly useful?

4   If a sample of grocery shops were selected randomly from the Yellow Pages in your town, would you necessarily have a representative sample?

5   Flip a coin four times. What is the probability of finding the particular sequence of outcomes you did?

6   If the coin were unbiased, would you obtain two heads and two tails if you threw it four times?

7   What is the probability of obtaining any sequence of two heads and two tails?

8   You have developed a test of general knowledge, which consists of a hundred statements, half of which are false and half of which are true. Each person is given one point for a correct answer. How many points is someone who has no general knowledge most likely to achieve on this test?

9   Fifty people are tested to see if they can tell margarine from butter. Half of them are given butter and the other half are given margarine. They have to say which of these two products they were given (i.e. there were no 'don't knows'). If people cannot discriminate between them, how many people on average are likely to guess correctly?

10 If we wanted to see if women were more talkative than men, what would the null hypothesis be?

11 What would the non-directional hypothesis be?

12 What is the 95 per cent confidence interval for **age** in the Job Survey?

Bivariate analysis: exploring differences between scores on two variables

IN THIS CHAPTER we will be looking at ways of determining whether the differences between the distributions of two variables are statistically significant. Thus, for example, when analysing data we may wish to know the answers to some of the following kinds of questions: Is the proportion of black to white workers the same among men as it is among women? Do women workers earn less than their male counterparts? Does job satisfaction change from one month to the next? Do the scores in one treatment group differ from those in another?

In looking at differences between two variables, the variable which we use to form our comparison groups usually has a small number of values or levels, say between two and six. We shall call this the comparison-group variable to distinguish it from the other one, which we shall refer to as the criterion variable. The comparison variable is sometimes known as the *independent* variable, and the criterion variable as the *dependent* one. An example of a comparison group variable would be gender if we wanted to compare men with women. This typically has two levels (i.e. men and women) which go to make up two comparison groups. Race or ethnic origin, on the other hand, may take on two or more levels (e.g. Caucasian, Negroid, Asian, and Mongolian), thereby creating two or more comparison groups. Other examples of comparison-group variables include different experimental treatments (for example, drugs versus psychotherapy in treating depression), different points in time (for example, two consecutive months), and the categorisation of participants into various levels on some variable (such as high, intermediate, and low job satisfaction). The other variable is the one that we shall use to make our comparison (for example, income or job satisfaction).

Criteria for selecting bivariate tests of differences

There are a relatively large number of statistical tests to determine whether a difference between two or more groups is significant. In deciding which is the most appropriate statistical test to use to analyse your data, it is necessary to bear the following considerations in mind.

Categorical data

If the data are of a categorical or nominal nature, where the values refer to the number or frequency of cases that fall within particular categories such as the number of black female workers, it is only possible to use what is referred to as a *non-parametric* test (see below for an explanation). Thus, for example, in trying to determine whether there are significantly more white than black female employees, it would be necessary to use a non-parametric test.

Ordinal and interval/ratio data

If the data are of a non-categorical nature, such as the rating of how skilled workers are or how much they earn, then it is necessary to decide whether it is more appropriate to use a *parametric* or a *non-parametric* test. Since this issue is a complex and controversial one, it will be discussed later in some detail.

Means or variances?

Most investigators who use parametric tests are primarily interested in checking for differences between means. Differences in *variances* are also normally carried out but only to determine the appropriateness of using such a test to check for differences in the means. Variance is an expression showing the spread or dispersion of data around the mean and is the square of the standard deviation. If the variances are found to differ markedly, then it may be more appropriate to use a non-parametric test. However, differences in variance (i.e. variability) may be of interest in their own right and so these tests have been listed separately. Thus, for example, it may be reasonable to suppose that the variability of job satisfaction of women will be greater than that of men, but that there will be no difference in their mean scores. In this case, it would also be necessary to pay attention to the differences between the variances to determine if this is so.

Related or unrelated comparison groups?

Which test you use also depends on whether the values that you want to compare come from different cases or from the same or similar ones. If, for example, you are comparing different groups of people such as men and women or people who have been assigned to different experimental treatments, then you are dealing with unrelated samples of participants. It is worth noting that this kind of situation or design is also referred to in some of the following other ways: *independent* or *uncorrelated* groups or samples; and *between-subjects* design. If, on the other hand, you are comparing the way that the same people have responded on separate occasions or under different conditions, then you are dealing with *related* samples of observations. This is also true of groups of people who are or have been *matched* or *paired* on one or more important characteristics such as, for example, husbands and wives, which may also make them more similar in terms of the criterion variable under study. Once again, there are a number of other terms used to describe related scores such as the following: *dependent* or *correlated* groups or samples; *repeated measures*; and *within-subjects* design.

Two or more comparison groups?

Different tests are generally used to compare two rather than three or more comparison groups.

The tests to be used given these criteria are listed in Table 7.1. Readers may wish to use this table as a guide to the selection of tests appropriate to their needs. Page numbers are inserted in the table cells to facilitate finding the appropriate tests.

Parametric versus non-parametric tests

One of the unresolved issues in data analysis is the question of when parametric rather than non-parametric tests should be used. Some writers have argued that it is only appropriate to use parametric tests when the data fulfil the following three conditions: (1) the level or scale of measurement is of equal interval or ratio scaling, that is, more than ordinal; (2) the distribution of the population scores is normal; and (3) the variances of both variables are equal or *homogeneous*. The term *parameter* refers to a measure which describes the distribution of the population such as the mean or variance. Since parametric tests are based on the assumption that we know certain characteristics of the population from which the sample is drawn, they are called *parametric tests*. Non-parametric or *distribution-free* tests are so named because they do not depend on assumptions about the precise form of the distribution of the sampled populations.

However, the need to meet these three conditions for using parametric tests has been strongly questioned. Some of the arguments will be mentioned here and these will be simply stated, with sources provided where further details can be found. As far as the first condition is concerned, level of measurement, it has been suggested that parametric tests can also be used with ordinal variables since tests apply to numbers and not to what those numbers signify (for example, Lord, 1953). Thus, for example, we apply these tests to determine if two scores differ. We know what these scores indicate, but the test obviously does not. Therefore, the data are treated as if they are of interval or ratio scaling. Furthermore, it can be argued that since many psychological and sociological variables such as attitudes are basically ordinal in nature (see p. 70), parametric tests should not be used to analyse them if this first condition is valid. However, it should be noted that parametric tests are routinely applied to such variables.

With respect to the second and third conditions, the populations being normally distributed and of equal variances, a number of studies have been carried out (for example, Boneau, 1960; Games and Lucas, 1966) where the values of the statistics used to analyse samples drawn from populations which have been artificially set up to violate these conditions have been found not to differ greatly from those for samples which have been drawn from populations which do not violate these conditions. Tests which are able to withstand such violations are described as being *robust*.

One exception to this general finding was where both the size of the samples and the variances were unequal, although some have argued that this exception applies even with equal sample sizes (Wilcox, 1987). Another exception was where both distributions of scores were non-normal. In such circumstances, it may be prudent to compare the results of a non-parametric test with those of a parametric test. Where the distributions of scores are not normal, it may also be worth running a parametric test on the scores as they are and after they have been transformed closer to normality. For more details on transforming scores to normality, see Mosteller and Tukey (1977). It may also be more desirable to use non-parametric tests when the size of the samples is small, say under 15, since in these circumstances it is more difficult to determine the extent to which these conditions have been met. A fuller description of non-parametric tests may be found in Siegel and Castellan (1988) or Conover (1980).

TABLE 7.1 Tests of differences

Nature of criterion variable	Type of test	Type of data	Number of comparison groups	Name of test	Page numbers
Categorical: nominal or frequency	Non-parametric	Unrelated	1	Binomial	148–50
			2+	Chi-square for one sample	150–4
			2+	Chi-square for more than one sample	154–7
		Related	2	McNemar	157–60
			3+	Cochran Q	160–1
Non-categorical:	Non-parametric	Unrelated	1–2	Kolmogorov–Smirnov	161–5
			2	Mann–Whitney U	167–9
			2+	Median	165–7
			3+	Kruskal–Wallis H	169–70

	Related	2	Sign	170–1
		2	Wilcoxon	171–2
		3+	Friedman	173
Parametric: means	Unrelated	1–2	t	174–80
		2+	One-way analysis of variance	180–6
		2+	Two-way analysis of variance	255–62
	Related	2	t	186–90
		2+	Single factor repeated measures	190–6
	Related and unrelated	2+	Two-way analysis of variance with repeated measures on one factor	269–74
		2+	One-way analysis of covariance	262–7
		2+	Three-way analysis of covariance with repeated measures on one factor	274–80
Parametric: variances	Unrelated	2+	Levene's test	177, 182–3, 185
	Related	2	t	190

Categorical variables and non-parametric tests

Binomial test for one dichotomous variable

The binomial test is used to compare the frequency of cases actually found in the two categories of a dichotomous variable with those which are expected on some basis. Suppose, for example, that we wanted to find out whether the ratio of female to male workers in the industry covered by our Job Survey was the same as that in the industry in general, which we knew to be 1:3. We could do this by carrying out a binomial test in which the proportion of women in our survey was compared with that of an expected proportion of 1:4 or one out of every four workers.

To do this with SPSS, we would use the following sequence:

→**Analyze** →**Nonparametric Tests** →**Binomial...** [opens **Binomial Test** dialog box shown in Box 7.1]

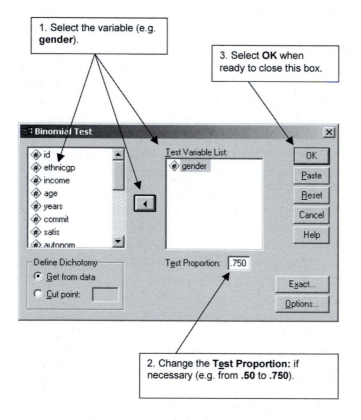

BOX 7.1   Binomial Test dialog box

➔**gender** ➔►button [puts **gender** under **Test Variable List:**]

➔box called **Test Proportion:** and type **.75** ➔**OK**

Since males have been coded as 1, they form the first category and the proportion of them becomes 3:4 or 0.75. The default value is 0.5. The two categories
compared are taken from the data by default (**Get from data**) so the lower
category (e.g. **1**) of a dichotomous variable such as **gender** forms one group
and the higher category (e.g. **2**) the other group. If there are more than two
groups (such as in **ethnicgp**) and we wish to compare two of them (such as
Asian and West Indian workers), we would have to select these two groups.
Sometimes it may be possible to define our two groups by using a cut-off
point. For instance, if we wished to determine if there were equal numbers
of black and white workers, we could do this by typing **1** in the box entitled
Cut point:. All cases equal to or less than this point form the first category,
while all the others form the second category.

The output for the first procedure is displayed in Table 7.2. (It should
be noted that there are no zeros before the decimal points; this reflects a
general tendency in SPSS that where the maximum value is one, there is no
zero before the decimal point.) As we can see, the number of males (thirty-
nine) is only slightly greater than that of females (thirty-one) and so it would
appear from an inspection of these figures that the ratio of males to females
is nearer 1:1 than 3:1. The hypothesis that the proportion of males to
females is 0.75 is rejected since the probability of obtaining this result by
chance is highly unlikely with p equal to 0.000. SPSS gives p to three decimal
places. Where, as in this case, p consists of three zeros, the fourth decimal place
is 5 or lower which means that p is at least 0.0005. Consequently, the difference
between the obtained and the hypothesized outcome is interpreted as being
statistically different. Therefore, we would conclude that the ratio of male to
female workers is not 3:1.

TABLE 7.2 Binomial test comparing proportion of men and women
(Job Survey)

Binomial Test

		Category	N	Observed Prop.	Test Prop.	Asymp. Sig. (1-tailed)
gender	Group 1	Men	39	.56	.75	.000[a,b]
	Group 2	Women	31	.44		
	Total		70	1.00		

a. Alternative hypothesis states that the proportion of cases in the first group < .75.

b. Based on Z Approximation.

The output for comparing the proportion of white and non-white workers is shown in Table 7.3. The number of white workers (thirty-six) is almost the same as that of non-white ones (thirty-four), so the ratio is close to 1:1. The hypothesis that there are equal numbers of white and non-white workers is accepted since the probability of obtaining this result by chance is high (i.e. $p = 0.90$). In other words, since there is no significant difference between the obtained and the hypothesised result, we would conclude that there are equal numbers of white and non-white workers.

Incidentally, the similarity of these examples to those used to illustrate the notion of significance testing in the previous chapter should be noted, except that there we were comparing the frequency of finding one tail (or one male) to every five heads (or five females) against an expected frequency or probability of 0.5. To work this out using SPSS, we would have to create a data file which consisted of one sequence of such a frequency and then carry out a binomial test on it.

Chi-square test for one sample

If we want to compare the observed frequencies of cases with those expected in a variable which has more than two categories, then we use a chi-square or χ^2 (pronounced 'kye-square') test rather than a binomial test. If, for instance, we wished to know whether there were equal numbers of workers from the four different ethnic groups coded in our Job Survey data, then we would use a chi-square test for one sample. We would use the following procedure to do this.

→**Analyze** →**Nonparametric Tests** →**Chi-Square...** [opens **Chi-Square Test** dialog box shown in Box 7.2]

TABLE 7.3 Binomial test comparing proportion of whites and non-whites (Job Survey)

Binomial Test

		Category	N	Observed Prop.	Test Prop.	Asymp. Sig. (2-tailed)
ethnic group	Group 1	<= 1	36	.51	.50	.905[a]
	Group 2	> 1	34	.49		
	Total		70	1.00		

a. Based on Z Approximation.

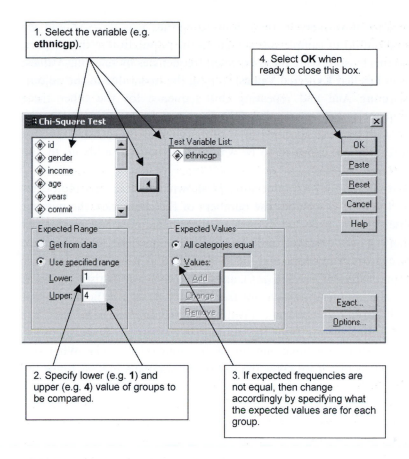

1. Select the variable (e.g. **ethnicgp**).

4. Select **OK** when ready to close this box.

2. Specify lower (e.g. **1**) and upper (e.g. **4**) value of groups to be compared.

3. If expected frequencies are not equal, then change accordingly by specifying what the expected values are for each group.

BOX 7.2   Chi-Square Test dialog box

→**ethnicgp** →▶button [puts **ethnicgp** under <u>T</u>**est Variable List:**] →**Use specified range** and type **1** [in box labelled <u>L</u>**ower:**] →box called <u>U</u>**pper:** and type **4** →**OK**

The range of categories to be examined needs to be specified if not all of them are to be included. In this example, we have chosen to exclude the 'other' category by listing categories one to four. This fifth category would have been included in this analysis by default if we had not specifically excluded it.

The expected frequencies are assumed to be equal, unless explicitly specified otherwise. In other words, in this case we are testing the hypothesis that the four categories will contain the same number of workers, or one in four. If we expect them to be different, then we need to list these expected frequencies. If, for example, we knew that in the industry covered by our Job

Survey the ratio of workers in these four categories was 95:2:2:1 and we wished to find out if our sample was similar to the population in this respect, we would do this by specifying these expected frequencies by selecting **Values:** (in the section labelled **Expected Values**), typing the first value in the adjoining box, selecting **Add** and repeating this sequence for the other three expected frequencies before selecting **OK**. Expected frequencies need to be greater than zero and are specified as a proportion of those listed. In this case, 95 out of 100 are expected to be white since the total adds up to 100 ($95 + 2 + 2 + 1$).

The output for the first procedure is shown in Table 7.4. Note that for this test, the display includes the numbers of the categories, the number of cases observed and expected in each of these categories, the residual or difference between the observed and the expected frequencies, the chi-square statistic, the degrees of freedom, and the level of significance.

The term *degrees of freedom* (*d.f.*), associated with any statistic, refers to the number of components which are free to vary. It is a difficult concept which is well explained elsewhere (Walker, 1940). In this case, they are calculated by subtracting 1 from the number of categories. Since there are four categories, there are three degrees of freedom (i.e. $4 - 1$). What this means essentially is that if we know the size of the sample and if we know the

TABLE 7.4   One-sample chi-square test comparing number of people in ethnic groups (Job Survey)

Frequencies

	Category	Observed N	Expected N	Residual
	ethnic group			
1	White	36	17.5	18.5
2	Asian	18	17.5	.5
3	West Indian	14	17.5	-3.5
4	African	2	17.5	-15.5
Total		70		

Test Statistics

	ethnic group
Chi-Square[a]	34.000
df	3
Asymp. Sig.	.000

a. 0 cells (.0%) have expected frequencies less than 5. The minimum expected cell frequency is 17.5.

observed frequencies in three of the four categories, then we can work out from this the observed frequencies in the remaining category. In other words, if we know one of the values, the other three are free to vary.

As we can see, the observed frequencies are significantly different ($p <$ 0.0005) from the expected ones of there being an equal number of cases in each of the four categories. In other words, since the probability of obtaining this result by chance is very low (at least 5 out of 10,000 times), we would conclude that the number of workers in each ethnic group is not equal.

There is a restriction on using chi-square when the expected frequencies are small. With only two categories (or one degree of freedom), the number of cases expected to fall in these categories should be at least five before this test can be applied. If the expected frequencies are less than five, then the binomial test should be used instead. With three or more categories (or more than one degree of freedom), chi-square should not be used when any expected frequency is smaller than 1, or when more than 20 per cent of the expected frequencies are smaller than 5. In these situations, it may be possible to increase the expected frequencies in a category by combining it with those of another.

An example of the latter case is the second statistical analysis we asked for, the output of which is presented in Table 7.5. Here, three of the expected frequencies fall below 2, one of which is below 1. We would need a much larger

TABLE 7.5 One-sample chi-square with insufficient cases (Job Survey)

Frequencies

	Category	Observed N	Expected N	Residual
		ethnic group		
1	White	36	66.5	-30.5
2	Asian	18	1.4	16.6
3	West Indian	14	1.4	12.6
4	African	2	.7	1.3
Total		70		

Test Statistics

	ethnic group
Chi-Square[a]	326.632
df	3
Asymp. Sig.	.000

a. 3 cells (75.0%) have expected frequencies less than 5. The minimum expected cell frequency is .7.

sample of participants to use a chi-square test on these data. If we had only two categories, whites and non-whites, we would require a minimum sample of 100 in order to have an expected frequency of 5 in the non-white category. Consequently, it would be necessary to use a binomial test to determine if the frequency of non-whites in the Job Survey is different from a hypothesised one of 5 per cent.

Chi-square test for two or more unrelated samples

If we wanted to compare the frequency of cases found in one variable in two or more unrelated samples or categories of another variable, we would also use the chi-square test. We will illustrate this test with the relatively simple example in which we have two dichotomous variables, gender (male and female) and ethnic group (white and non-white), although it can also be applied to two variables which have three or more categories. Suppose, for instance, we wished to find out whether the proportion of male to female workers was the same in both white and black workers.

First of all, we have to recode the category of ethnic group, so that all the non-whites are coded as 2. If we wanted to assign value labels, we would have to provide new ones for the two groups. Second, because the chi-square test for two or more unrelated samples is only available as part of the SPSS procedure for generating tables which show the distribution of two or more variables, we have to use the relevant options in this **Crosstabs** procedure. Further details on it can be found in the next chapter, where its operation is described more fully. In order not to replicate this information, only the basic steps for generating chi-square will be outlined here, which for this analysis are as follows:

➔**Analyze** ➔**Descriptive Statistics** ➔**Crosstabs...** [opens **Crosstabs** dialog box shown in Box 7.3]

➔**gender** ➔▶button [puts **gender** under **Row[s]:**] ➔**ethncgpc** ➔▶button [puts **ethncgpc** under **Column[s]:**] ➔**Cells...** [opens **Crosstabs: Cell Display** subdialog box shown in Box 7.4]

➔**Expected** [in **Counts** section] ➔**Unstandardised** [in **Residuals** section] ➔**Continue** [closes **Crosstabs: Cell Display** subdialog box]

➔**Statistics...** [opens **Crosstabs: Statistics** subdialog box shown in Box 7.5]

➔**Chi-square** ➔**Continue** [closes **Crosstabs: Statistics** subdialog box]

➔**OK**

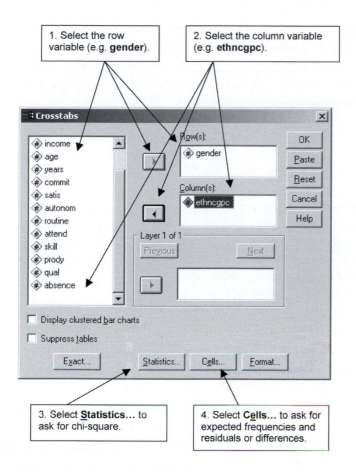

1. Select the row variable (e.g. **gender**).

2. Select the column variable (e.g. **ethncgpc**).

3. Select **Statistics...** to ask for chi-square.

4. Select **Cells...** to ask for expected frequencies and residuals or differences.

BOX 7.3 **Crosstabs** dialog box

Since chi-square is based on comparing the expected with the observed frequency in each cell, it is useful to have a display of the expected frequencies and the difference (the unstandardised residual) between the expected and the observed frequencies.

The output from this procedure is shown in Table 7.6 which includes a table of the expected and observed frequencies in each cell, their difference, the Pearson chi-square statistic, the degrees of freedom, the significance level and the minimum expected frequency. This last value is useful when the degrees of freedom are larger than one, because as in the case of a one-sample chi-square, this test should not be used if any cell has an expected frequency of less than 1 or if 20 per cent or more of the cells have an expected frequency of less than 5. As the minimum expected frequency in any one cell is 15.1

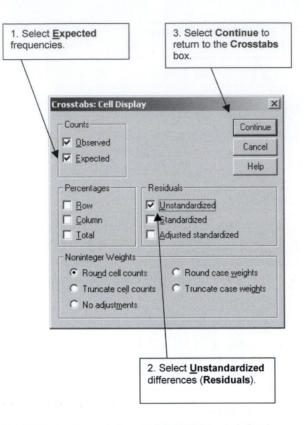

1. Select **Expected** frequencies.

3. Select **Continue** to return to the **Crosstabs** box.

2. Select **Unstandardized** differences (**Residuals**).

BOX 7.4 **Crosstabs: Cell Display** subdialog box

(for non-white females) and there are no cells with an expected frequency of less than 5, it is appropriate to use this test. The degrees of freedom are calculated by subtracting 1 from the number of categories in each of the two variables and multiplying the remaining values (i.e. $(2 - 1)(2 - 1) = 1$). The observed frequencies are displayed above the expected ones in each of the cells. Thus, the observed frequency of white males is 22, while the expected one is 20.1. The residual or difference is 1.9. Two chi-squares are given. The first chi-square is the uncorrected value while the second incorporates Yates's correction which assumes that the frequencies can be non-integral (i.e. consist of whole numbers and fractions or decimals). Yates's correction is only given for 2×2 tables and may no longer be needed (Cramer, 1998). Since the value of chi-square is not significant, this means that the proportion of male to female workers is the same for both whites and non-whites.

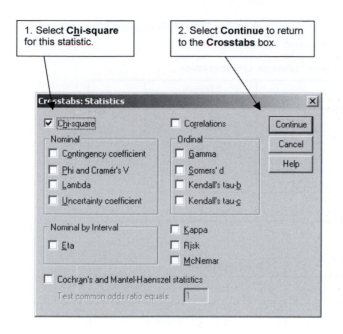

1. Select **Chi-square** for this statistic.

2. Select **Continue** to return to the **Crosstabs** box.

BOX 7.5 Crosstabs: Statistics subdialog box

McNemar test for two related samples

This test is used to compare the frequencies of a dichotomous variable from the same cases at two points in time, in two treatments, or from two samples which have been matched to be similar in certain respects such as having the same distributions of age, gender, and socio-economic status. Suppose, for example, we wanted to find out if there had been any changes in the attendance of workers at a firm's monthly meetings in two consecutive months (**attend1** and **attend2**). The use of tests to analyse information from two or more related samples will be illustrated with the small set of data in Table 7.7. This consists of one example of the three kinds of variables (categorical, ordinal and interval/ratio) measured at three consecutive monthly intervals on twelve workers. The categorical variable is their attendance at the firm's monthly meeting (**attend1** to **attend3**), the ordinal one is the quality of their work as rated by their supervisor (**qual1** to **qual3**), while the interval/ratio one is their self-expressed job satisfaction (**satis1** to **satis3**). A study in which data are collected from the same individuals at two or more points is known as a *prospective, longitudinal,* or *panel* design. Consequently, this example will be referred to as the Panel Study.

TABLE 7.6 Chi-square test produced by **Crosstabs** comparing number of white and non-white men and women

gender * ethncgpc Crosstabulation

			ethncgpc		Total
			White	Non-white	
gender	Men	Count	22	17	39
		Expected Count	20.1	18.9	39.0
		Residual	1.9	-1.9	
	Women	Count	14	17	31
		Expected Count	15.9	15.1	31.0
		Residual	-1.9	1.9	
Total		Count	36	34	70
		Expected Count	36.0	34.0	70.0

Chi-Square Tests

	Value	df	Asymp. Sig. (2-sided)	Exact Sig. (2-sided)	Exact Sig. (1-sided)
Pearson Chi-Square	.875[b]	1	.350		
Continuity Correction[a]	.483	1	.487		
Likelihood Ratio	.876	1	.349		
Fisher's Exact Test				.471	.244
Linear-by-Linear Association	.862	1	.353		
N of Valid Cases	70				

a. Computed only for a 2x2 table.

b. 0 cells (.0%) have expected count less than 5. The minimum expected count is 15.06.

To conduct a McNemar test comparing **attend1** and **attend2** we use the following SPSS procedure:

→**A**nalyze →**N**onparametric Tests →**2** Related Samples... [opens **Two-Related-Samples Tests** dialog box shown in Box 7.6]

→**attend1** [puts **attend1** beside **Variable 1:** in **Current Selections** section] →**attend2** [puts **attend2** beside **Variable 2:** in **Current Selections** section] →►button [puts the **attend1** and **attend2** under **T**est Pair[s] List:] →**W**ilcoxon [to de-select] →**M**cNemar →**OK**

The output for this procedure is presented in Table 7.8. The table shows the number of people whose attendance changed or remained the same from the first to the second month. Since attendance is coded as 1 and non-attendance as 2, we can see that six workers attended the first but not the

TABLE 7.7 The Panel Study data

Id	Attend1	Qual1	Satis1	Attend2	Qual2	Satis2	Attend3	Qual3	Satis3
01	1	5	17	1	4	18	1	5	16
02	1	4	12	2	3	9	2	2	7
03	2	3	13	1	4	15	2	3	14
04	2	4	11	2	5	14	2	3	8
05	2	2	7	2	3	10	1	3	9
06	1	4	14	1	4	15	2	3	10
07	1	3	15	2	1	6	1	4	12
08	2	4	12	1	3	9	1	4	13
09	1	4	13	2	5	14	1	3	15
10	1	1	5	2	2	4	2	3	9
11	1	3	8	2	3	7	1	3	6
12	1	4	11	2	4	13	1	3	10

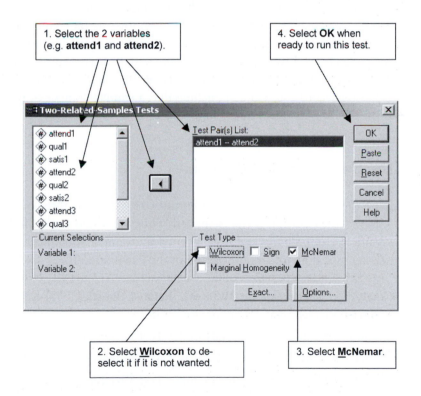

BOX 7.6   Two-Related-Samples Tests dialog box

159

TABLE 7.8 McNemar test comparing attendance across two months (Panel Study)

attend1 & attend2

attend1	attend2	
	1	2
1	2	6
2	2	2

Test Statistics[b]

	attend1 & attend2
N	12
Exact Sig. (2-tailed)	.289[a]

a. Binomial distribution used.

b. McNemar Test.

second meeting and that two attended the second but not the first one. If fewer than 26 cases change from one sample to another as they did here, the binomial test is computed. Otherwise, the one-sample chi-square test is used. As the two-tailed level of probability is greater than 0.05, this means that there was no significant change in attendance between the first and the second meeting. In other words, we would conclude that a similar number of people attended the first and the second meeting.

Cochran Q test for three or more related samples

To compare the distribution of a dichotomous variable across three or more related samples, the Cochran Q test is applied. Thus, we would use the following procedure to compute this test if we wanted to examine attendance at the firm's meeting over the three-month period in the Panel Study:

→**Analyze** →**Nonparametric Tests** →**K Related Samples…** [opens **Tests for Several Related Samples** dialog box shown in Box 7.7]

→**attend1** →▶button [puts **attend1** under **Test Variables:**]

→**attend2** →button [puts **attend2** under **Test Variables:**]

→**attend3** →▶button [puts **attend3** under **Test Variables:**]

→**Friedman** [to de-select] →**Cochran's Q** →**OK**

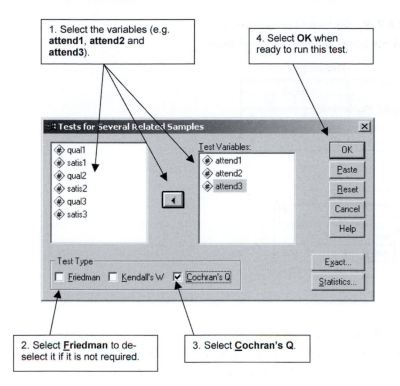

1. Select the variables (e.g. **attend1**, **attend2** and **attend3**).

4. Select **OK** when ready to run this test.

2. Select **F**riedman to de-select it if it is not required.

3. Select **C**ochran's **Q**.

BOX 7.7 **Tests for Several Related Samples** dialog box

This procedure produced the output in Table 7.9. This shows the number of people who did and did not attend the three meetings. Once again, as the probability level is above 0.05, this indicates there is no significant difference in attendance over the three meetings.

Non-categorical variables and non-parametric tests

Kolmogorov–Smirnov test for one sample

This test is used to compare the observed frequencies of the values of an ordinal variable, such as rated quality of work, against some specified theoretical distribution. It determines the statistical significance of the largest difference between them. In SPSS, the theoretical distribution can be **Normal, Uniform, Poisson** or **Exponential**. These are the keywords which must be used to specify which one of these four options is to be selected. Thus, for example, if

TABLE 7.9 Cochran Q test comparing attendance across three months (Panel Study)

Frequencies

	Value	
	1	2
attend1	8	4
attend2	4	8
attend3	7	5

Test Statistics

N	12
Cochran's Q	2.600[a]
df	2
Asymp. Sig.	.273

a. 1 is treated as a success.

we expected the five degrees of rated quality of work (i.e. very poor, poor, average, good, and very good) in the Job Survey to appear equally often (i.e. as a uniform distribution), we would use the following procedure:

→**A**nalyze →**N**onparametric Tests →**1**-Sample K-S... [opens **One-Sample Kolmogorov-Smirnov Test** dialog box shown in Box 7.8]

→**qual** →► button [puts **qual** under **T**est Variable List:]

→**N**ormal [to de-select] →**U**niform [under **Test Distribution**]

→**OK**

The lowest and the highest values in the sample data will be used. In other words, if the lowest rating was 2 and the highest 4, then SPSS will compare the distribution of this range of values. The sample mean and standard deviation are used for the normal distribution and the sample mean for the Poisson distribution.

The second table in the output from this procedure is displayed in Table 7.10. The largest absolute, positive and negative differences between the observed and theoretical distributions are printed, together with the Kolmogorov–Smirnov Z statistic and its probability value. The largest absolute difference is simply the largest difference, regardless of its direction. Since p is well below the two-tailed 0.05 level, the difference is significant. This means the number of cases at each of the five levels is not equal.

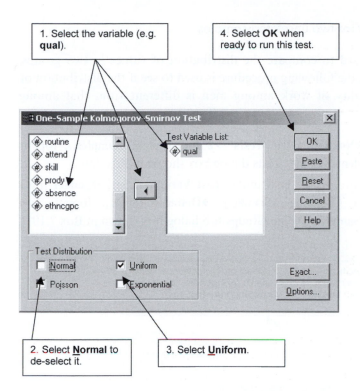

1. Select the variable (e.g. **qual**).

4. Select **OK** when ready to run this test.

2. Select **Normal** to de-select it.

3. Select **Uniform**.

BOX 7.8   One-Sample Kolmogorov-Smirnov Test dialog box

TABLE 7.10   One-sample Kolmogorov–Smirnov test comparing distribution of quality of work (Job Survey)

One-Sample Kolmogorov-Smirnov Test

		qual
N		70
Uniform Parameters[a,b]	Minimum	1
	Maximum	5
Most Extreme Differences	Absolute	.207
	Positive	.129
	Negative	-.207
Kolmogorov-Smirnov Z		1.733
Asymp. Sig. (2-tailed)		.005

a. Test distribution is Uniform.

b. Calculated from data.

Kolmogorov–Smirnov test for two unrelated samples

This test is also used to compare the distribution of values in two groups. Thus, for example, the following procedure is used to see if the distribution of the ratings of quality of work among men is different from that among women:

→**Analyze** →**Nonparametric Tests** →**2 Independent Samples...** [opens **Two-Independent-Samples Tests** dialog box shown in Box 7.9]

→**qual** →▶▶button [puts **qual** under **Test Variable List:**] →**gender** [puts **gender** under **Grouping Variable:**] →**Define Groups...** [opens **Two Independent Samples: Define Groups** subdialog box shown in Box 7.10]

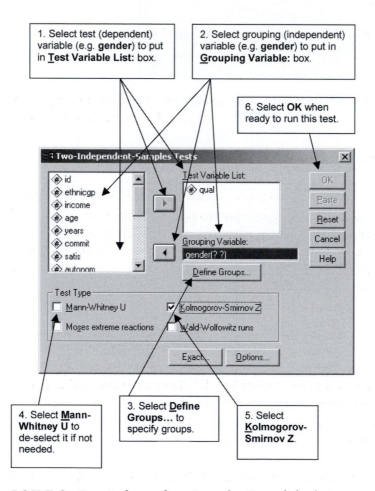

BOX 7.9 Two-Independent-Samples Tests dialog box

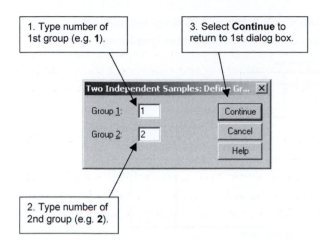

1. Type number of
1st group (e.g. **1**).

3. Select **Continue** to
return to 1st dialog box.

2. Type number of
2nd group (e.g. **2**).

BOX 7.10   Two Independent Samples: Define Groups subdialog box

→in box beside **Group 1:** type **1** →box beside **Group 2:** and type **2** →
Continue [closes **Two Independent Samples: Define Groups** subdialog
box]
→**M**ann-Whitney U [to de-select] →**K**olmogorov-Smirnov Z →**OK**

This procedure produced the output in Table 7.11. Once again, the largest
absolute, positive and negative differences are shown, together with the *Z*
statistic. The number of cases or participants in each of the two groups being
compared is also shown. As *p* is well above the two-tailed 0.05 level, this means
there is no difference in the distribution of quality of work ratings for men and
women.

Median test for two or more unrelated samples

The median test is used to determine if the distribution of values either side of
a common median differs for two or more unrelated samples. If we wanted to
determine if the distribution of rated quality of work was similar for men and
women, we would use the following procedure:

→**A**nalyze →**N**onparametric Tests →**K** Independent Samples... [opens
Tests for Several Independent Samples dialog box shown in Box 7.11]

TABLE 7.11 Two-sample Kolmogorov–Smirnov test comparing distribution of quality of work in men and women (Job Survey)

Frequencies

	gender	N
qual	Men	39
	Women	31
	Total	70

Test Statistics[a]

		qual
Most Extreme Differences	Absolute	.126
	Positive	.017
	Negative	-.126
Kolmogorov-Smirnov Z		.522
Asymp. Sig. (2-tailed)		.948

a. Grouping Variable: gender.

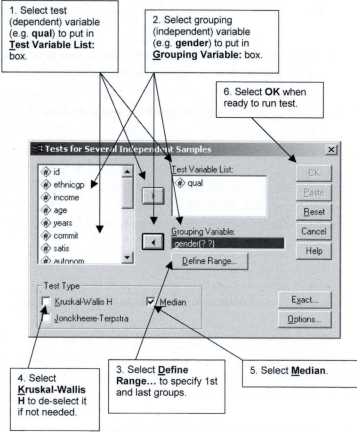

1. Select test (dependent) variable (e.g. **qual**) to put in **Test Variable List:** box.

2. Select grouping (independent) variable (e.g. **gender**) to put in **Grouping Variable:** box.

6. Select **OK** when ready to run test.

4. Select **Kruskal-Wallis H** to de-select it if not needed.

3. Select **Define Range...** to specify 1st and last groups.

5. Select **Median**.

BOX 7.11 Tests for Several Independent Samples dialog box

→**qual** →▶button [puts **qual** under **Test Variable List:**] →**gender** [puts **gender** under **Grouping Variable:**] →**Define Range…** [opens a **Define Range** subdialog box shown in Box 7.12]

→in box beside **Minimum:** type **1** →box beside **Maximum:** and type **2** →**Continue** [closes **Several Independent Samples: Define Range** subdialog box]

→**Kruskal-Wallis H** [to de-select] →**Median** →**OK**

This procedure gave the output in Table 7.12. It has a 2×2 table showing the number of cases above the median and less than or equal to it for males and females. We can see that there are twenty men above the median and nineteen below or equal to it. Also given is the median value which is 3, the chi-square statistic (uncorrected and corrected for continuity) and its significance. Because p is greater than 0.05 (for both values) and therefore not significant, the median rating of work quality does not differ for men and women.

Mann–Whitney U test for two unrelated samples

The Mann–Whitney test is more powerful than the median test because it compares the number of times a score from one of the samples is ranked higher than a score from the other sample rather than the number of scores which are above the median. If the two groups are similar, then the number of

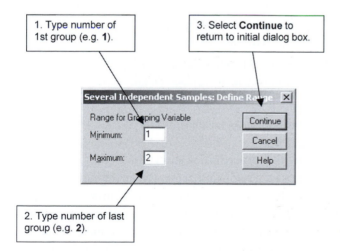

1. Type number of 1st group (e.g. **1**).

3. Select **Continue** to return to initial dialog box.

2. Type number of last group (e.g. **2**).

BOX 7.12 **Several Independent Samples: Define Range** subdialog box

TABLE 7.12 Median test comparing quality of work in men and women (Job Survey)

Frequencies

		gender	
		Men	Women
qual	> Median	20	12
	<= Median	19	19

Test Statistics[a]

		qual
N		70
Median		3.00
Chi-Square		1.100
df		1
Asymp. Sig.		.294
Yates' Continuity	Chi-Square	.652
Correction	df	1
	Asymp. Sig.	.419

a. Grouping Variable: gender.

times this happens should also be similar for the two groups. The procedure for comparing the rated quality of work for men and women is:

→**Analyze** →**Nonparametric Tests** →**2 Independent Samples...** [opens **Two-Independent-Samples Tests** dialog box shown in Box 7.9]

→**qual** →►button [puts **qual** under **Test Variable List:**] →**gender** [puts **gender** under **Grouping Variable:**] →**Define Groups...** [opens **Two Independent Samples: Define Groups** subdialog box shown in Box 7.10]

→in box beside **Group 1:** type **1** →box beside **Group 2:** and type **2** → **Continue** [closes **Two Independent Samples: Define Groups** subdialog box]

[→**Mann–Whitney** U unless already selected] →**OK**

The output produced by this procedure is shown in Table 7.13. It gives the mean rank of the ratings for men and women (as well as the sum of ranks), the number of cases on which these are based, the Mann–Whitney U statistic, and the Wilcoxon W (which is the sum of the ranks of the smaller group and which we can ignore). Since it is necessary to correct for the number of scores which receive, or tie for, the same rank, it does this by giving the Z statistic and its significance level. Although the significance of U is not shown here,

TABLE 7.13 Mann–Whitney test comparing quality of work in men and women (Job Survey)

Ranks

	GENDER	N	Mean Rank	Sum of Ranks
QUAL	Men	39	36.94	1440.50
	Women	31	33.69	1044.50
	Total	70		

Test Statistics[a]

	QUAL
Mann-Whitney U	548.500
Wilcoxon W	1044.500
Z	-.680
Asymp. Sig. (2-tailed)	.496

a. Grouping Variable: GENDER.

correcting for ties increases the value of Z slightly. As the Z statistic is still not significant (i.e. p is greater than 0.05), there is no difference between men and women in the mean ranking of the rated quality of their work.

Kruskal–Wallis *H* test for three or more unrelated samples

The Kruskal–Wallis H test is similar to the Mann–Whitney U test in that the cases in the different samples are ranked together in one series. However, unlike the Mann–Whitney U test, it can be used to compare scores in more than two groups. To compare the rated quality of work for people in the four ethnic groups, we use the following procedure:

→**Analyze** →**Nonparametric Tests** →**K Independent Samples...** [opens **Tests for Several Independent Samples** dialog box shown in Box 7.11]

→**qual** →▶ button [puts **qual** under **Test Variable List:**] →**ethnicgp** [puts **ethnicgp** under **Grouping Variable:**] →**Define Range...** [opens a **Define Range** subdialog box shown in Box 7.12]

→in box beside **Minimum:** type **1** →box beside **Maximum:** and type **4** →**Continue** [closes **Several Independent Samples: Define Range** subdialog box]

→**Kruskal–Wallis** →**OK**

This procedure produced the output in Table 7.14. It shows the mean rank for each group, the number of cases in them, and the chi-square statistic and its significance level corrected for rank ties. Since the significance level is greater than 0.05, this indicates there is no difference between workers of the four ethnic groups in the mean ranking of the rated quality of their work.

Sign test for two related samples

The sign test compares the number of positive and negative differences between two scores from the same or similar (i.e. matched) samples such as those in the Panel Study, and ignores the size of these differences. If the two samples are similar, then the number of these differences should be similar. Thus, for example, we could compare the rated quality of work at two of the times (say, **qual1** and **qual2**) in the Panel Study. If the number of positive differences (i.e. decreases in ratings) was similar to the number of negative ones (i.e. increases in ratings), this would mean that there was no change in one particular direction between the two occasions. To compute this comparison, we use the following procedure:

→**Analyze** →**Nonparametric Tests** →**2 Related Samples...** [opens **Two-Related-Samples Tests** dialog box shown in Box 7.6]

TABLE 7.14 Kruskal–Wallis test comparing quality of work between ethnic groups (Job Survey)

Ranks

	ethnicgp	N	Mean Rank
qual	White	36	34.99
	Asian	18	33.47
	West Indian	14	37.71
	African	2	47.50
	Total	70	

Test Statistics[a,b]

	qual
Chi-Square	1.121
df	3
Asymp. Sig.	.772

a. Kruskal-Wallis Test.

b. Grouping Variable: ethnicgp.

→**qual1** [puts **qual1** beside **Variable 1:** in **Current Selections** section]
→**qual2** [puts **qual2** beside **Variable 2:** in **Current Selections** section]
→▶button [puts **qual1** and **qual2** under **Test Pair[s] List:**] →**Wilcoxon** [to de-select] →**Sign** →**OK**

This procedure produced the output in Table 7.15. It displays the number of negative, positive and zero (ties) differences. There are three ties, five positive differences and four negative ones. Since fewer than twenty-six differences were found, it gives the binomial significance level. If more than twenty-five differences had been obtained, it would have given the significance level for the Z statistic. With almost equal numbers of positive and negative differences, it is not surprising that the test is non-significant. In other words, there is no change in rated quality of work over the two months.

Wilcoxon matched-pairs signed-ranks test for two related samples

This test, like the Mann–Whitney, takes account of the size of the differences between two sets of related scores by ranking and then summing those with the same sign. If there are no differences between the two samples, then the

TABLE 7.15 Sign test comparing quality across two months (Panel Study)

Frequencies

		N
qual2 - qual1	Negative Differences[a]	4
	Positive Differences[b]	5
	Ties[c]	3
	Total	12

a. qual2 < qual1.

b. qual2 > qual1.

c. qual2 = qual1.

Test Statistics[b]

	qual2 - qual1
Exact Sig. (2-tailed)	1.000[a]

a. Binomial distribution used.

b. Sign Test.

mean rank of positive differences should be similar to that of the negative one. This test would be used, for example, to determine if the rated quality of work in the Panel Study was the same in the first and second month (**qual1** and **qual2**). To do this we would use the following procedure:

→**A**nalyze →**N**onparametric Tests →**2 Re**lated Samples... [opens **Two-Related-Samples Tests** dialog box shown in Box 7.6]

→**qual1** [puts **qual1** beside **Variable 1:** in **Current Selections** section]

→**qual2** [puts **qual2** beside **Variable 2:** in **Current Selections** section]

→▶button [puts **qual1** and **qual2** under **T**est Pair[s] List:] →**W**ilcoxon

→**OK**

Table 7.16 contains the output for this procedure. It presents the mean rank and sum of ranks for the negative and positive ranks, the number of cases on which these are based together with the number of tied ranks, the test statistic Z, and its significance level. We obtain the same result with this test. The mean rank of rated quality of work does not differ between the two months.

TABLE 7.16 Wilcoxon matched-pairs signed-ranks test comparing job quality across first two months (Panel Study)

Ranks

		N	Mean Rank	Sum of Ranks
qual2 - qual1	Negative Ranks	4[a]	5.63	22.50
	Positive Ranks	5[b]	4.50	22.50
	Ties	3[c]		
	Total	12		

a. qual2 < qual1.

b. qual2 > qual1.

c. qual2 = qual1.

Test Statistics[b]

	qual2 - qual1
Z	.000[a]
Asymp. Sig. (2-tailed)	1.000

a. The sum of negative ranks equals the sum of positive ranks.

b. Wilcoxon Signed Ranks Test.

Friedman test for three or more related samples

If we wanted to compare the scores of three or more related samples, such as the rated quality of work across all three months rather than just two of them, we would use the Friedman two-way analysis of variance test. It ranks the scores for each of the cases and then calculates the mean rank score for each sample. If there are no differences between the samples, their mean ranks should be similar. We would use the following procedure to compare the quality of work over the three months in the Panel Study:

→**Analyze** →**Nonparametric Tests** →**K Related Samples...** [opens **Tests for Several Related Samples** dialog box shown in Box 7.7]

→**qual1** →►button [puts **qual1** under **Test Variables:**] →**qual2** →►button [puts **qual2** under **Test Variables:**] →**qual3** →►button [puts **qual3** under **Test Variables:**] →**Friedman** →**OK**

The output produced by this procedure is shown in Table 7.17. It contains the mean rank for the three samples, the number of cases in them, the chi-square statistic, its degrees of freedom (which is the number of samples minus 1), and its significance level. The non-significant chi-square means there is no difference in the mean ranks of rated quality of work across the three months.

TABLE 7.17 Friedman test comparing job quality across three months (Panel Study)

Ranks

	Mean Rank
qual1	2.04
qual2	2.13
qual3	1.83

Test Statistics[a]

N	12
Chi-Square	.684
df	2
Asymp. Sig.	.710

a. Friedman Test.

Non-categorical variables and parametric tests

t test for one sample

This test is used to determine if the mean of a sample is similar to that of the population. If, for example, we knew that the mean score for job satisfaction for workers in the industry covered in the Job Survey was 10 and we wanted to find out if the mean of our sample was similar to it, we would carry out a *t* test. To do this with SPSS, we carry out the following procedure.

→**Analyze** →**Compare Means** →**One-Sample T Test...** [opens **One-Sample T Test** dialog box shown in Box 7.13]

→**satis** →▶button [puts **satis** under **Test Variable(s):**] →type **10** in box beside **Test Value:** →**OK**

The output for this procedure is shown in Table 7.18. We see that there is a significant difference between the population mean of 10 and the sample mean of 10.84 at the two-tailed probability level of 0.04.

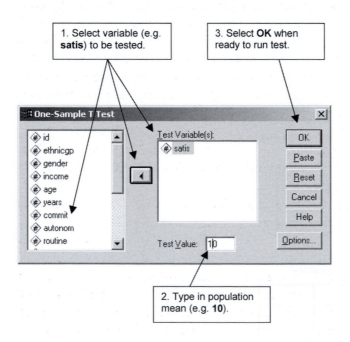

BOX 7.13   One-Sample T Test dialog box

TABLE 7.18 One-sample *t* test for job satisfaction (Job Survey)

One-Sample Statistics

	N	Mean	Std. Deviation	Std. Error Mean
satis	68	10.84	3.304	.401

One-Sample Test

	Test Value = 10					
					95% Confidence Interval of the Difference	
	t	df	Sig. (2-tailed)	Mean Difference	Lower	Upper
satis	2.092	67	.040	.838	.04	1.64

Standard error of the mean

It is necessary to outline more fully what the *standard error of the mean* is since this important idea also constitutes the basis of other parametric tests such as the analysis of variance. One of the assumptions of many parametric tests is that the population of the variable to be analysed should be normally distributed. The errors of most distributions are known to take this form. For example, if a large group of people were asked to guess today's temperature, the distribution of their guesses would approximate that of a normal distribution, even if the temperature does not itself represent a normal distribution. In addition, it has been observed that the distribution of certain characteristics also takes this form. If, for example, you plot the distribution of the heights of a large group of adult human beings, it will be similar to that of a normal distribution.

If we draw samples from a population of values which is normally distributed, then the means of those samples will also be normally distributed. In other words, most of the means will be very similar to that of the population, although some of them will vary quite considerably. The standard error of the mean represents the standard deviation of the sample means. The one-sample *t* test compares the mean of a sample with that of the population in terms of how likely it is that that difference has arisen by chance. The smaller this difference is, the more likely it is to have resulted from chance.

t test for two unrelated means

This test is used to determine if the means of two unrelated samples differ. It does this by comparing the difference between the two means with the standard error of the difference in the means of different samples:

$$t = \frac{\text{sample one mean} - \text{sample two mean}}{\text{standard error of the difference in means}}$$

The *standard error of the difference in means*, like the standard error of the mean, is also normally distributed. If we draw a large number of samples from a population whose values are normally distributed and plot the differences in the means of each of these samples, the shape of this distribution will be normal. Since the means of most of the samples will be close to the mean of the population and therefore similar to one another, if we subtract them from each other the differences between them will be close to zero. In other words, the nearer the difference in the means of two samples is to zero, the more likely it is that this difference is due to chance.

To compare the means of two samples, such as the mean job satisfaction of male and female workers in the Job Survey, we would use the following procedure:

→**Analyze** →**Compare Means** →**Independent-Samples T Test...** [opens **Independent-Samples T Test** dialog box shown in Box 7.14]

→**satis** →►button [puts **satis** under **Test Variable[s]:**] →**gender** [puts **gender** under **Grouping Variable:**] →**Define Groups...** [opens **Define Groups** subdialog box shown in Box 7.15]

→in box beside **Group 1:** type **1** →box beside **Group 2:** and type **2** → **Continue** [closes **Define Groups** subdialog box]

→**OK**

There are two ways of defining the two groups. First, we can define them in terms of their two codes (**1** and **2**) as has been done above. Second, one of the values can be used as a cut-off point, at or above which all the values constitute one group while those below form the other group. In this instance, the cut-off point is 2 which would be placed in parentheses after gender.

The output for this procedure is displayed in Table 7.19. The number of cases in the two groups, together with their means, standard deviations and standard errors is listed. Since we do not know what the standard error of the

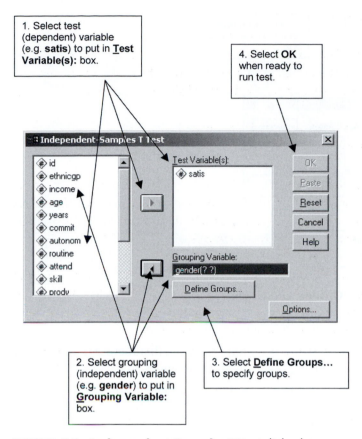

1. Select test (dependent) variable (e.g. **satis**) to put in **Test Variable(s):** box.

4. Select **OK** when ready to run test.

2. Select grouping (independent) variable (e.g. **gender**) to put in **Grouping Variable:** box.

3. Select **Define Groups...** to specify groups.

BOX 7.14 Independent-Samples T Test dialog box

difference in means is of the population in question, we have to estimate it. How this is done depends on whether the difference in the variances of the two samples is statistically significant. This information is provided by Levene's test for equality of variances. Levene's test is a one-way analysis of variance on the absolute (i.e. ignoring the minus sign) deviation scores of the groups where the group mean is subtracted from each of the individual scores within that group. A one-way analysis of variance for three or more groups is described below. In this case the one-way analysis would be done on only two groups. If Levene's test is significant (i.e. has a probability of 0.05 or less), then the variances are unequal and so the *separate* variance estimate is used to calculate the *t* value. If the variances are equal, the *pooled* variance estimate is employed for this purpose. In Table 7.19, the variances are not statistically different since the *p* value of Levene's test is 0.733. Consequently, we look at the *t* value based on equal variances. This is non-significant with a two-tailed

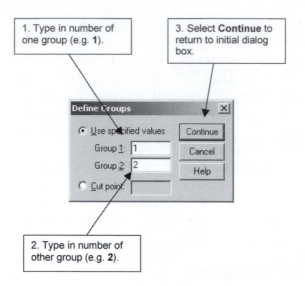

1. Type in number of one group (e.g. **1**).

3. Select **Continue** to return to initial dialog box.

2. Type in number of other group (e.g. **2**).

BOX 7.15 Define Groups subdialog box

p value of 0.771. In other words, we would conclude that there is no significant difference in mean job satisfaction between males and females. The two-tailed test of significance is provided by default. To calculate the one-tailed level of significance, divide the two-tailed one by 2, which in this case would still be non-significant at 0.386 (0.771/2).

TABLE 7.19 Unrelated *t* test comparing job satisfaction in men and women (Job Survey)

Group Statistics

	gender	N	Mean	Std. Deviation	Std. Error Mean
satis	Men	37	10.95	3.325	.547
	Women	31	10.71	3.329	.598

Independent Samples Test

		Levene's Test for Equality of Variances		t-test for Equality of Means						95% Confidence Interval of the Difference	
		F	Sig.	t	df	Sig. (2-tailed)	Mean Difference	Std. Error Difference	Lower	Upper
satis	Equal variances assumed	.117	.733	.292	66	.771	.236	.810	-1.381	1.853
	Equal variances not assumed			.292	63.904	.771	.236	.810	-1.382	1.855

It should be pointed out that the variance, the standard deviation and the standard error of a sample are related. The *variance* or mean squared deviation is calculated by subtracting the mean of the sample from each of its scores (to provide a measure of their deviation from the mean), squaring them, adding them together and dividing them by one less than the number of cases. Since the deviations would sum to zero, they are squared to make the negative deviations positive. The *standard deviation* is simply the square root of the variance. The advantage of the standard deviation over the variance is that it is expressed in the original values of the data. For example, the standard deviation of job satisfaction is described in terms of the points on this scale. The *standard error* is the standard deviation divided by the square root of the number of cases. The relationships between these three measures can be checked out on the statistics shown in Table 7.19.

Unrelated *t* test and ordinal data

Some people have argued that parametric tests should only be used on interval/ratio data (for example, Stevens, 1946). Others, as we have mentioned earlier, have reasoned that such a restriction is unnecessary. In view of this controversy, it may be interesting to see whether the use of an unrelated *t* test on an ordinal variable such as rated quality of work gives very dissimilar results to that of the Mann–Whitney previously used. According to Siegel and Castellan (1988), the Mann–Whitney test is about 95 per cent as powerful as the *t* test. What this means is that the *t* test requires 5 per cent fewer participants than the Mann–Whitney test to reject the null hypothesis when it is false. The following procedure was used to generate the output in Table 7.20:

→**Analyze** →**Compare Means** →**Independent-Samples T Test...** [opens **Independent-Samples T Test** dialog box shown in Box 7.14]

→**qual** →▶button [puts **qual** under **Test Variable[s]:**] →**gender** [puts **gender** under **Grouping Variable:**] →**Define Groups...** [opens **Define Groups** subdialog box shown in Box 7.15]

→in box beside **Group 1:** type **1** →box beside **Group 2:** and type **2** → **Continue** [closes **Define Groups** subdialog box]

→**OK**

As can be seen, this test also indicates that there is no significant difference between men and women in the mean of their rated quality of work.

TABLE 7.20 *t* test comparing quality of work in men and women (Job Survey)

Group Statistics

	gender	N	Mean	Std. Deviation	Std. Error Mean
qual	Men	39	3.28	1.213	.194
	Women	31	3.06	1.340	.241

Independent Samples Test

		Levene's Test for Equality of Variances		t-test for Equality of Means						
									95% Confidence Interval of the Difference	
		F	Sig.	t	df	Sig. (2-tailed)	Mean Difference	Std. Error Difference	Lower	Upper
qual	Equal variances assumed	.000	.987	.712	68	.479	.218	.306	-.393	.828
	Equal variances not assumed			.703	61.277	.484	.218	.309	-.401	.836

One-way analysis of variance for three or more unrelated means

To compare the means of three or more unrelated samples, such as the mean job satisfaction of the four ethnic groups in the Job Survey, it is necessary to compute a one-way analysis of variance. This is essentially an *F* test in which an estimate of the *between-groups* variance (or *mean-square* as the estimate of the variance is referred to in analysis of variance) is compared with an estimate of the *within-groups* variance by dividing the former by the latter:

$$F = \frac{\text{between-groups estimated variance or mean-square}}{\text{within-groups estimated variance or mean-square}}$$

The total amount of variance in the dependent variable (i.e. job satisfaction) can be thought of as comprising two elements: that which is due to the independent variable (i.e. ethnic group) and that which is due to other factors. This latter component is often referred to as *error* or *residual* variance. The variance that is due to the independent variable is frequently described as *explained* variance. If the between-groups (i.e. explained) estimated variance is considerably larger than that within-groups (i.e. error or residual), then the value of the *F* ratio will be higher, which implies that the differences between the means are unlikely to be due to chance.

The within-groups mean-square or estimated variance is its sum-of-squares divided by its degrees of freedom. These degrees of freedom are the sum of the number of cases minus one in each group (i.e. [the number of cases in group one − 1] + [the number of cases in group two − 1] and so on).

The sum-of-squares is the sum of squared differences between each score in a group and its mean, summed across all groups. The between-groups sum-of-squares, on the other hand, is obtained by subtracting each group's mean from the overall (total or grand) mean, squaring them, multiplying them by the number of cases in each group, and summing the result. It can also be calculated by subtracting the within-groups sum-of-squares from the total sum-of-squares since the total sum-of-squares is the sum of the between- and within-groups sum-of-squares:

$$
\begin{array}{ccccc}
 & \text{total} & & \text{between-groups} & \text{within-groups} \\
\text{sum-of-squares} & = & \text{(i.e. explained)} & + & \text{(i.e. error)} \\
 & & \text{sum-of-squares} & & \text{sum-of-squares}
\end{array}
$$

The between-groups mean-square or estimated variance is its sum-of-squares divided by its degrees of freedom. These degrees of freedom are the number of groups minus one. The degrees of freedom for the total sum-of-squares are the sum of those for the within- and between-groups sum-of-squares or the total number of participants minus one. Although this test may sound complicated, the essential reasoning behind it is that if the groups or samples come from the same population, then the between-groups estimate of the population's variance should be similar to the within-groups estimated variance.

To compare the mean job satisfaction of the four ethnic groups in the Job Survey, we first have to define the groups we want to analyse. As there are no participants identified as 'Other', we only have four groups. If we had a fifth group which we wanted to exclude, we would have to define that group as missing. We then carry out the following procedure:

→ **Analyze** → **Compare Means** → **One-Way ANOVA...** [opens **One-Way ANOVA** dialog box shown in Box 7.16]

→**satis** →▶ button [puts **satis** under **Dependent List:**]

→**ethnicgp** [puts **ethnicgp** under **Factor:**]

→**OK**

The output for this procedure is displayed in Table 7.21. The F ratio, which is the between-groups mean square divided by the within-groups one ($2.912/11.289 = 0.258$), is non-significant. Consequently, there is no significant difference in job satisfaction between the four ethnic groups.

The number of cases in each group, their means, standard deviations and the other statistics shown in Table 7.22 are produced by selecting

181

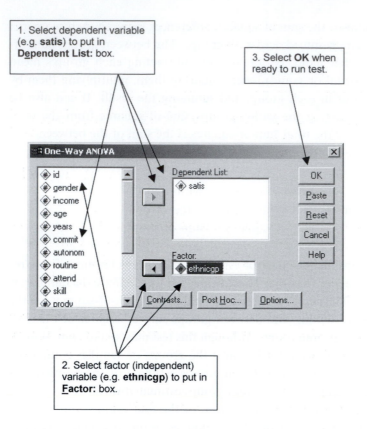

1. Select dependent variable (e.g. **satis**) to put in **Dependent List:** box.

3. Select **OK** when ready to run test.

2. Select factor (independent) variable (e.g. **ethnicgp**) to put in **Factor:** box.

BOX 7.16   One-Way ANOVA dialog box

Options... (which opens the **One-Way ANOVA: Options** subdialog box shown in Box 7.17) and **Descriptive**.

If we select **Homogeneity of variance test** in the **Options** subdialog box, Levene's test for homogeneity of variance is produced as shown in Table 7.23. The variances for the four groups do not differ significantly as the significance

TABLE 7.21   A one-way analysis of variance table comparing job satisfaction across ethnic groups (Job Survey)

ANOVA

satis

	Sum of Squares	df	Mean Square	F	Sig.
Between Groups	8.737	3	2.912	.258	.855
Within Groups	722.484	64	11.289		
Total	731.221	67			

TABLE 7.22 Descriptive group statistics with one-way analysis of variance comparing job satisfaction across ethnic groups (Job Survey)

Descriptives

satis

	N	Mean	Std. Deviation	Std. Error	95% Confidence Interval for Mean		Minimum	Maximum
					Lower Bound	Upper Bound		
White	35	10.54	3.284	.555	9.41	11.67	5	19
Asian	17	10.94	3.596	.872	9.09	12.79	6	16
West Indian	14	11.29	3.292	.880	9.39	13.19	6	15
African	2	12.00	2.828	2.000	-13.41	37.41	10	14
Total	68	10.84	3.304	.401	10.04	11.64	5	19

level is greater than 0.05. If the number of participants in each group and the variances were unequal, it would be necessary to transform the scores so that the variances were equal (see Chapter 9). If it was not possible to make the variance equal, a non-parametric test such as the median or Kruskal–Wallis *H* test should be used instead.

The *F* test or ratio only tells us whether there is a significant difference between one or more of the groups. It does not inform us where this difference lies. To determine this, we need to carry out further statistical tests. Which tests

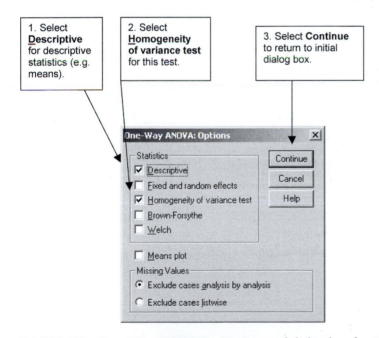

BOX 7.17 One-Way ANOVA: Options subdialog box for Release 13 (which differs slightly from Releases 10 and 11)

TABLE 7.23 Levene's test of homogeneity of variance (Job Survey)

Test of Homogeneity of Variances

satis

Levene Statistic	df1	df2	Sig.
.432	3	64	.731

we use depends on whether or not we predicted where the differences would be. If, for example, we *predicted* that whites would be less satisfied than Asians, then we would carry out an unrelated *t* test as described above using a one-tailed level of significance. We could also do this by selecting the **Contrasts** option which opens the **One-Way ANOVA: Contrasts** subdialog box displayed in Box 7.18. In this option, for instance, we can specify any two groups by defining one of them (i.e. whites) as minus one (−1), the other one (i.e. Asians) as one (**1**), and the remaining ones (i.e. West Indians and African) as zeros. To do this, we type −1 in the box beside **Coefficients:**, select **Add**, type **1** in the box beside **Coefficients:**, select **Add**, type **0** in the box beside **Coefficients:**, select **Add**, type **0** in the box beside **Coefficients:**, select **Add**, type **0** and then **Continue**.

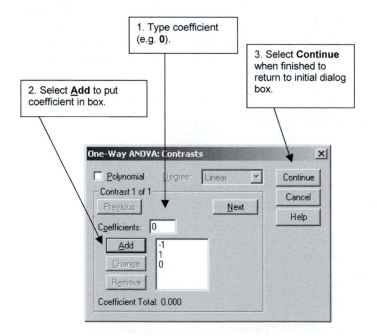

BOX 7.18 One-Way ANOVA: Contrasts subdialog box

The output for this option is shown in Table 7.24. This gives the value for the contrast, its standard error, and both the pooled and separate variance estimates. However, to determine which of these to use, we need to know whether the variances of the two groups differ. To do this, we obtain the standard deviations as reported in Table 7.22, convert them to variances by squaring them, divide the larger variance by the smaller one ($F = 12.934/10.785 = 1.20$) and look up the result in a table of critical values for F. Alternatively we can do this using Levene's test on the **t-test** procedure. Because the value of the F test is non-significant, we use the pooled variance estimate. The difference in job satisfaction between whites and those of Asian ethnic origin is non-significant.

If, however, we had not expected any differences, then we would need to take into account the fact that if we carried out a large number of comparisons some of these would be significant just by chance. Indeed, at the 5 per cent level of significance, 5 per cent or one in twenty comparisons could be expected to be significant by definition. A number of tests which take account of this fact have been developed and are available on the **Post Hoc** option which opens the **One-Way ANOVA: Post Hoc Multiple Comparisons** subdialog box presented in Box 7.19.

Because these tests are carried out after the data have been initially analysed, they are referred to as *post hoc* or *a posteriori* tests. One of these, the Scheffé test, will be briefly outlined. This test is the most conservative in the sense that it is least likely to find significant differences between groups or, in other words, to make a Type I error. It is also exact for unequal numbers of participants in the groups. To conduct a Scheffé test to compare job satisfaction between every possible pair of ethnic group, we select **Scheffe** and then **Continue**.

TABLE 7.24 Statistics provided by a one-way contrast comparing job satisfaction in groups 1 and 2 (Job Survey)

Contrast Coefficients

Contrast	White	Asian	West Indian	African
			ethnicgp	
1	-1	1	0	0

Contrast Tests

		Contrast	Value of Contrast	Std. Error	t	df	Sig. (2-tailed)
satis	Assume equal variances	1	.40	.993	.401	64	.690
	Does not assume equal	1	.40	1.034	.385	29.322	.703

185

1. Select **Scheffe**.

2. Select **Continue** to return to initial dialog box.

BOX 7.19 One-Way ANOVA: Post Hoc Multiple Comparisons subdialog box

The output for this test is shown in Table 7.25. This shows that there were no significant differences between any of the groups, taken two at a time.

Levene's test for three or more unrelated variances

As we have seen, Levene's test is used to determine whether the variances, rather than the means, of three or more unrelated samples are different.

t test for two related means

To compare the means of the same participants in two conditions or at two points in time, we would use a related *t* test. We would also use this test to compare participants who had been matched to be similar in certain respects. The advantage of using the same participants or matched participants is that the amount of error deriving from differences between participants is reduced. The related *t* test compares the mean difference between pairs of scores within

TABLE 7.25   Statistics provided by a one-way Scheffé test comparing job satisfaction across ethnic groups (Job Survey)

Multiple Comparisons

Dependent Variable: satis
Scheffe

(I) ethnicgp	(J) ethnicgp	Mean Difference (I-J)	Std. Error	Sig.	95% Confidence Interval	
					Lower Bound	Upper Bound
White	Asian	-.398	.993	.983	-3.25	2.45
	West Indian	-.743	1.062	.921	-3.79	2.31
	African	-1.457	2.443	.949	-8.47	5.56
Asian	White	.398	.993	.983	-2.45	3.25
	West Indian	-.345	1.213	.994	-3.83	3.14
	African	-1.059	2.512	.981	-8.27	6.15
West Indian	White	.743	1.062	.921	-2.31	3.79
	Asian	.345	1.213	.994	-3.14	3.83
	African	-.714	2.540	.994	-8.01	6.58
African	White	1.457	2.443	.949	-5.56	8.47
	Asian	1.059	2.512	.981	-6.15	8.27
	West Indian	.714	2.540	.994	-6.58	8.01

Homogeneous Subsets

satis

Scheffe[a,b]

ethnicgp	N	Subset for alpha = .05
		1
White	35	10.54
Asian	17	10.94
West Indian	14	11.29
African	2	12.00
Sig.		.903

Means for groups in homogeneous subsets are displayed.

a. Uses Harmonic Mean Sample Size = 6.071.

b. The group sizes are unequal. The harmonic mean of the group sizes is used. Type I error levels are not guaranteed.

the sample with that of the population in terms of the standard error of the difference in means:

$$t = \frac{\text{sample mean differences} - \text{population mean differences}}{\text{standard error of the difference in means}}$$

Since the population mean difference is zero, the closer the sample mean difference is to zero, the less likely it is that the two sets of scores differ significantly from one another.

The difference between a related and an unrelated *t* test lies essentially in the fact that two scores from the same person are likely to vary less than two scores from two different people. For example, if we weigh the same person on two occasions, the difference between those two weights is likely to be less than the weights of two separate individuals. This fact is reflected in the different way in which the standard error of the difference in means is calculated for the two tests, which we do not have time to go into here. The variability of the standard error for the related *t* test is less than that for the unrelated one, as illustrated in Figure 7.1. In fact, the variability of the standard error of the difference in means for the related *t* test will depend on the extent to which the pairs of scores are similar or related. The more similar they are, the less the variability will be of their estimated standard error.

To compare two related sets of scores such as job satisfaction in the first two months (**satis1** and **satis2**) in the Panel Study, we would use the following procedure:

→**Analyze** →**Compare Means** →**Paired-Samples T Test...** [opens **Paired-Samples T Test** dialog box shown in Box 7.20]

→**satis1** [puts **satis1** beside **Variable 1:** in **Current Selections** section]

→**satis2** [puts **satis2** beside **Variable 2:** in **Current Selections** section]

→►button [puts **satis1** and **satis2** under **Paired Variables:**] →**OK**

This procedure produces the output in Table 7.26. The mean, standard deviation, and standard error are given for the two sets of scores as well as for

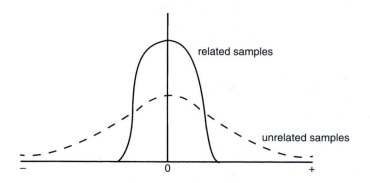

FIGURE 7.1 A comparison of the distribution of the standard error of the differences in means for related and unrelated samples

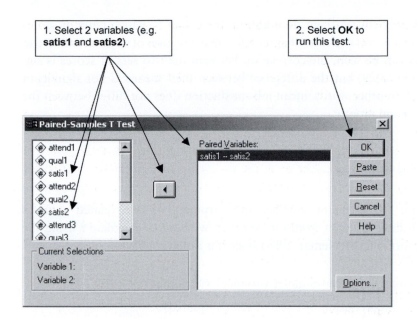

BOX 7.20   Paired-Samples T Test dialog box

TABLE 7.26   Related *t* test comparing job satisfaction across first two months (Panel Study)

Paired Samples Statistics

		Mean	N	Std. Deviation	Std. Error Mean
Pair 1	satis1	11.50	12	3.425	.989
	satis2	11.17	12	4.282	1.236

Paired Samples Correlations

		N	Correlation	Sig.
Pair 1	satis1 & satis2	12	.626	.029

Paired Samples Test

| | Paired Differences | | | | | | | |
	Mean	Std. Deviation	Std. Error Mean	95% Confidence Interval of the Difference Lower	Upper	t	df	Sig. (2-tailed)
Pair 1 satis1 - satis2	.333	3.420	.987	-1.840	2.506	.338	11	.742

the difference between them. In addition, the extent to which pairs of scores are similar or correlated (see Chapter 8 for an exposition of correlation) is also shown. As can be seen, the correlation between the two sets of scores is significant ($p = 0.029$) but the difference between their means is not significant ($p = 0.742$). In other words, mean job satisfaction does not differ between the first and second month.

t test for two related variances

If we want to determine whether the variances of two related samples are significantly different from one another, we have to calculate t using the following formula (McNemar, 1969) since it is not available on SPSS:

$$t = \frac{(\text{larger variance} - \text{smaller variance}) \times \sqrt{(\text{number of cases} - 2)}}{\sqrt{(1 - \text{correlation of 2 sets of scores squared})} \times \atop (4 \times \text{larger variance} \times \text{smaller variance})}$$

To apply this formula to the job satisfaction variances in the above example, we would first have to calculate their variances which is the square of their standard deviations (i.e. 18.34 and 11.73). Substituting the appropriate values in the above equation, we arrive at a t value of 0.91, which with 10 degrees of freedom is not significant with a two-tailed test. To have been significant at this level, we would have needed a t value of 2.228 or greater.

Analysis of variance for three or more related means

The following section deals with a cluster of procedures that are highly complex and which relate to an application that many readers are unlikely to encounter in the normal course of events. Consequently, this section may either be omitted or returned to after having read Chapter 9.

To compare three or more means from the same or matched participants, such as job satisfaction during three consecutive months, we would need to carry out an analysis of variance test which has one within-subjects or *repeated-measures* variable. This variable, job satisfaction, is called a *factor* and has three *levels* since it is repeated three times. This design is referred to variously as a single group (or factor) repeated-measures and treatments-by-subjects design. To conduct it on the present example, we would use the following procedure:

→**Analyze** → **General Linear Model** → **Repeated Measures...** [opens **Repeated Measures Define Factor(s)** subdialog box shown in Box 7.21]

→highlight **factor1** type **month** in box beside **Within-Subject Factor Name:** →box beside **Number of Levels:** and type **3** →**Add** →**Define** [opens **Repeated Measures** subdialog box shown in Box 7.22]

→**satis1** →▶button [puts **satis1** under **Within-Subjects Variables [month]:**] →**satis2** → ▶button →**satis3** →▶button →**Options** [opens **Repeated Measures: Options** subdialog box shown in Box 7.23] →**Descriptive statistics** →**Continue** [closes **Repeated Measures: Options** subdialog box]

→**OK**

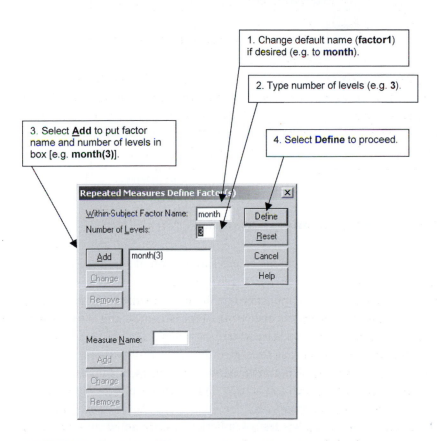

BOX 7.21   Repeated Measures Define Factor(s) dialog box

1. Select within-subject variables (e.g. **satis1**, **satis2** and **satis3**) to put in this box.

3. When **Options...** selected, select OK to run this test.

Repeated Measures

attend1
qual1
attend2
qual2
attend3
qual3
satis3

Within-Subjects Variables   (month):

satis1(1)
satis2(2)
__?__(3)

OK
Paste
Reset
Cancel
Help

Between-Subjects Factor(s):

Covariates:

Model... | Contrasts... | Plots... | Post Hoc... | Save... | Options...

2. Select **Options**....

BOX 7.22   Repeated Measures subdialog box

The means and standard deviations of job satisfaction at the three times are shown in Table 7.27.

The multivariate tests are presented in Table 7.28. Four multivariate tests are provided to assess the significance of the repeated-measures effect. These are Pillai's criterion, Hotelling's trace criterion, Wilks' Lambda, and Roy's *gcr* criterion. In many cases, all four tests give the same results (Stevens, 1979). Provided that the number of participants in each group is equal or almost equal, it does not matter which test is used. Where this is not the case, Pillai's criterion may be the most appropriate.

The output for Mauchly's test of sphericity is presented in Table 7.29. Because this test is not significant we assume sphericity and look at the output

1. Select **Descriptive statistics** for descriptive statistics (e.g. means).

2. Select **Continue** to proceed.

BOX 7.23 **Repeated Measures: Options** subdialog box

in the first line of the table in Table 7.31. If the test had been significant, the significance of the F ratio needs to be adjusted with one of the three adjustments offered.

The univariate tests are for the two transformed variables, T2 and T3, shown in Table 7.30. It is important to note that T2 and T3 do not refer to the original variables having those names, but to the two transformed variables.

TABLE 7.27 Repeated measures means and standard deviations for job satisfaction (Panel Study)

Descriptive Statistics

	Mean	Std. Deviation	N
satis1	11.50	3.425	12
satis2	11.17	4.282	12
satis3	10.75	3.223	12

TABLE 7.28 Repeated measures multivariate tests (Panel Study)

Multivariate Tests[b]

Effect		Value	F	Hypothesis df	Error df	Sig.
month	Pillai's Trace	.075	.404[a]	2.000	10.000	.678
	Wilks' Lambda	.925	.404[a]	2.000	10.000	.678
	Hotelling's Trace	.081	.404[a]	2.000	10.000	.678
	Roy's Largest Root	.081	.404[a]	2.000	10.000	.678

a. Exact statistic.

b. Design: Intercept
Within Subjects Design: month

TABLE 7.29 Repeated measures Mauchly's test of sphericity (Panel Study)

Mauchly's Test of Sphericity[b]

Measure: MEASURE_1

Within Subjects Effect	Mauchly's W	Approx. Chi-Square	df	Sig.	Epsilon[a]		
					Greenhouse e-Geisser	Huynh-Feldt	Lower-bound
month	.882	1.253	2	.535	.895	1.000	.500

Tests the null hypothesis that the error covariance matrix of the orthonormalized transformed dependent variables is proportional to an identity matrix.

a. May be used to adjust the degrees of freedom for the averaged tests of significance. Corrected tests are displayed in the Tests of Within-Subjects Effects table.

b. Design: Intercept
Within Subjects Design: month

TABLE 7.30 Repeated measures univariate tests of significance for transformed variables (Panel Study)

Tests of Within-Subjects Contrasts

Measure: MEASURE_1

Source	month	Type III Sum of Squares	df	Mean Square	F	Sig.
month	Linear	3.375	1	3.375	.881	.368
	Quadratic	.014	1	.014	.002	.966
Error(month)	Linear	42.125	11	3.830		
	Quadratic	81.153	11	7.378		

When comparing three related scores, it is only necessary to test the statistical significance of the differences between two of them (e.g. **satis1 – satis2** and **satis2 – satis3**) since the remaining difference (i.e. **satis1 – satis3**) can be worked out if the other two differences are known [(**satis1 – satis3**) = (**satis1 – satis2**) + (**satis2 – satis3**)]. The number of unrelated comparisons is always one less than the number of variables being compared. Unless requested otherwise, SPSS automatically transforms the variables in a repeated-measures design so that the comparisons are statistically independent. The nature of these transformations can be determined by examining the transformation matrix. However, this is normally done only when the univariate tests are significant, which is not the case here. The values for both the multivariate and univariate tests are not significant. In other words, there is no difference in mean job satisfaction over the three months.

The result of the averaged univariate test is presented in Table 7.31, which is also not significant.

As was the case for the one-way analysis of variance test, the F test only tells us whether there is a significant difference between the three related scores but does not inform us where this difference lies. If we had predicted a difference between two scores, then we can determine if this prediction was confirmed by conducting a related t test as described above. If we had not predicted a difference, then we need to use a *post hoc* test, of which there are a number (Maxwell, 1980). Since these are not available on SPSS, they have to be calculated separately. If the scores are significantly correlated, the Bonferroni inequality test is recommended, whereas if they are not, the Tukey test is advocated.

The Bonferroni test is based on the related t test but modifies the significance level to take account of the fact that more than one comparison is being made. To calculate this, work out the total number of possible comparisons between any two groups, divide the chosen significance level (which is usually 0.05) by this number, and treat the result as the appropriate significance level for comparing more than three groups. In the case of three groups, the total number of possible comparisons is 3 which means the appropriate significance level is 0.017 (0.05/3).

TABLE 7.31 Repeated measures averaged test of significance (Panel Study)

Tests of Within-Subjects Effects

Measure: MEASURE_1

Source		Type III Sum of Squares	df	Mean Square	F	Sig.
month	Sphericity Assumed	3.389	2	1.694	.302	.742
	Greenhouse-Geisser	3.389	1.789	1.894	.302	.719
	Huynh-Feldt	3.389	2.000	1.694	.302	.742
	Lower-bound	3.389	1.000	3.389	.302	.593
Error(month)	Sphericity Assumed	123.278	22	5.604		
	Greenhouse-Geisser	123.278	19.683	6.263		
	Huynh-Feldt	123.278	22.000	5.604		
	Lower-bound	123.278	11.000	11.207		

The calculation for the Tukey test is more complicated (Stevens, 1996). The difference between any two means is compared against the value calculated by multiplying the square root of the repeated measures within-cells mean-square error term (divided by the number of cases) with the studentised range statistic, a table of which can be found in Stevens (1996). If the difference between any two means is greater than this value, then this difference is a significant one. The within-cells mean-square error term is presented in the output in Table 7.31 and is about 5.6. The square root of this divided by the number of cases is 0.68 ($\sqrt{5.6/12}$). The appropriate studentised range value with 3 groups and 22 degrees of freedom for the error term is 3.58. This multiplied by 0.68 gives 2.43. If any two means differed by more than this, they would be significant at the 0.05 level.

Exercises

1   Suppose you wanted to find out whether there had been a statistically significant change in three types of books (classified as romance, crime and science fiction) sold by two shops. What test would you use?

2   What would the null hypothesis be?

3   If the SPSS names were **book** for the type of book sold and **shop** for the two shops, what would be the procedure for running this test?

4   Would you use a one- or a two-tailed level of significance?

5   If the probability level of the result of this test were 0.25, what would you conclude about the number of books sold?

6   Would a finding with a probability level of 0.0001 mean that there was a greater change in the number of books sold than one with a probability level of 0.037?

7   If the value of this test were statistically significant, how would you determine if there had been a significant change between any two cells, say romance books, for the two shops?

8   Would you use a one- or a two-tailed level of significance to test the expectation that the first shop should sell more romance books than the second?

9   How would you determine a one-tailed level of significance from a two-tailed one of, say, 0.084?

10 If you wanted to find out if more men than women reported having fallen in love at first sight, would it be appropriate to test for this difference using a binomial test in which the number of men and women saying that they had had this experience was compared?

11 What test would you use to determine if women reported having a greater number of close friends than men?

12 When would you use the pooled rather than the separate variance estimates in interpreting the results of a *t* test?

13 What test would you use if you wanted to find out if the average number of books sold by the same ten shops had changed significantly in the three months of October, November and December?

Chapter 8

Bivariate analysis: exploring relationships between two variables

THIS CHAPTER FOCUSES on relationships between pairs of variables. Having examined the distribution of values for particular variables through the use of frequency tables, histograms, and associated statistics as discussed in Chapter 5, a major strand in the analysis of a set of data is likely to be bivariate analysis – how two variables are related to each other. The analyst is unlikely to be satisfied with the examination of single variables alone, but will probably be concerned to demonstrate whether variables are related. The investigation of relationships is an important step in explanation and consequently contributes to the building of theories about the nature of the phenomena in which we are interested. The emphasis on relationships can be contrasted with the material covered in the previous chapter, in which the ways in which cases or subjects may differ in respect to a variable were described. The topics covered in the present chapter bear some resemblance to those examined in Chapter 7, since the researcher in both contexts is interested in exploring variance and its connections with other variables. Moreover, if we find that members of different ethnic groups differ in regard to a variable, such as income, this may be taken to indicate that there is a relationship between ethnic group and income. Thus, as will be seen, there is no hard-and-fast distinction between the exploration of differences and of relationships.

What does it mean to say that two variables are related? We say that there is a relationship between two variables when the distribution of values for one variable is associated with the distribution exhibited by another variable. In other words, the variation exhibited by one variable is patterned in such a way that its variance is not randomly distributed in relation to the other variable. Examples of relationships that are frequently encountered are: middle-class individuals are more likely to vote Conservative than members of the working class; infant mortality is higher among countries with a low per capita income than those with a high per capita income; work alienation is greater in routine, repetitive work than in varied work. In each case, a relationship between two variables is indicated: between social class and voting behaviour; between the infant mortality rate and one measure of a nation's prosperity (per capita income); and between work alienation and job characteristics. Each of these examples implies that the variation in one variable is patterned, rather than randomly distributed, in relation to the other variable. Thus, in saying that there is a relationship between social class and voting behaviour from the above example, we are saying that people's tendency to vote Conservative is not randomly distributed across categories of social class. Middle-class individuals are more likely to vote for this party; if there was no relationship we would not be able to detect such a tendency since there would be no evidence that the middle and working classes differed in their propensity to vote Conservative.

Crosstabulation

In order to provide some more flesh to these ideas the notion of *crosstabulation* will be introduced in conjunction with an example. Crosstabulation is one of the simplest and most frequently used ways of demonstrating the presence or absence of a relationship. To illustrate its use, consider the hypothetical data on thirty individuals that are presented in Table 8.1. We have data on two variables: whether each person exhibits job satisfaction and whether they have been absent from work in the past six months. For ease of presentation, each variable can assume either of two values – yes or no. In order to examine the relationship between the two variables, individuals will be allocated to one of the four possible combinations that the two variables in conjunction can assume. Table 8.2 presents these four possible combinations, along with the frequency of their occurrence (as indicated from the data in Table 8.1). This procedure is very similar to that associated with frequency tables (see Chapter 5). We are trying to summarise and reduce the amount of information with which we are confronted to make it readable and analysable. Detecting a pattern in the relationship between two variables as in Table 8.1 is fairly easy when there are only thirty subjects and the variables are dichotomous; with larger data sets and more complex variables the task of seeing patterns without the employment of techniques for examining relationships would be difficult and probably lead to misleading conclusions.

The crosstabulation of the two variables is presented in Table 8.3. This kind of table is often referred to as a *contingency table*. Since there are four possible combinations of the two variables, the table requires four cells, in which the frequencies listed in Table 8.2 are placed. The following additional information is also presented. First, the figures to the right of the table are called the *row marginals* and those at the bottom of the table are the *column marginals*. These two items of information help us to interpret frequencies in the cells. Also, if the frequencies for each of the two variables have not been presented previously in a report or publication, the row and column marginals provide this information. Second, a percentage in each cell is presented. This

TABLE 8.1 Data for thirty individuals on job satisfaction and absenteeism

Subject	Job satisfaction	Absent in past 6 months
1	Yes	No
2	Yes	Yes
3	No	Yes
4	Yes	Yes
5	No	Yes
6	No	Yes
7	Yes	No
8	Yes	No
9	No	No
10	Yes	No
11	No	No
12	No	Yes
13	No	Yes
14	No	No
15	No	Yes
16	Yes	No
17	Yes	Yes
18	No	No
19	Yes	No
20	No	Yes
21	No	No
22	Yes	No
23	No	Yes
24	No	Yes
25	Yes	No
26	Yes	Yes
27	Yes	No
28	No	Yes
29	Yes	No
30	Yes	No

allows any patterning to be easily detectable, a facility that becomes especially helpful and important when tables with large numbers of cells are being examined. The percentages presented in Table 8.3 are *column percentages*, that

TABLE 8.2 Four possible combinations

Job satisfaction	Absent	N
Yes	Yes	4
Yes	No	10
No	Yes	11
No	No	5

TABLE 8.3 The relationship between job satisfaction and absenteeism

	Job satisfaction		
	Yes	No	Row marginals
Absenteeism Yes	1 4 29%	2 11 69%	15
Absenteeism No	3 10 71%	4 5 31%	15
Column marginals	14	16	30

is, the frequency in each cell is treated as a percentage of the column marginal for that cell. Thus, for cell 1 the frequency is 4 and the column marginal is 14; the column percentage is $(4/14) \times 100$, that is 28.6 (rounded up to 29 per cent).

What then does the contingency table show? Table 8.3 suggests that there is a relationship between job satisfaction and absence. People who express job satisfaction tend not to have been absent from work (cell 3), since the majority (71 per cent) of the fourteen individuals who express satisfaction have not been absent; on the other hand, of the sixteen people who are not satisfied, a majority of 69 per cent have been absent from work (cell 2). Thus, a relationship is implied; satisfied individuals *are* considerably less likely to be absent from work than those who are not satisfied.

In saying that a relationship exists between job satisfaction and absence, we are not suggesting that the relationship is perfect; some satisfied individuals *are* absent from work (cell 1) and some who are not satisfied have not been absent (cell 4). A relationship does not imply a perfect correspondence between the two variables. Such relationships are not specific to the social sciences – everyone has heard of the relationship between lung cancer and smoking, but no one believes that it implies that everyone who smokes will contract lung cancer or that lung cancer only afflicts those who smoke. If there had been a perfect relationship between satisfaction and absence, the contingency table presented in Table 8.4(a) would be in evidence; if there was no relationship, the crosstabulation in Table 8.4(b) would be expected. In the case of Table 8.4(a), all individuals who express satisfaction would be in the 'No' category, and all who are not satisfied would be in the absence category. With Table 8.4(b), those who are not satisfied are equally likely to have been absent as not absent.

As noted above, the percentages in Tables 8.2 to 8.4 are column percentages. Another kind of percentage that might have been preferred is a row percentage. With this calculation, the frequency in each cell is calculated in terms of the row totals, so that the percentage for cell 1 would be $(4/15) \times 100$, that is, 27 per cent. The row percentages for cells 2, 3 and 4 respectively would be 73 per cent, 67 per cent and 33 per cent. In taking row percentages, we would be emphasising a different aspect of the table, for example, the percentage of those who have been absent who are satisfied (27 per cent in cell 1) and the percentage who are not satisfied with their jobs (73 per cent in cell 2). The question of whether to use row or column percentages in part depends on what aspects of the data you want to highlight. It is sometimes suggested that the decision depends on whether the independent variable is across the top or along the side of the table: if the former, column percentages should be used;

TABLE 8.4   Two types of relationship

(a) A perfect relationship

Job satisfaction

		Yes	No	
Absenteeism	Yes	0	16 100%	16
	No	14 100%	0	14
		14	16	30

(b) No relationship

Job satisfaction

		Yes	No	
Absenteeism	Yes	7 50%	8 50%	15
	No	7 50%	8 50%	15
		14	16	30

if the latter, row percentages should be employed. Typically, the independent variable will go across the table, in which case column percentages should be used. However, this suggestion implies that there is a straightforward means of identifying the independent and dependent variables, but this is not always the case and great caution should be exercised in making such an inference for reasons that will be explored below. It may appear that job satisfaction is the independent and absence the dependent variable, but it is hazardous to make such an attribution.

SPSS can produce tables without percentages, though such tables are unlikely to be very helpful, and can produce output with either row or column percentages or both.

Crosstabulation with SPSS

Crosstabulations can easily be created with SPSS. Let us turn now to the Job Survey data. Imagine that we want to examine the relationship between **skill** and **gender** and that we want the following information in the table: counts (i.e. the frequency for each cell); the row percentages; the column percentages; and a chi-square test. This last piece of information will be dealt with in detail below. Let us also say that we want the dependent variable, **skill**, to go down the table and the independent variable, **gender**, to go across. To produce such output (see Table 8.5), the following sequence should be followed:

> →**Analyze** →**Descriptive Statistics** →**Crosstabs...** [opens **Crosstabs** dialog box shown in Box 8.1]
>
> →**skill** →▶ button [puts **income** in **Row[s]:** box] →**gender** →▶ button [puts **gender** in **Column[s]:** box] →**Statistics** [opens **Crosstabs: Statistics...** subdialog box shown in Box 8.2]
>
> →**Chi-square** → **Continue** [closes **Crosstabs: Statistics** dialog box]
>
> →**Cells...** [opens **Crosstabs: Cell Display** subdialog box shown in Box 8.3]
>
> [ensure **Observed** beneath **Counts** has been selected. Under **Percentages** ensure **Row** and **Column** have been selected.] →**Continue**
>
> →**OK**

If only column percentages were required, you need only click at the appropriate point. In fact, it is likely that only column percentages would be used since **gender** has been identified as the independent variable and goes

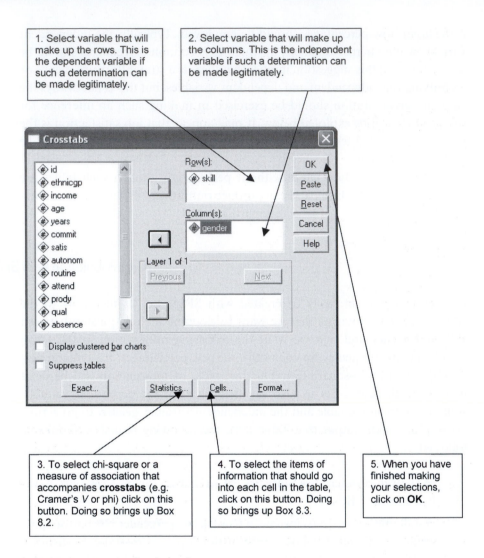

1. Select variable that will make up the rows. This is the dependent variable if such a determination can be made legitimately.

2. Select variable that will make up the columns. This is the independent variable if such a determination can be made legitimately.

3. To select chi-square or a measure of association that accompanies **crosstabs** (e.g. Cramer's *V* or phi) click on this button. Doing so brings up Box 8.2.

4. To select the items of information that should go into each cell in the table, click on this button. Doing so brings up Box 8.3.

5. When you have finished making your selections, click on **OK**.

BOX 8.1 Crosstabs dialog box

across the table; the row percentages are requested and presented here for illustrative purposes. Table 8.5 provides the output deriving from these.

Crosstabulation and statistical significance: the chi-square (χ^2) test

As the discussion of statistical significance in Chapter 6 implies, a problem that is likely to be of considerable concern is the question of whether there

1. To select a chi-square test to accompany a contingency table, click here.

2. When you have finished making your selections, click on **Continue**, which takes you back to Box 8.1.

Crosstabs: Statistics

☒ Chi-square   ☐ Correlations   Continue

Nominal   Ordinal   Cancel
☐ Contingency coefficient   ☐ Gamma   Help
☐ Phi and Cramér's V   ☐ Somers' d
☐ Lambda   ☐ Kendall's tau-b
☐ Uncertainty coefficient   ☐ Kendall's tau-c

Nominal by Interval   ☐ Kappa
☐ Eta   ☐ Risk
                       ☐ McNemar

☐ Cochran's and Mantel-Haenszel statistics
   Test common odds ratio equals: [1]

BOX 8.2   Crosstabs: Statistics subdialog box

really is a relationship between the two variables or whether the relationship has arisen by chance, for example as a result of sampling error having engendered an idiosyncratic sample. If the latter were the case, concluding that there is a relationship would mean that an erroneous inference was being made: if we find a relationship between two variables from an idiosyncratic sample, we would infer a relationship even though the two variables are *independent* (i.e. not related) in the population from which the sample was taken. Even though the sample may have been selected randomly, sampling error may have engendered an idiosyncratic sample, in which case the findings cannot be generalised to the population from which the sample was selected. What we need to know is the probability that there *is* a relationship between the two variables in the population from which a random sample was derived. In order to establish this probability, the chi-square (χ^2) test is widely used in conjunction with contingency tables. This is a test of statistical significance, meaning that it allows the researcher to ascertain the probability that the observed relationship between two variables may have arisen by chance. In the case of Table 8.3, it might be that there is no relationship between job satis-faction and absence in the company as a whole, and that the relationship

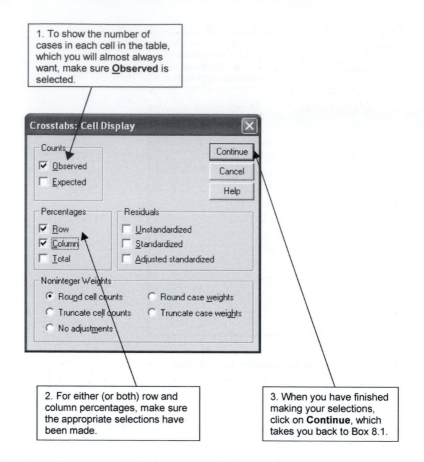

1. To show the number of cases in each cell in the table, which you will almost always want, make sure **Observed** is selected.

2. For either (or both) row and column percentages, make sure the appropriate selections have been made.

3. When you have finished making your selections, click on **Continue**, which takes you back to Box 8.1.

BOX 8.3 Crosstabs: Cell Display subdialog box

observed in our sample is a product of sampling error (i.e. the sample is in fact unrepresentative).

The starting point for the administration of a chi-square test, as with tests of statistical significance in general, is a *null hypothesis* of no relationship between the two variables being examined. In seeking to discern whether a relationship exists between two variables in the population from which a random sample was selected, the null hypothesis would need to be rejected. If the null hypothesis is confirmed, the proposition that there is a relationship must be rejected. The chi-square statistic is then calculated. This statistic is calculated by comparing the observed frequencies in each cell in a contingency table with those that would occur if there were no relationship between the two variables. These are the frequencies that would occur if the values associated with each of the two variables were randomly distributed in relation

TABLE 8.5 Contingency table: **skill** by **gender** (SPSS output)

Each **skill** by **gender** cell shows the number of cases (here 5 men who are unskilled), the row percentage below it (35.7% of unskilled workers are men), and the column percentage (12.8% of men are unskilled).

This column contains the *row* totals and percentages. Thus, 14 members of the sample are unskilled and make up 20% of the total sample.

SKILL * GENDER Crosstabulation

| | | | GENDER | | |
			men	women	Total
SKILL	unskilled	Count	5	9	14
		% within SKILL	35.7%	64.3%	100.0%
		% within GENDER	12.8%	29.0%	20.0%
	semi-skilled	Count	11	7	18
		% within SKILL	61.1%	38.9%	100.0%
		% within GENDER	28.2%	22.6%	25.7%
	fairly skilled	Count	11	10	21
		% within SKILL	52.4%	47.6%	100.0%
		% within GENDER	28.2%	32.3%	30.0%
	highly skilled	Count	12	5	17
		% within SKILL	70.6%	29.4%	100.0%
		% within GENDER	30.8%	16.1%	24.3%
Total		Count	39	31	70
		% within SKILL	55.7%	44.3%	100.0%
		% within GENDER	100.0%	100.0%	100.0%

This row shows the *column* totals and percentages. Thus, 39 members of the sample are men and make up 55.7% of the sample.

This is the calculated value of the chi-square test for this table.

Number of *degrees of freedom*.

Shows the level of statistical significance. A *p* value of .251 is higher than the conventional cut-off level of .05, so the relationship is not statistically significant.

Chi-Square Tests

	Value	df	Asymp. Sig. (2-sided)
Pearson Chi-Square	4.101[a]	3	.251
Likelihood Ratio	4.157	3	.245
Linear-by-Linear Association	2.591	1	.107
N of Valid Cases	70		

a. 0 cells (.0%) have expected count less than 5. The minimum expected count is 6.20.

to each other. In other words, the chi-square test entails a comparison of actual frequencies with those which would be expected to occur on the basis of chance alone (often referred to as the *expected frequencies*). The greater the difference between the observed and the expected frequencies, the larger the ensuing chi-square value will be; if the observed frequencies are very close to the expected frequencies, a small value is likely to occur.

The next step is for the researcher to decide what *significance level* to accept. This means that the researcher must decide what is an acceptable risk that the null hypothesis may be incorrectly rejected (i.e. a Type I error). The null hypothesis would be incorrectly rejected if, for example, there was in fact no relationship between job satisfaction and absence in the population, but our sample data (see Table 8.3) suggested that there was such a relationship. The significance level relates to the probability that we might be making such a false inference. If we say that the computed chi-square value is significant at the 0.05 level of statistical significance, we are saying that we would expect that a maximum of 5 in every 100 possible randomly selected samples that could be drawn from a population might appear to yield a relationship between two variables when in fact there is no relationship between them in that population. In other words, there is a 1 in 20 chance that we are rejecting the null hypothesis of no relationship when we should in fact be confirming it. If we set a more stringent qualification for rejection, the 0.01 level of significance, we are saying that we are only prepared to accept a chi-square value that implies a maximum of 1 sample in every 100 showing a relationship where none exists in the population. The probability estimate here is important – the probability of your having a deviant sample (i.e. one suggesting a relationship where none exists in the population) is greater if the 0.05 level is preferred to the 0.01 level. With the former, there is a 1 in 20 chance, but with the latter a 1 in 100 chance, that the null hypothesis will be erroneously rejected. An even more stringent test is to take the 0.001 level which implies that a maximum of 1 in 1000 samples might constitute a deviant sample. These three significance levels – 0.05, 0.01, 0.001 – are the ones most frequently encountered in reports of research results.

The calculated chi-square value must therefore be related to a significance level, but how is this done? It is *not* the case that a larger chi-square value implies a higher significance level. For one thing, the larger a table is, that is, the more cells it has, the larger a chi-square value is likely to be. This is because the value is computed by taking the difference between the observed and the expected frequencies for each cell in a contingency table and then adding all the differences. It would hardly be surprising if a contingency table comprising four cells exhibited a lower chi-square value than one with twenty cells. This would be a ridiculous state of affairs, since larger tables would always be more likely to yield statistically significant results than smaller ones. In order to relate the chi-square value to the significance level it is necessary to establish the number of degrees of freedom associated with a crosstabulation. This is calculated as follows:

(number of columns – 1)(number of rows – 1)

In Table 8.3, there are two columns and two rows (excluding the column and row marginals which are of no importance in calculating the degrees of freedom), implying that there is one degree of freedom, that is, $(2 - 1)(2 - 1)$. In addition to calculating the chi-square value, SPSS will calculate the degrees of freedom associated with a crosstabulation. In order to generate such output with SPSS, simply click on the **Statistics** button in the **Crosstabs** dialog box (Box 8.1) and in the **Crosstabs: Statistics** subdialog box click on **Chi-square** (Box 8.2), as suggested on page 205.

Table 8.5 provides the SPSS output for **skill** by **gender**. SPSS generates three types of chi-square value. The first of these – Pearson chi-square – is the statistic that is discussed in the text. The chi-square value is 4.101 with three degrees of freedom and the significance level is 0.25. This last figure suggests that there is unlikely to be a relationship between the two variables: although, for example, men (1) are more likely than women (2) to work on higher skill jobs (4), the respective column percentages being 30.8 per cent and 16.1 per cent, the chi-square value is not sufficiently large for us to be confident that the relationship could not have arisen by chance. There is a 25 per cent or 1 in 4 possibility that the there is no relationship between the two variables in the population. In other words, the null hypothesis of independence between the two variables is confirmed. By contrast, the contingency table presented in Table 8.3 generates a chi-square value of 4.82 which is significant at the 0.05 level, implying that we could have confidence in a relationship between the two variables in the population.

If desired, SPSS can also provide the expected values from which the calculation of a chi-square value is derived. This additional information can be useful in order to provide a stronger 'feel' for the degree to which the observed frequencies (the counts) differ from the distribution that would occur if chance alone were operating. This additional information can aid the understanding and interpretation of a relationship but would not normally be used in tables presented to readers. To generate expected frequencies, simply click on **Expected** in the **Crosstabs: Cell Display** subdialog box (see Box 8.3), as well as on **Observed**.

When presenting a contingency table and its associated chi-square test for a report or publication, some attention is needed to its appearance and to what is conveyed. Table 8.6 presents a 'cleaned' table of the output provided in Table 8.5. A number of points should be noted. First, only column marginals have been presented. Second, observed and expected frequencies are not included. Some writers prefer to include observed frequencies as well as

TABLE 8.6 Rated **skill** by **gender**

		Gender	
		Male %	Female %
Rated skill	Unskilled	13	29
	Semi-skilled	28	23
	Fairly skilled	28	32
	Highly skilled	31	16
	Total	$N = 39$	$N = 31$

Note: $\chi^2 = 4.10$ NS, $p > .05$.

column percentages, but if as in Table 8.6 the column marginals are included, observed frequencies can be omitted. Percentages have been rounded. Strictly speaking, this should only be done for large samples (e.g. in excess of 200), but rounding is often undertaken on smaller samples since it simplifies the understanding of relationships. The chi-square value is inserted at the bottom with the associated level of significance. In this case, the value is not significant at the 0.05 level, the usual minimum level for rejecting the null hypothesis. This is often indicated by NS (i.e. non-significant) and an indication of the significance level employed. Thus, $p > 0.05$ means that the chi-square value is below that necessary for achieving the 0.05 level, meaning that there is more than a 5 per cent chance that there is no relationship in the population. If the chi-square value exceeds that necessary for achieving the 0.05 level, one would write $p < 0.05$.

A number of points about chi-square should be registered in order to facilitate an understanding of its strengths and limitations, as well as some further points about its operation. First, chi-square is not a strong statistic in that it does not convey information about the *strength* of a relationship. This notion of strength of relationship will be examined in greater detail below when correlation is examined. By strength is meant that a large chi-square value and a correspondingly strong significance level (e.g. $p < 0.001$) cannot be taken to mean a closer relationship between two variables than when chi-square is considerably smaller but moderately significant (e.g. $p < 0.05$). What it is telling us is how confident we can be that there is a relationship between two variables. Second, the combination of a contingency table and chi-square is most likely to occur when either both variables are nominal (categorical) or when one is nominal and the other is ordinal. When both variables are ordinal or interval/ratio other approaches to the elucidation of relationships, such as correlation which allows strength of relationships to be examined and which therefore conveys more information, are likely to be preferred. When one variable is nominal and the other interval, such as the relationship between voting preference and age, the latter variable will need to be 'collapsed' into ordinal groupings (i.e. 20–29, 30–39, 40–49, etc.) in order to allow a contingency table and its associated chi-square value to be provided.

Third, chi-square should be adapted for use in relation to a 2×2 table, such as Table 8.3. A different formula is employed, using something called 'Yates' Correction for Continuity'. It is not necessary to go into the technical reasons for this correction, save to say that some writers take the view that the conventional formula results in an overestimate of the chi-square value when applied to a 2×2 table. When SPSS is used to calculate the chi-square value for such a table, two sets of computations are provided – one with and one before Yates' correction. Normally, the results of the former should be used. If Yates' correction has been used in the computation of the chi-square statistic, this should be clearly stated when the data are presented for publication.

Some writers suggest that the phi coefficient (ϕ) can be preferable to chi-square as a test of association between two dichotomous variables. This statistic, which is similar to the correlation coefficient (see below) in that it varies between 0 and plus or minus 1 to provide an indication of the strength of a relationship, can easily be generated in SPSS by clicking at the appropriate point in the **Crosstabs: Statistics** subdialog box (see Box 8.2). The statistical significance of the value of phi is given in the SPSS output.

Fourth, chi-square can be unreliable if expected cell frequencies are less than five, although like Yates' correction for 2×2 tables, this is a source of some controversy. SPSS prints the number and percentage of such cells.

Correlation

The idea of correlation is one of the most important and basic in the elaboration of bivariate relationships. Unlike chi-square, measures of correlation indicate both the strength and the direction of the relationship between a pair of variables. Two types of measure can be distinguished: measures of linear correlation using interval variables and measures of rank correlation using ordinal variables. While these two types of measure of correlation share some common properties, they also differ in some important respects which will be examined after the elucidation of measures of linear correlation.

Linear correlation: relationships between interval variables

Correlation entails the provision of a yardstick whereby the intensity or strength of a relationship can be gauged. To provide such estimates, *correlation coefficients* are calculated. These provide succinct assessments of the closeness of a relationship among pairs of variables. Their widespread use in the social sciences has meant that the results of tests of correlation have become easy to recognise and interpret. When variables are interval/ratio, by far the most common measure of correlation is *Pearson's Product Moment Correlation Coefficient*, often referred to as Pearson's *r*. This measure of correlation presumes that interval variables are being used, so that even ordinal variables are not supposed to be employed, although this is a matter of some debate (e.g. O'Brien, 1979).

In order to illustrate some of the fundamental features of correlation, *scatter diagrams* (often called 'scattergrams' or 'scatterplots') will be employed. A scatter diagram plots each individual case on a graph, thereby representing for each case the points at which the two variables intersect. Thus, each point on the scatter diagram represents each respondent's position in relation to each of these two variables. Let us say that we want to examine the relationship between two Job Survey variables – **satis** and **routine**. In Figure 8.1, the data for these two variables are plotted to form a scatter diagram. Thus, case number 3, which has a **satis** score of 15 and a **routine** score of 8, is positioned at the intersection of these two values on the graph. This case has an arrow pointing to it in the figure.

Initially, the nature of the relationship between two variables can be focused upon. It should be apparent that the pattern of the points moves downwards from left to right. This pattern implies a *negative relationship*, meaning that as one variable increases the other decreases: higher **routine** levels are associated with lower levels of job satisfaction; lower levels of **routine** with higher levels of job satisfaction. In Figure 8.2 a different kind of relationship between two variables is exhibited. Here, there is a *positive relationship*, with higher values on one variable (**satis**) being associated with higher values on the other (**autonom**). In Figure 8.2, case number 3 again has an arrow pointing to it. Notice how in neither case is the relationship between the two variables a perfect one. If there was a perfect linear relationship, all of the points in the scatter diagram would be on a straight line (see Figure 8.3), a situation which almost never occurs in the social sciences. Instead, we tend to have, as in Figures 8.1 and 8.2, a certain amount of scatter, though a pattern is often visible, such as the negative and positive relationships each figure respectively exhibits. If there is a large amount of scatter, so that no patterning

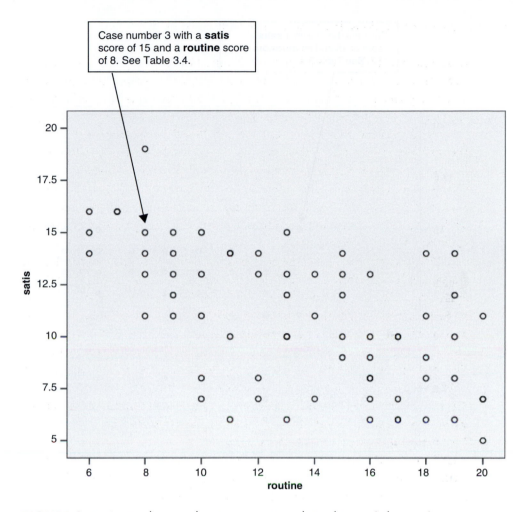

Case number 3 with a **satis** score of 15 and a **routine** score of 8. See Table 3.4.

FIGURE 8.1 Scatter diagram showing a negative relationship: **satis** by **routine**

is visible, we can say that there is no or virtually no relationship between two variables (see Figure 8.4).

In addition to positive and negative relationships we sometimes find *curvilinear relationships*, in which the shape of the relationship between two variables is not straight, but curves at one or more points. Figure 8.5 provides three different types of curvilinear relationship. The relationship between organisational size and organisational properties, like the amount of special-isation, often takes a form similar to diagram (c) in Figure 8.5 (Child, 1973). When patterns similar to those exhibited in Figure 8.5 are found, the relationship is *non-linear*, that is it is not straight, and it is not appropriate

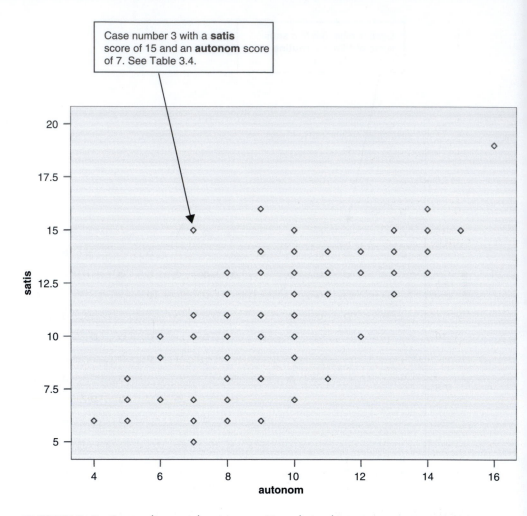

Case number 3 with a **satis** score of 15 and an **autonom** score of 7. See Table 3.4.

FIGURE 8.2 Scatter diagram showing a positive relationship

to employ a measure of linear correlation like Pearson's *r*. When scatter diagrams are similar to the patterns depicted in Figure 8.5 (b) and (c), researchers often transform the independent variable into a logarithmic scale, which will usually engender a linear relationship and hence will allow the employment of Pearson's *r*. Here we see an important reason for investigating scatter diagrams before computing *r* – if there is a non-linear relationship the computed estimate of correlation will be meaningless, but unless a scatter diagram is checked it is not possible to determine whether the relationship is not linear.

Scatter diagrams allow three aspects of a relationship to be discerned:

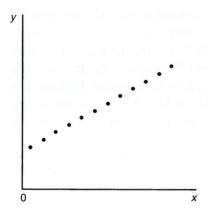

FIGURE 8.3   A perfect relationship

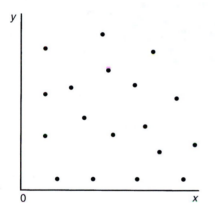

FIGURE 8.4   No relationship or virtually no relationship

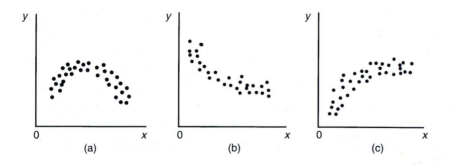

FIGURE 8.5   Three curvilinear relationships

whether it is linear; the direction of the relationship (i.e. whether positive or negative); and the strength of the relationship. The amount of scatter is indicative of the strength of the relationship. Compare the pairs of positive and negative relationships in Figures 8.6 and 8.7 respectively. In each case the right-hand diagram exhibits more scatter than the left-hand diagram. The left-hand diagram exhibits the stronger relationship: the greater the scatter (with the points on the graph departing more and more from being positioned on a straight line as in Figure 8.3), the weaker the relationship.

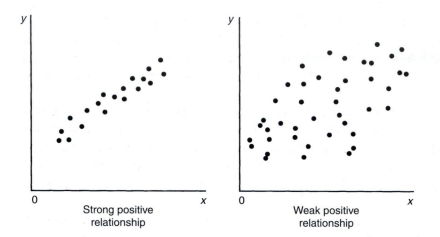

FIGURE 8.6 Two positive relationships

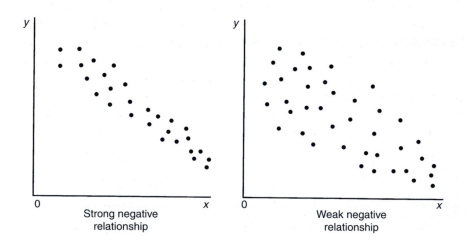

FIGURE 8.7 Two negative relationships

Scatter diagrams are useful aids to the understanding of correlation. Pearson's r allows the strength and direction of linear relationships between variables to be gauged. Pearson's r varies between -1 and $+1$. A relationship of -1 or $+1$ would indicate a perfect relationship, negative or positive respectively, between two variables. Thus, Figure 8.4 would denote a perfect positive relationship of $+1$. The complete absence of a relationship would engender a computed r of zero. The closer r is to 1 (whether positive or negative), the stronger the relationship between two variables. The nearer r is to zero (and hence the further it is from $+1$ or -1), the weaker the relationship. These ideas are expressed in Figure 8.8. If r is 0.82, this would indicate a strong positive relationship between two variables, whereas 0.24 would denote a weak positive relationship. Similarly, -0.79 and -0.31 would be indicative of strong and weak negative relationships respectively. In Figures 8.6 and 8.7, the left-hand diagrams would be indicative of larger computed rs than those on the right.

What is a large correlation? Cohen and Holliday (1982) suggest the following: 0.19 and below is very low; 0.20 to 0.39 is low; 0.40 to 0.69 is modest; 0.70 to 0.89 is high; and 0.90 to 1 is very high. However, these are rules of thumb and should not be regarded as definitive indications, since there are hardly any guidelines for interpretation over which there is substantial consensus.

Further, caution is required when comparing computed coefficients. We can certainly say that an r of -0.60 is larger than one of -0.30, but we cannot say that the relationship is twice as strong. In order to see why not, a useful aid to the interpretation of r will be introduced – the *coefficient of determination* (r^2). This is simply the square of r multiplied by 100. It provides us with an indication of how far variation in one variable is accounted for by the other. Thus, if $r = -0.6$, then $r^2 = 36$ per cent. This means that 36 per cent of the variance in one variable is due to the other. When $r = -0.3$, then r^2 will be 9 per cent. Thus, although an r of -0.6 is twice as large as one of -0.3, it cannot indicate that the former is twice as strong as the latter, because *four* times more variance is being accounted for by an r of -0.6 than one of -0.3. Thinking about the coefficient of determination can have a salutary effect on one's

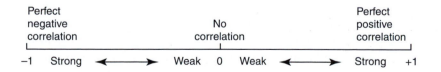

FIGURE 8.8 The strength and direction of correlation coefficients

interpretation of r. For example, when correlating two variables, x and y, an r of 0.7 sounds quite high, but it would mean that less than half of the variance in y can be attributed to x (i.e. 49 per cent). In other words, 51 per cent of the variance in y is due to variables other than x.

A word of caution is relevant at this point. In saying that 49 per cent of the variation in y is attributable to x, we must recognise that this also means that 49 per cent of the variation in x is due to y. Correlation is not the same as cause. We cannot determine from an estimate of correlation that one variable causes the other, since correlation provides estimates of covariance, that is, that two variables are related. We may find a large correlation of 0.8 between job satisfaction and organisational commitment, but does this mean that 64 per cent of the variation in job satisfaction can be attributed to commitment? This would suggest that organisational commitment is substantially caused by job satisfaction. But the reverse can also hold true: 64 per cent of the variation in organisational commitment may be due to job satisfaction. It is not possible from a simple correlation between these two variables to arbitrate between the two possibilities. Indeed, as Chapter 10 will reveal, there may be reasons other than not knowing which causes which for needing to be cautious about presuming causality.

Another way of expressing these ideas is through Venn diagrams (see Figure 8.9). If we treat each circle as representing the amount of variance exhibited by each of two variables, x and y, Figure 8.9 illustrates three conditions: in the top diagram we have independence in which the two variables do not overlap, that is, a correlation of zero as represented by Figure 8.4 or in terms of a contingency table by Table 8.4(b); in the middle diagram there is a perfect relationship in which the variance of x and y coincides perfectly, that is, a correlation of 1 as represented by Figure 8.3 or the contingency table in Table 8.4(a); and the bottom diagram which points to a less than perfect, though strong, relationship between x and y, that is, as represented by the left-hand diagrams in Figures 8.6 and 8.7. Here only parts of the two circles intersect, that is, the shaded area, which represents just over 67 per cent of the variance shared by the two variables; the unshaded area of each circle denotes a sphere of variance for each variable that is unrelated to the other variable.

It is possible to provide an indication of the statistical significance of r. This is described in the next section. The way in which the significance of r is calculated is strongly affected by the number of cases for which there are pairs of data. For example, if you have approximately 500 cases, r only needs to be 0.088 or 0.115 to be significant at the 0.05 and 0.01 levels respectively. If you have just eighteen cases (as in Table 8.6), r will need to be at least 0.468 or 0.590 respectively. Some investigators only provide information about the sig-

(a) Independence: the two variables are totally unrelated

(b) A perfect relationship

(c) A relationship

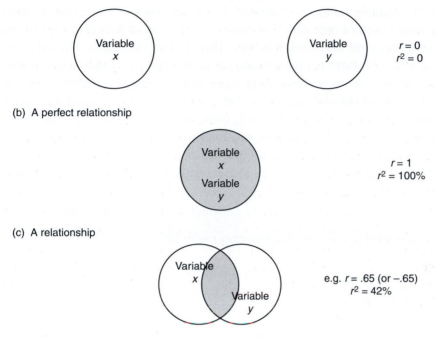

FIGURE 8.9 Types of relationship

nificance of relationships. However, this is a grave error since what is and is not significant is profoundly affected by the number of cases. What statistical significance does tell us is the likelihood that a relationship of at least this size could have arisen by chance. It is necessary to interpret both r and the significance level when computing correlation coefficients. For example, a correlation of 0.17 in connection with a random sample of 1,000 individuals would be significant at the 0.001 level, but would indicate that this weak relationship is unlikely to have arisen by chance and that we can be confident that a relationship of at least this size holds in the population. Consider an alternative scenario of a correlation of 0.43 based on a sample of 42. The significance level would be 0.01, but it would be absurd to say that the former correlation was more important than the latter simply because the correlation of 0.17 is more significant. The second coefficient is larger, though we have to be somewhat more circumspect in this second case than in the first in inferring that the relationship could not have arisen by chance. Thus, the size of r and the significance level must by considered in tandem. The test of statistical significance tells us whether a correlation could have arisen by chance (i.e. sampling error) or whether it is likely to exist in the population from which the sample was selected. It tells us how likely it is that we might conclude from sample data that there is a relationship between two variables when there is no relationship between them in the population. Thus, if $r = 0.7$ and $p < 0.01$, there is only one chance in 100 that we could have selected a sample that shows a relationship when none exists in the population. We would almost certainly conclude that the relationship is statistically significant. However, if $r = 0.7$ and $p = 0.1$, there are ten chances in 100 that we have selected a sample which shows a relationship when none exists in the population. We would probably decide that the risk of concluding that there is a relationship in the population is too great and conclude that the relationship is non-significant.

Generating scatter diagrams and computing *r* with SPSS

Taking the Job Survey data, if you wanted to plot **satis** and **routine**, assuming that the latter variable was to form the horizontal axis, the following sequence would be used:

→**Graphs** →**Scatter/Dot** [opens **Scatter/Dot** dialog box shown in Box 8.4]

→**Simple Scatter** →**Define** [opens **Simple Scatterplot** subdialog box shown in Box 8.5]

→**satis** →▶button [puts **satis** in box **Y** **Axis:**] →**routine** →▶button [puts **routine** in box by **X** **Axis:**] →**OK**

Examples of SPSS scatter diagram output can be found in Figures 8.1 and 8.2. The appearance of the points in the diagram can be varied by

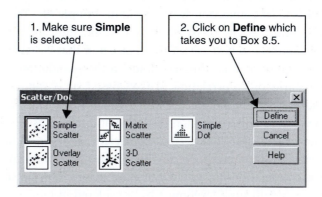

BOX 8.4 **Scatter/Dot** dialog box

BOX 8.5 Simple Scatterplot subdialog box

double-clicking anywhere in the scatterplot. This brings up the **SPSS Chart Editor**. A smaller version of this will appear in the **Chart Editor**. Click once on any circle in the figure in the **Chart Editor** (dark double circles will appear). Then, double click on any of these double circles and a **Properties** dialog box will appear. Click on the downward pointing arrow next to **Type**, click on your preferred choice and then click on **Apply** and **Close**. It is also possible to vary the size of the points. Figures 8.1 and 8.2 illustrate two different types of marker. The colour of the scatterplot points can be changed by clicking on **Format** on the **Chart Editor** menu bar and then selecting **Color...** .

In order to generate correlation coefficients for the variables **routine, autonom** and **satis**, the following sequence should be followed:

→**Analyze** →**Correlate** →**Bivariate...** [opens **Bivariate Correlations** dialog box shown in Box 8.6]

→**autonom** →►button →**routine** →►button →**satis** →►button [puts

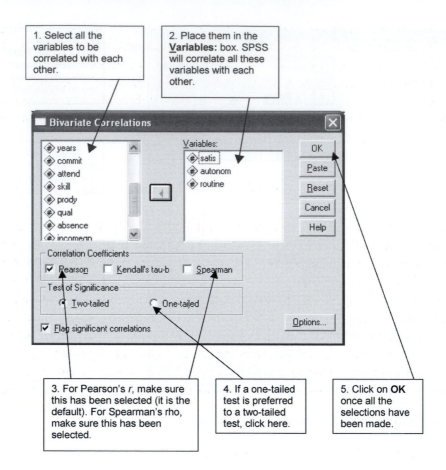

1. Select all the variables to be correlated with each other.

2. Place them in the **Variables:** box. SPSS will correlate all these variables with each other.

3. For Pearson's *r*, make sure this has been selected (it is the default). For Spearman's rho, make sure this has been selected.

4. If a one-tailed test is preferred to a two-tailed test, click here.

5. Click on **OK** once all the selections have been made.

BOX 8.6   Bivariate Correlations dialog box

autonom, **routine** and **satis** in **Variables:** box] →**Pearson** [*if* not already selected] →**One tailed** [*if* preferred to **Two-tailed**] →**OK**

SPSS will delete missing cases on a *pairwise* basis, meaning that missing cases will only be excluded for each pair of variables. With *listwise* deletion of missing cases, the correlation coefficients will only be produced on those cases for which data are all available for all three variables. If listwise deletion is preferred, before clicking on **OK**:

→**Options…** [opens **Bivariate Correlations: Options** subdialog box]

→**Exclude cases listwise** → Continue [closes **Bivariate Correlations: Options** subdialog box]

→**OK**

A matrix of correlation coefficients will be generated, as in Table 8.7. This table includes both the levels of statistical significance achieved for each coefficient and the number of cases. If pairwise deletion has been selected, the number of cases may vary from pair to pair (as in Table 8.7), but if list-wise deletion of missing cases was selected, the numbers of cases will be the same. All coefficients are quite large and all achieve a high level of statistical significance at $p < 0.000$ (which means $p < 0.0005$).

Rank correlation: relationships between ordinal variables

In order to employ Pearson's r, variables must be interval and the relationship must be linear. When variables are at the ordinal level, an alternative measure of correlation can be used called *rank correlation*. Two prominent methods for examining the relationship between pairs of ordinal variables are available – Spearman's rho (ρ) and Kendall's tau (τ) – the former probably being more common in reports of research findings. The interpretation of the results of either method is identical to Pearson's r, in that the computed coefficient will vary between -1 and $+1$. Thus, it provides information on the strength *and* direction of relationships. Moreover, unlike Pearson's r, rho and tau are non-parametric methods which means that they can be used in a wide

TABLE 8.7 *Matrix of Pearson product moment correlation coefficients (SPSS output)*

Each cell shows: the level of correlation (in this case .733 between **autonom** and **satis**); the significance level (.000, which is much better than the conventional cut-off of .05, suggesting that the relationship is definitely statistically significant); and the number of cases on which the calculation was performed (68).

Correlations

		satis	autonom	routine
satis	Pearson Correlation	1	.733**	-.580**
	Sig. (2-tailed)	.	.000	.000
	N	68	68	68
autonom	Pearson Correlation	.733**	1	-.487**
	Sig. (2-tailed)	.000	.	.000
	N	68	70	70
routine	Pearson Correlation	-.580**	-.487**	1
	Sig. (2-tailed)	.000	.000	.
	N	68	70	70

**. Correlation is significant at the 0.01 level (2-tailed).

variety of contexts since they make fewer assumptions about variables. Obviously, the formulae for the two methods of measuring correlation differ, but the areas of divergence need not concern us here. Kendall's tau usually produces slightly smaller correlations, but since rho is more commonly used by researchers, it is probably preferable to report this statistic unless there are obvious reasons for thinking otherwise. One possible reason that is sometimes suggested for preferring tau is that it deals better with tied ranks – for example, where two or more people are at the same rank. Thus, if there seems to be quite a large proportion of tied ranks, tau may be preferable.

Let us say that we want to correlate **skill**, **prody** and **qual**, each of which is an ordinal measure. Even though these are ordinal variables, they have to be rank ordered. SPSS allows both tau and rho to be computed. The procedure is essentially identical to that used above for generating Pearson's *r*, except that it is necessary to select Kendall's tau or Spearman's rho or both. Thus the sequence is:

> →**Analyze** →**Correlate** →**Bivariate...** [opens **Bivariate Correlations** dialog box shown in Box 8.6]
>
> →**qual** →▶ button →**prody** →▶ button →**skill** →▶ button [puts **qual**, **prody** and **skill** into **Variables** box] →**Kendall's tau-b** [*if* not already selected] or **Spearman** or both →**One tailed** [*if* preferred to **Two-tailed**]
>
> →**OK**

It will also be necessary to decide whether to exclude missing cases on a listwise or pairwise basis through the **Options** button. Table 8.8 shows the output for Spearman's rho only. All of the correlations reported in Table 8.8 are low, the largest being the correlation between **prody** and **skill** (0.24 rounded up). This is the only one of the three correlations that achieves statistical significance at $p < 0.05$. Thus, there is a tendency for better skilled workers to be more productive.

Although rank correlation methods are more flexible than Pearson's *r*, the latter tends to be preferred because interval/ratio variables comprise more information than ordinal ones. One of the reasons for the widespread use in the social sciences of questionnaire items which are built up into scales or indices (and which are then treated as interval variables) is probably that stronger approaches to the investigation of relationships like Pearson's *r* (and regression – see below) can be employed.

TABLE 8.8   Matrix of Spearman's rho correlation coefficients

Correlations

Spearman's rho			skill	prody	qual
skill	Correlation Coefficient		1.000	.239*	.013
	Sig. (2-tailed)		.	.048	.913
	N		70	69	70
prody	Correlation Coefficient		.239*	1.000	.171
	Sig. (2-tailed)		.048	.	.160
	N		69	69	69
qual	Correlation Coefficient		.013	.171	1.000
	Sig. (2-tailed)		.913	.160	.
	N		70	69	70

*. Correlation is significant at the 0.05 level (2-tailed).

Other approaches to bivariate relationships

Up to now, the approach to the examination of relationships has been undertaken within a framework in which the nature of the variables has been the most important factor: crosstabulation and chi-square are most likely to occur in conjunction with nominal variables; Pearson's r presumes the use of interval variables; and when examining pairs of ordinal variables, rho or tau should be employed. However, what if, as can easily occur in the social sciences, pairs of variables are of different types, for example, nominal plus ordinal or ordinal plus interval? There are methods for the elucidation of relationships which can deal with such eventualities. Freeman (1965), for example, catalogues a vast array of methods that can be used in such circumstances. There are problems with many of these methods. First, they are unfamiliar to most readers, who would therefore experience great difficulty in understanding and interpreting the results of calculations. Second, while particular statistical methods should not be followed fetishistically, the notion of learning a new statistical method each time a particular combination of circumstances arises is also not ideal. Third, for many unusual methods, software is not available, even within a wide-ranging package like SPSS.

One rule of thumb that can be recommended is to move downwards in measurement level when confronted with a pair of different variables. Thus, if you have an ordinal and an interval variable, a method of rank correlation could be used. If you have an ordinal and a nominal variable, you should use crosstabulation and chi-square. This may mean collapsing ranks into groups (for example, 1–5, 6–10, 11–15, and so on) and assigning ranks to the groupings (for example, 1–5 = 1, 6–10 = 2, 11–15 = 3, and so on), using the

Recode procedure. If you have a nominal and an interval variable, again the combination of a contingency table and chi-square is likely to be used. As suggested in the discussion of crosstabulation, the interval variable will need to be collapsed into groups. The chief source of concern with collapsing values of an ordinal or interval variable is that the choice of cut-off points is bound to be arbitrary and will have a direct impact on the results obtained. Accordingly, it may be better to use more than one method of grouping or to employ a fairly systematic procedure such as quartiles as a means of collapsing cases into four groups.

When pairs of variables are dichotomous, the phi coefficient should be given serious consideration. Its interpretation is the same as Pearson's r, in that it varies between 0 and +1 or −1. A description of a test of statistical significance for phi was provided in the section on crosstabulation. As such, it can measure both the strength and direction of relationships among pairs of dichotomous variables.

Statistics textbooks often present a host of methods for examining relationships which are rarely seen in reports of research. It is not proposed to provide such a catalogue here, but two methods are particularly worthy of attention. First, in order to provide a measure of the strength of the relationship between two variables from a contingency table, Cramer's V can be recommended. This test, whose calculation in large part derives from chi-square, provides results which vary between 0 and +1. Moreover, in a 2×2 table, phi and Cramer's V will yield the same result. For the data in Table 8.5, which analysed the relationship between **skill** and **gender**, Cramer's V is 0.24 (rounded down), suggesting a weak relationship. Phi can be generated in SPSS through the **Crosstabs...** procedure by ensuring that in the **Crosstabs: Statistics** subdialog box (see Box 8.2), **Phi and Cramer's V** has been selected. This will provide both phi and Cramer's V. The former should be used for 2×2 tables; Cramer's V should be used for larger tables in which the number of both rows and columns is greater than 2.

Second, when the researcher is confronted with an interval dependent variable and an independent variable that is either nominal or ordinal, the eta coefficient warrants consideration. Like Cramer's V, it can only vary between 0 and +1 and can be computed through the **Crosstabs** procedure by ensuring that in the **Crosstabs: Statistics** subdialog box (see Box 8.2), **Phi and Cramer's V** has been activated (i.e. has a tick by it). A common derivation of eta is eta-squared, which is similar to r^2 in its underlying interpretation. Thus, eta-squared refers to the amount of variation in the dependent (i.e. interval) variable that is accounted for by the independent (i.e. nominal or ordinal) variable. Both eta and eta-squared are also produced by SPSS when an analysis of variance is requested in association with the **Means...** procedure, which is described below. Eta can be regarded as a useful test which provides a measure of strength of relationship in the contexts cited above. However, because it forces the researcher to commit him- or herself to which variable is independent, eta may be sensible to avoid when such decisions are particularly difficult.

The SPSS **Means...** procedure provides an interesting way of analysing pairs of variables when the dependent variable is interval and the independent variable is either nominal, ordinal, or dichotomous. This procedure is very similar to **Crosstabs**, except that with **Means...** the dependent variable is broken down in terms of the independent variable and the mean and standard deviation of the dependent variable for each subgroup of the independent variable are computed. Thus, if we knew the incomes and ethnic group membership for a sample of individuals, we could examine the mean income of each of the ethnic groups identified, as well as the standard deviations for each subgroup mean. This allows the impact of the independent variable on the dependent variable to be examined. Earlier it was suggested that if we have an interval and an ordinal variable, we should examine the relationship between them using rank correlation. However, if the ordinal variable has relatively few categories and the interval variable has many values, it is likely to be more appropriate to use **Means...**. If rank correlation is used in such a context, the contrast between the two variables is considerable and makes the ensuing statistic difficult to interpret.

Let us say that we wish to look at the relationship between **satis** and **skill** (which only has four categories) in the Job Survey data. The following sequence should be followed:

> **Analyze →Compare Means →Means...** [opens **Means** dialog box shown in Box 8.7]
>
> **→satis →▶**button by **Dependent List:** [puts **satis** in **Dependent List:** box]
>
> **→skill →▶** button by **Independent List:** [puts **skill** in **Independent List:** box] **→Options** [opens **Means: Options** subdialog box shown in Box 8.8]
>
> [ensure **Mean**, **Standard Deviation** and **Number of Cases** appear in the **Cell Statistics:** box] **→ Anova table and eta** in the **Statistics for First Layer** box
>
> **→Continue** [closes **Means: Options** subdialog box]
>
> **→OK**

An analysis of variance table will be produced along with the F ratio (which provides a test of statistical significance), and eta and eta-squared.

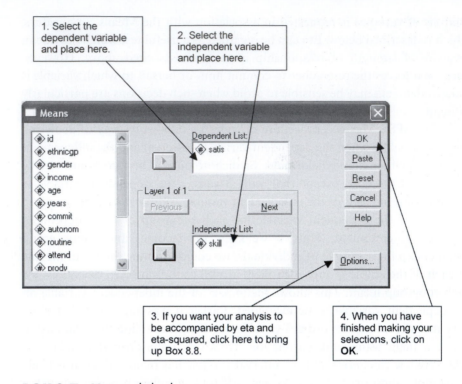

BOX 8.7 Means dialog box

Table 8.9 provides SPSS output from this set of commands. As this output shows, job satisfaction varies by skill (with lower **satis** means for lower **skill** levels) and the *F* ratio of 6.782 is significant at the 0.0005 level, suggesting a strong probability of a relationship in the population. The eta-squared suggests that about one-quarter of the variance of **satis** can be attributed to **skill**. Thus, **Means...** can be considered a useful tool for examining relationships when there is an interval dependent variable and a nominal, dichotomous, or short ordinal variable. However, it only makes sense if the interval variable can be unambiguously recognised as the dependent variable.

Regression

Regression has become one of the most widely used techniques in the analysis of data in the social sciences. It is closely connected to Pearson's *r*, as will become apparent at a number of points. Indeed, it shares many of the same

Means: Options

Statistics:

Median
Grouped Median
Std. Error of Mean
Sum
Minimum
Maximum
Range
First
Last
Variance
Kurtosis
Std. Error of Kurtosis
Skewness
Std. Error of Skewne
Harmonic Mean

Cell Statistics:

Mean
Number of Cases
Standard Deviation

Statistics for First Layer
☑ Anova table and eta
☐ Test for linearity

Continue   Cancel   Help

1. Click here for eta.
An analysis of
variance will also be
performed.

2. Click on **Continue**,
which takes you back
to Box 8.7.

BOX 8.8   Means: Options subdialog box

assumptions as *r*, such as that relationships between variables are linear and that variables are interval. In this section, the use of regression to explore relationships between pairs of variables will be examined. It should become apparent that regression is a powerful tool for summarising the nature of the relationship between variables and for making predictions of likely values of the dependent variable.

At this point, it is worth returning to the scatter diagrams encountered in Figures 8.1 and 8.2. Each departs a good deal from Figure 8.3 in which all of the points are on a straight line, since the points in Figures 8.1 and 8.2 are more scattered. The idea of regression is to summarise the relationship between two variables by producing a line which fits the data closely. This line is called the *line of best fit*. Only one line will minimise the deviations of all of the dots in a scatter diagram from the line. Some points will appear above the line, some below and a small proportion may actually be on the line. Because only one line can meet the criterion of line of best fit, it is unlikely that it can

TABLE 8.9 Means output for **satis** by **skill**

Case Processing Summary

	Cases					
	Included		Excluded		Total	
	N	Percent	N	Percent	N	Percent
satis * skill	68	97.1%	2	2.9%	70	100.0%

Report

satis

skill	Mean	N	Std. Deviation
unskilled	8.64	14	2.499
semi-skilled	9.67	18	2.401
fairly skilled	11.79	19	3.376
highly skilled	12.82	17	3.264
Total	10.84	68	3.304

Shows the mean level of **satis** for each category of **skill** along with the number of cases in each category and the standard deviation.

This is an analysis of variance table which provides an *F* test for the data and shows that the significance level associated with the *F* test is .000, which is a very high level.

ANOVA Table

			Sum of Squares	df	Mean Square	F	Sig.
satis * skill	Between Groups	(Combined)	176.378	3	58.793	6.782	.000
	Within Groups		554.843	64	8.669		
	Total		731.221	67			

Measures of Association

	Eta	Eta Squared
satis * skill	.491	.241

This part of the output shows eta and therefore the strength of relationship between **skill** and **satis**.

accurately be drawn by visual inspection. This is where regression comes in. Regression procedures allow the precise line of best fit to be computed. Once we know the line of best fit, we can make predictions about likely values of the dependent variable, for particular values of the independent variable.

In order to understand how the line of best fit operates, it is necessary to get to grips with the simple equation that governs its operation and how we make predictions from it. The equation is

$$y = a + bx + e$$

In this equation, y and x are the dependent and independent variables respectively. The two elements, a and b, refer to aspects of the line itself. First, a is known as the intercept, which is the point at which the line cuts the vertical axis. Second, b is the slope of the line of the best fit and is usually referred to as the regression coefficient. By the 'slope' is meant the rate at which changes in values of the independent variable (x) affect values of the dependent variable (y). In order to predict y for a given value of x, it is necessary to

1   multiply the value of x by the regression coefficient, b, and
2   add this calculation to the intercept, a.

Finally, e is referred to as an *error term* which points to the fact that a proportion of the variance in the dependent variable, y, is unexplained by the regression equation. In order to simplify the following explanation of regression, for the purposes of making predictions the error term is ignored and so will not be referred to below.

Consider the following example. A researcher may want to know whether managers who put in extra hours after the normal working day tend to get on better in the organisation than others. The researcher finds out the average amount of time a group of twenty new managers in a firm spend working on problems after normal working hours. Two years later the managers are re-examined to find out their annual salaries. Individuals' salaries are employed as an indicator of progress, since incomes often reflect how well a person is getting on in a firm. Moreover, for these managers, extra hours of work are not rewarded by overtime payments, so salaries are a real indication of progress. Let us say that the regression equation which is derived from the analysis is

$$y = 7500 + 500x$$

The line of best fit is drawn in Figure 8.10.

The intercept, a, is 7,500, that is, £7,500; the regression coefficient, b, is 500, that is, £500. The latter means that each extra hour worked produces an extra £500 on a manager's annual salary. We can calculate the likely annual salary of someone who puts in an extra 7 hours per week as follows:

$$y = 7500 + (500)(7)$$

which becomes

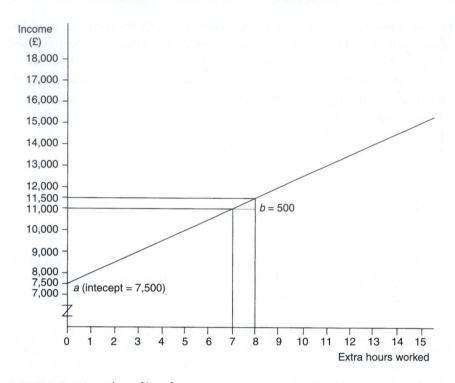

FIGURE 8.10 A line of best fit

$$y = 7500 + 3500$$

which becomes

$$y = 11000 \text{ (i.e. £11,000)}$$

For someone who works an extra 8 hours per week, the likely salary will be £11,500, that is, 7500 + (500)(8). If a person does not put in any extra work, the salary is likely to be £7,500, that is, 7500 + (500)(0). Thus, through regression, we are able to show how y changes for each additional increment of x (because the regression coefficient expresses how much more of y you get for each extra increment of x) and to predict the likely value of y for a given value of x. When a relationship is negative, the regression equation for the line of best fit will take the form $y = a - bx$ (see Figure 8.11). Thus, if a regression equation is $y = 50 - 2x$, each extra increment of x produces a decrease in y. If we wanted to know the likely value of y when $x = 12$, we would substitute as follows:

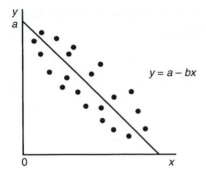

FIGURE 8.11   Regression: a negative relationship

$$y = 50 - 2x$$
$$y = 50 - (2)(12)$$
$$y = 50 - 24$$
$$y = 26$$

When a line of best fit shows a tendency to be vertical and to intersect with the horizontal axis, the intercept, a, will have a minus value. This is because it will cut the horizontal axis and when extended to the vertical axis it will intercept it at a negative point (see Figure 8.12). In this situation the regression equation will take the form:

$$y = -a + bx$$

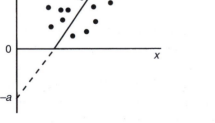

FIGURE 8.12   Regression: a negative intercept

Supposing the equation were $y = -7 + 23x$, if we wanted to know the likely value of y when $x = 3$, we would substitute as follows

$$y = -7 + 23x$$
$$y = -7 + (23)(3)$$
$$y = -7 + 69$$
$$y = 69 - 7$$
$$y = 62$$

As suggested at the start of this section, correlation and regression are closely connected. They make identical assumptions that variables are interval/ratio and that relationships are linear. Further, r and r^2 are often employed as indications of how well the regression line fits the data. For example, if $r = 1$, the line of best fit would simply be drawn straight through all of the points (see Figure 8.13). Where points are more scattered, the line of best fit will provide a poorer fit with the data. Accordingly, the more scatter there is in a scatter diagram, the less accurate the prediction of likely y values will be. Thus, the closer r is to 1, the less scatter there is and, therefore, the better the fit between the line of best fit and the data. If the two scatter diagrams in Figures 8.6 and 8.7 are examined, the line of best fit for the left-hand diagram in each case will constitute a superior fit between data and line and will permit more accurate predictions. This can be further illustrated by reference to Figure 8.14. If we take a particular value of x, that is, x_n, then we can estimate the likely value of y ($\hat{y}_n$) from the regression line. However, the corresponding y value for a particular case may be y_n, which is different from y. In other words, the latter provides an estimate of y, which is likely not to be totally accurate. Clearly, the further the points are from the line, the less accurate estimates are likely to be. Therefore, where r is low, scatter will be greater and the regression equation

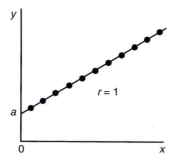

FIGURE 8.13 Regression: a perfect relationship

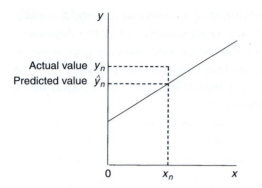

FIGURE 8.14   The accuracy of the line of best fit

will provide a less accurate representation of the relationship between the two variables.

On the other hand, although correlation and regression are closely connected, it should be remembered that they serve different purposes. Correlation is concerned with the degrees of relationship between variables and regression with making predictions. But they can also be usefully used in conjunction, since, unlike correlation, regression can express the character of relationships. Compare the two scatter diagrams in Figure 8.15. The pattern of dots is identical and each would reveal an identical level of correlation (say 0.75), but the slope of the dots in (a) is much steeper than in (b). This difference would be revealed in a larger regression coefficient for (a) and a larger intercept for (b).

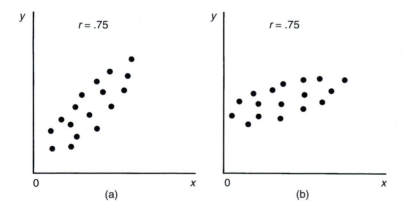

FIGURE 8.15   Scatter diagrams for two identical levels of correlation

The r^2 value is often used as an indication of how well the model implied by the regression equation fits the data. If we conceive of y, the dependent variable, as exhibiting variance which the independent variable goes some of the way in explaining, then we can say that r^2 reflects the proportion of the variation in y explained by x. Thus, if r^2 equals 0.74, the model is providing an explanation of 74 per cent of the variance in y.

Although we have been talking about y as the dependent and x as the independent variable, in many instances it makes just as much sense to treat x as dependent and y as independent. If this is done, the regression equation will be different. Two other words of caution should be registered. First, regression assumes that the dispersion of points in a scatter diagram is *homoscedastic*, or where the pattern of scatter of the points about the line shows no clear pattern. When the opposite is the case, and the pattern exhibits *heteroscedasticity*, where the amount of scatter around the line of best fit varies markedly at different points, the use of regression is questionable. An example of hetero-scedasticity is exhibited in Figure 8.16, which suggests that the amount of unexplained variation exhibited by the model is greater at the upper reaches of x and y. Homoscedasticity is also a precondition of the use of Pearson's r.

Second, the size of a correlation coefficient and the nature of a regression equation will be affected by the amount of variance in either of the variables concerned. For example, if one variable has a restricted range and the other a wider range, the size of the correlation coefficient may be reduced, compared with if both were of equally wide variance.

Third, *outliers*, that is extreme values of x or y, can exert an excessive influence on the results of both correlation and regression. Consider the data in Table 8.10. We have data on twenty firms regarding their size (as measured

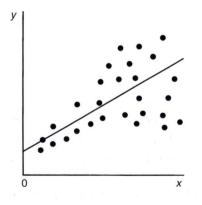

FIGURE 8.16 Heteroscedasticity

TABLE 8.10 The impact of an outlier: the relationship between size of firm and number of specialist functions

Case number	Size of firm (number of employees)	Number of specialist functions
1	110	3
2	150	2
3	190	5
4	230	8
5	270	5
6	280	6
7	320	7
8	350	5
9	370	8
10	390	6
11	420	9
12	430	7
13	460	3
14	470	9
15	500	12
16	540	9
17	550	13
18	600	14
19	640	11
20	2,700	16

Notes:
When case 20 is included, Pearson's $r = 0.67$ and the regression equation is: specialisation $= 5.55 + 0.00472$size.
When case 20 is excluded, Pearson's $r = 0.78$ and the regression equation is: specialisation $= 0.78 + 0.0175$size.

by the number of employees) and the number of specialist functions in the organisation (that is, the number of specialist areas, such as accounting, personnel, marketing, or public relations, in which at least one person spends 100 per cent of his or her time). The article by Child (1973) presents a similar variable with a maximum score of 16, which formed the idea for this example. In Table 8.10, we have an outlier – case number 20 – which is much larger than all of the other firms in the sample. It is also somewhat higher in terms of the number of specialist functions than the other firms. In spite of the fact that this is only one case its impact on estimates of both correlation and regression is quite pronounced. The Pearson's r is 0.67 and the regression equation is $y = 5.55 + 0.00472\text{size}$. If the case with the outlier is excluded, the magnitude of r rises to 0.78 and the regression equation is $y = 0.78 + 0.0175\text{size}$. Such a difference can have a dramatic effect on predictions. If we wanted to know the likely value of y (number of specialist functions) for an organisation of 340 employees with all twenty cases, the prediction would be 7.15; with the outlying case omitted the prediction is 6.73. Thus, this one outlying case can have an important impact upon the predictions that are generated. When such a situation arises, serious consideration has to be given to the exclusion of such an outlying case.

The purpose of this section has been to introduce the general idea of regression. In Chapter 10, it will receive a much fuller treatment, when the use of more than one independent variable will be examined, an area in which the power of regression is especially evident.

Generating basic regression analysis with SPSS

SPSS can generate a host of information relating to regression. However, much of this information is too detailed for present purposes; only some of it will be examined in Chapter 10. It is proposed to postpone a detailed treatment of generating regression information until this later chapter. The following discussion should allow the user to generate basic regression information relating to the relationship between two variables. Imagine that we want to undertake a simple regression analysis of **routine** and **satis**, with the latter as the implied dependent variable. The following sequence should be followed:

→<u>S</u>tatistics →<u>R</u>egression →<u>L</u>inear... [opens **Linear Regression** dialog box shown in Box 8.9]

→**satis** →► button [puts **satis** in **Dependent:** box] →**routine** →►button [puts **routine** in **Independent[s]:** box] →**OK**

The regression equation can be found below **Variables in the Equation** in the resulting output (see Table 8.11). The equation is:

satis $= 17.094 - 0.464$**routine**

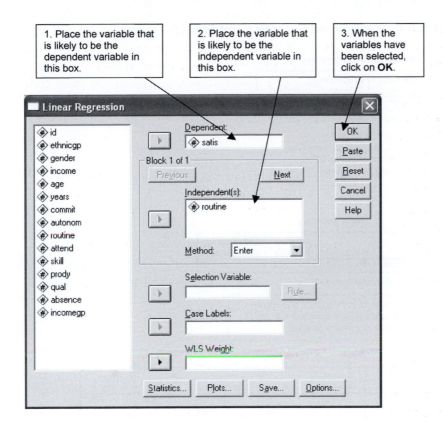

1. Place the variable that is likely to be the dependent variable in this box.

2. Place the variable that is likely to be the independent variable in this box.

3. When the variables have been selected, click on **OK**.

BOX 8.9 Linear Regression dialog box

which can be rounded to

> **satis** = 17.09 − 0.46**routine**

This implies that for every increment of **routine**, **satis** declines by 0.46. We are also given quite a large amount of extra information. We are given the coefficient of determination, r^2, which is 0.336 (see **R Square**), which implies that 33.6 per cent of the variance in **satis** is explained by **routine**. Other basic useful information includes an estimation of the statistical significance of the coefficients relating to the constant in the equation and to **routine** using the t value and an analysis of variance which provides an F test for the equation. The p values suggest that the coefficients and the equation itself achieve a high level of statistical significance.

A scatter diagram along with a fitted regression line and basic regression information can be generated in SPSS. To generate this output, a scatter

TABLE 8.11 Regression analysis: **satis** by **routine** (SPSS output)

Variables Entered/Removed[b]

Model	Variables Entered	Variables Removed	Method
1	routine[a]	.	Enter

a. All requested variables entered.

b. Dependent Variable: satis.

Shows the amount of the variation in **satis** explained by **routine**.

Model Summary

Model	R	R Square	Adjusted R Square	Std. Error of the Estimate
1	.580[a]	.336	.326	2.711

a. Predictors: (Constant), routine.

Provides an *F* test for the equation and shows that the significance level associated with the *F* test is .000, which is a very high level.

ANOVA[b]

Model		Sum of Squares	df	Mean Square	F	Sig.
1	Regression	246.036	1	246.036	33.469	.000[a]
	Residual	485.184	66	7.351		
	Total	731.221	67			

a. Predictors: (Constant), routine.

b. Dependent Variable: satis.

This is the value of the constant (intercept) in the regression equation for the line of best fit.

These are *t* tests with significance levels for the constant (a) and the regression coefficient (b) and in both cases are very statistically significant.

Coefficients[a]

Model		Unstandardized Coefficients		Standardized Coefficients	t	Sig.
		B	Std. Error	Beta		
1	(Constant)	17.094	1.130		15.125	.000
	routine	-.464	.080	-.580	-5.785	.000

a. Dependent Variable: satis.

This is the value of the regression coefficient in the regression equation for the line of best fit.

diagram needs to be produced as above, using the sequence previously followed:

→**Graphs** →**Scatter/Dot** [opens **Scatter/Dot** dialog box shown in Box 8.4]

→**Simple** →**Define** [closes **Scatter/Dot** dialog box and opens **Simple Scatterplot** subdialog box shown in Box 8.5]

→**satis** →▶button [puts **satis** in box by **Y** Axis:] →**routine** →▶button [puts **routine** in box by **X** Axis:] →**OK**

When the diagram has appeared

double-click anywhere in the scatterplot [opens **SPSS Chart Editor**] **Elements** →**Fit Line at Total** [opens the **Properties** box] → x at top right corner of **Chart Editor** to close.

A regression line will be drawn onto the scatter diagram. Figure 8.17 provides an example of a scatter diagram with a line of best fit produced with SPSS.

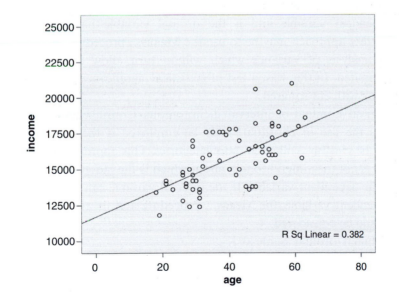

FIGURE 8.17 SPSS scatter diagram with a line of best fit (Job Survey data)

Overview of types of variable and methods of examining relationships

The following rules of thumb are suggested for the various types of combination of variable that may occur.

1 Nominal–nominal. Contingency-table analysis in conjunction with chi-square as a test of statistical significance can be recommended. To test for strength of association, Cramer's V can be used.

2 Ordinal–ordinal. Spearman's rho or Kendall's tau and their associated significance tests.

3 Interval–interval. Pearson's r and regression for estimates of the strength and character of relationships respectively. Each can generate tests of statistical significance, but more detail in this regard for regression is provided in Chapter 10.

4 Dichotomous–dichotomous. Same as under 1 for nominal–nominal, except that phi should be used instead of Cramer's V (and will be generated by SPSS instead of V).

5 Interval–ordinal. If the ordinal variable assumes quite a large number of categories, it will probably be best to use rho or tau. Contingency-table analysis may be used if there are few categories in both the ordinal and interval variables (or if categories can meaningfully be 'grouped'). If the interval variable can be relatively unambiguously identified as the dependent variable and if the ordinal variable has few categories, another approach may be to use the **Means...** procedure and to request an analysis of variance which will in turn allow an F ratio to be computed. In this way, a test of statistical significance can be provided, along with eta-squared.

6 Interval–nominal or interval–dichotomous. Contingency-table analysis plus the use of chi-square may be employed if the interval variable can be sensibly 'collapsed' into categories. This approach is appropriate if it is not meaningful to talk about which is the independent and which is the dependent variable. If the interval variable can be identified as a dependent variable, the **Means...** procedure and its associated statistics should be considered.

7 Nominal–ordinal. Same as 1.

Exercises

1. (a) Using SPSS, how would you create a contingency table for the relationship between **gender** and **prody**, with the former variable going across, along with column percentages (Job Survey data)?
   (b) How would you assess the statistical significance of the relationship with SPSS?
   (c) In your view, is the relationship statistically significant?
   (d) What is the percentage of women who are described as exhibiting 'good' productivity?

2. A researcher carries out a study of the relationship between ethnic group and voting behaviour. The relationship is examined through a contingency table, for which the researcher computes the chi-square statistic. The value of chi-square turns out to be statistically significant at $p < 0.01$. The researcher concludes that this means that the relationship between the two variables is important and strong. Assess this reasoning.

3. (a) Using SPSS, how would you generate a matrix of Pearson's r correlation coefficients for **income**, **years**, **satis** and **age** (Job Survey data)?
   (b) Conduct an analysis using the commands from question 3 (a). Which pair of variables exhibits the largest correlation?
   (c) Taking this pair of variables, how much of the variance in one variable is explained by the other?

4. A researcher wants to examine the relationship between social class and number of books read in a year. The first hundred people are interviewed as they enter a public library in the researcher's home town. On the basis of the answers given, the sample is categorised in terms of a fourfold classification of social class: upper middle class/lower middle class/ upper working class/ lower working class. Using Pearson's r, the level of correlation is found to be 0.73 which is significant at $p < 0.001$. The researcher concludes that the findings have considerable validity, especially since 73 per cent of the variance in number of books read is explained by social class. Assess the researcher's analysis and conclusions.

5. A researcher finds that the correlation between income and a scale measuring interest in work is 0.55 (Pearson's r) which is non-significant since p is greater than 0.05. This finding is compared to another study using the same variables and measures which found the correlation to be

0.46 and $p < 0.001$. How could this contrast arise? In other words, how could the larger correlation be non-significant and the smaller correlation be significant?

6 (a) What statistic or statistics would you recommend to estimate the strength of the relationship between **prody** and **commit** (Job Survey data)?
    (b) What SPSS commands would you use to generate the relevant estimates?
    (c) What is the result of using these commands?

7 The regression equation for the relationship between **age** and **autonom** (with the latter as the dependent variable) is

$$\textbf{autonom} = 6.964 + 0.06230\textbf{age} \qquad r = 0.28$$

    (a) Explain what 6.964 means.
    (b) Explain what 0.06230 means.
    (c) How well does the regression equation fit the data?
    (d) What is the likely level of **autonom** for someone aged 54?
    (e) Using SPSS, how would you generate this regression information?

Chapter 9

Multivariate analysis: exploring differences among three or more variables

IN MOST STUDIES in the social sciences we collect information on more than just two variables. Although it would be possible and more simple to examine the relationships between these variables just two at a time, there are serious disadvantages to restricting oneself to this approach, as we shall see. It is preferable initially to explore these data with multivariate rather than bivariate tests. The reasons for looking at three or more variables vary according to the aims and design of a study. Consequently, we will begin by outlining four design features which only involve three variables at a time. Obviously these features may include more than three variables and the features themselves can be combined to form more complicated designs, but we shall discuss them largely as if they were separate designs. However, as has been done before, we will use one set of data to illustrate their analysis, all of which can be carried out with a general statistical model called the *general linear model*. Although the details of the model are difficult to understand and to convey simply (and so will not be attempted here), its basic principles are similar to those of other parametric tests we have previously discussed such as the *t* test, one-way analysis of variance, and simple regression.

Multivariate designs

Factorial design

We are often interested in the effect of two variables on a third, particularly if we believe that the two variables may influence one another. To take a purely hypothetical case, we may expect the gender of the patient to interact with the kind of treatment they are given for feeling depressed. Women may respond more positively to psychotherapy where they have an opportunity to talk about their feelings while men may react more favourably to being treated with an antidepressant drug. In this case, we are anticipating that the kind of treatment will *interact* with gender in alleviating depression. An interaction is when the effect of one variable is not the same under all the conditions of the other variable. It is often more readily understood when it is depicted in the form of a graph as in Figure 9.1. However, whether these effects are statistically significant can only be determined by testing them and not just by

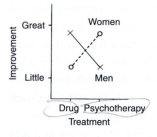

FIGURE 9.1 An example of an interaction between two variables

visually inspecting them. The vertical axis shows the amount of improvement in depression that has taken place after treatment, while the horizontal one can represent either of the other two variables. In this case it reflects the kind of treatment received. The effects of the third variable, gender, is depicted by two different kinds of points and lines in the graph itself. Men are indicated by a cross and a continuous line while women are signified by a small circle and a broken line.

An interaction is indicated when the two lines representing the third variable are not parallel. Consequently, a variety of interaction effects can exist, three of which are shown in Figure 9.2 as hypothetical possibilities. In Figure 9.2(a), men show less improvement with psychotherapy than with drugs while women derive greater benefit from psychotherapy than from the drug treatment. In Figure 9.2(b), men improve little with either treatment, while women, once again, benefit considerably more from psychotherapy than from drugs. Finally, in Figure 9.2(c), both men and women improve more with psychotherapy than with drugs, but the improvement is much greater for women than it is for men.

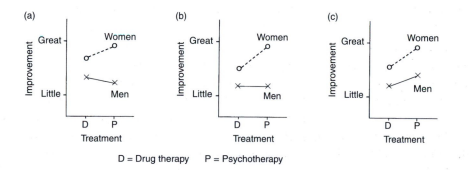

FIGURE 9.2 Examples of other interactions

The absence of an interaction can be seen by the lines representing the third variable remaining more or less parallel to one another, as is the case in the three examples in Figure 9.3. In Figure 9.3(a), both men and women show a similar degree of improvement with both treatments. In Figure 9.3(b), women improve more than men under both conditions while both treatments are equally effective. In Figure 9.3(c), women show greater benefit than men with both treatments, and psychotherapy is better than drugs.

The results of treatment and gender on their own are known as *main effects*. In these situations, the influence of the other variable is disregarded. If, for example, we wanted to examine the effect of gender, we would only look at improvement for men and women, ignoring treatment. If we were interested in the effect of the kind of treatment, we would simply compare the outcome of patients receiving psychotherapy with those being given drugs, paying no heed to gender.

The variables which are used to form the comparison groups are termed *factors*. The number of groups which constitute a factor are referred to as the *levels* of that factor. Since gender consists of two groups, it is called a two-level factor. The two kinds of treatment also create a two-level factor. If a third treatment had been included such as a control group of patients receiving neither drugs nor psychotherapy, we would have a three-level factor. Studies which investigate the effects of two or more factors are known as *factorial* designs. A study comparing two levels of gender and two levels of treatment is described as a 2×2 factorial design. If three rather than two levels of treatment had been compared, it would be a 2×3 factorial design. A study which only looks at one factor is called a one-way or single-factor design.

The factors in these designs may be ones that are *manipulated*, such as differing dosages of drugs, different teaching methods, or varying levels of

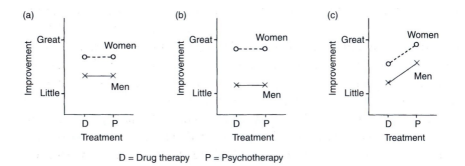

FIGURE 9.3 Examples of no interactions

induced anxiety. Where they have been manipulated and where participants have been randomly assigned to different levels, the factors may also be referred to as *independent* variables since they are more likely to be unrelated to, or independent of, other features of the experimental situation such as the personality of the participants. Variables which are used to assess the effect of these independent variables are known as *dependent* variables since the effect on them is thought to depend on the level of the variable which has been manipulated. Thus, for example, the improvement in the depression experienced by patients (i.e. the dependent variable) is believed to be partly the result of the treatment they have received (i.e. the independent variable). Factors can also be variables which have not been manipulated, such as gender, age, ethnic origin, and social class. Because they cannot be separated from the individual who has them, they are sometimes referred to as *subject* variables. A study which investigated the effect of such subject variables would also be called a factorial design.

One of the main advantages of factorial designs, other than the study of interaction effects, is that they generally provide a more sensitive or powerful statistical test of the effect of the factors than designs which investigate just one factor at a time. To understand why this is the case, it is necessary to describe how a one-way and a two-way (i.e. a factorial) analysis of variance differ. In one-way analysis of variance, the variance in the means of the groups (or levels) is compared with the variance within them combined for all the groups:

$$F = \frac{\text{variance between groups}}{\text{variance within groups}}$$

The between-groups variance is calculated by comparing the group mean with the overall or grand mean, while the within-groups variance is worked out by comparing the individual scores in the group with its mean. If the group means differ, then their variance should be greater than the average of those within them. This situation is illustrated in Figure 9.4 where the means of the three groups (M_1, M_2, and M_3) are quite widely separated, causing a greater spread of between-groups variance (V_B) while the variance within the groups (V_1, V_2, and V_3) is considerably less when combined (V_W).

Now the variance within the groups is normally thought of as error since this is the only way in which we can estimate it, while the between-groups variance is considered to consist of the effect of the factor which is being investigated. While some of the within-groups variance may be due to error, such as that of measurement and of procedure, the rest of it will be due

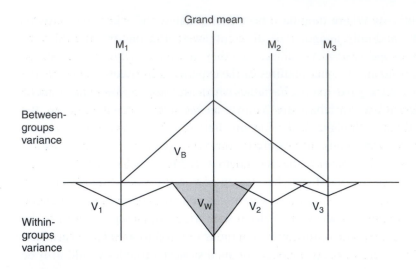

FIGURE 9.4 Schematic representation of a significant one-way effect

to factors which we have not controlled, such as gender, age, and motivation. In other words, the within-groups variance will contain error as well as variance due to other factors, and so will be larger than if it just contained error variance. Consequently, it will provide an overestimate of error. In a two-factor design, on the other hand, the variance due to the other factor can be removed from this overestimate of the error variance, thereby giving a more accurate calculation of it. If, for example, we had just compared the effectiveness of the drug treatment with psychotherapy in reducing depression, then some of the within-groups variance would have been due to gender but treated as error, and may have obscured any differential effect due to treatment.

Covariate design

Another way of reducing error variance is by removing the influence of a non-categorical variable (i.e. one which is not nominal) which we believe to be biasing the results. This is particularly useful in designs where participants are not randomly assigned to factors, such as in the Job Survey study, or where random assignment did not result in the groups being equal in terms of some other important variable, such as how depressed patients were before being treated. A covariate is a variable which is linearly related to the one we are most directly interested in, usually called the *dependent* or *criterion* variable.

We will give two examples of the way in which the effect of covariates may be controlled. Suppose, for instance, we wanted to find out the relationship between job satisfaction and the two factors of gender and ethnic group in the Job Survey data and we knew that job satisfaction was positively correlated with income, so that people who were earning more were also more satisfied with their jobs. It is possible that both gender and ethnic group will also be related to income. Women may earn less than men and non-white workers may earn less than their white counterparts. If so, then the relationship of these two factors to job satisfaction is likely to be biased by their association with income. To control for this, we will remove the influence of income by covarying it out. In this case, income is the covariate. If income was not correlated with job satisfaction, then there would be no need to do this. Consequently, it is only advisable to control a covariate when it has been found to be related to the dependent variable.

In true experimental designs, we try to control the effect of variables other than the independent ones by randomly assigning participants to different treatments or conditions. However, when the number of participants allocated to treatments is small (say, about ten or less), there is a stronger possibility that there will be chance differences between them. If, for example, we are interested in comparing the effects of drugs with psychotherapy in treating depression, it is important that the patients in the two conditions should be similar in terms of how depressed they are before treatment begins (i.e. at *pre-test*). If the patients receiving the drug treatment are found at pre-test to be more depressed than those having psychotherapy despite random assignment, then it is possible that because they are more depressed to begin with, they will show less improvement than the psychotherapy patients. If pre-test depression is positively correlated with depression at the end of treatment (i.e. at *post-test*), then the effect of these initial differences can be removed statistically by covarying them out. The covariate in this example would be the pre-test depression scores.

Three points need to be made about the selection of covariates. First, as mentioned before, they should only be variables which are related to the dependent variable. Variables which are unrelated to it do not require to be covaried out. Second, if two covariates are strongly correlated with one another (say 0.8 or above), it is only necessary to remove one of them since the other one seems to be measuring the same variable(s). And third, with small numbers of participants only a few covariates at most should be used, since the more covariates there are in such situations, the less powerful the statistical test becomes.

Multiple-measures design

In many designs we may be interested in examining differences in more than one dependent or criterion measure. For example, in the Job Survey study, we may want to know how differences in gender and ethnic group are related to job autonomy and routine as well as satisfaction. In the depression study, we may wish to assess the effect of treatment in more than one way. How depressed the patients themselves feel may be one measure. Another may be how depressed they appear to be to someone who knows them well, such as a close friend or informant. One of the advantages of using multiple measures is to find out how restricted or widespread a particular effect may be. In studying the effectiveness of treatments for depression, for instance, we would have more confidence in the results if the effects were picked up by a number of similar measures rather than just one. Another advantage is that although groups may not differ on individual measures, they may do so when a number of related individual measures are examined jointly. Thus, for example, psychotherapy may not be significantly more effective than the drug treatment when outcome is assessed by either the patients themselves or by their close friends, but it may be significantly better when these two measures are analysed together. This analysis is sometimes referred to as a multivariate analysis of variance (MANOVA).

Mixed between–within design

The multiple-measures design needs to be distinguished from the repeated-measures design which we encountered at the end of Chapter 7. A multiple-measures design has two or more dependent or criterion variables such as two separate measures of depression. A repeated-measures design, on the other hand, consists of one or more factors being investigated on the same group of participants. Measuring job satisfaction or depression at two or more points in time would be an example of such a factor. Another would be evaluating the effectiveness of drugs and psychotherapy on the same patients by giving them both treatments. If we were to do this, we would have to make sure that half the patients were randomly assigned to receiving psychotherapy first and the drug treatment second, while the other patients would be given the two treatments in the reverse order. It is necessary to counterbalance the sequence of the two conditions to control for *order effects*. It would also be advisable to check that the sequence in which the treatments were administered did not affect the results. The order effect would constitute a between-subjects factor since any one participant would only receive one of the two orders. In other words, this design would become a mixed one which included both a between-subjects factor (order) and a within-subjects one (treatment). One of the advantages of this design is that it restricts the amount of variance due to individuals, since the same treatments are compared on the same participants.

Another example of a mixed between–within design is where we assess the dependent variable before as well as after the treatment, as in the study on depression comparing the effectiveness of psychotherapy with drugs. This design has two advantages. The first is that the pre-test enables us to determine whether the groups were similar in terms of the dependent variable before the treatment began. The second is that it allows us to determine if there has been any change in the dependent variable before and after the treatment has been given. In other words, this design enables us to discern whether any improvement has taken place as a result of the treatment and whether this improvement is greater for one group than the other.

Combined design

As was mentioned earlier, the four design features can be combined in various ways. Thus, for instance, we can have two independent factors (gender and treatment for depression), one covariate (age), two dependent measures (assessment of depression by patient and informant), and one repeated measure (pre- and post-test). These components will form the basis of the following illustration, which shall be referred to as the Depression Project. The data for it are shown in Table 9.1.

There are three treatments: a no treatment control condition (coded 1 and with eight participants); a psychotherapy treatment (coded 2 and with ten participants); and a drug treatment (coded 3 and with twelve participants). Females are coded as 1 and males as 2. A high score on depression indicates a greater degree of it. The patient's assessment of their depression before and after treatment is referred to as **patpre** and **patpost** respectively, while the assessment provided by an informant before and after treatment is known as **infpre** and **infpost**. We shall now turn to methods of analysing the results of this kind of study using the general linear model.

Multivariate analysis

The example we have given is the more common one in which there are unequal numbers of cases on one or more of the factors. Although it is

TABLE 9.1 The Depression Project data

Id	Treat	Gender	Age	Patpre	Infpre	Patpost	Infpost
01	1	1	27	25	27	20	19
02	1	2	30	29	26	25	27
03	1	1	33	26	25	23	26
04	1	2	36	31	33	24	26
05	1	1	41	33	30	29	28
06	1	2	44	28	30	23	26
07	1	1	47	34	30	30	31
08	1	2	51	35	37	29	28
09	2	1	25	21	24	9	15
10	2	2	27	20	21	9	12
11	2	1	30	23	20	10	8
12	2	2	31	22	28	14	18
13	2	1	33	25	22	15	17
14	2	2	34	26	23	17	16
15	2	1	35	24	26	9	13
16	2	2	37	27	25	18	20
17	2	1	38	25	21	11	8
18	2	2	42	29	30	19	21
19	3	1	30	34	37	23	25
20	3	2	33	31	27	15	13
21	3	1	36	32	35	20	21
22	3	2	37	33	35	20	18
23	3	1	39	40	38	33	35
24	3	2	41	34	31	18	19
25	3	1	42	34	36	23	27
26	3	2	44	37	31	14	11
27	3	1	45	36	38	24	25
28	3	2	47	38	35	25	27
29	3	1	48	37	39	29	28
30	3	2	50	39	37	23	24

possible to equalise them by randomly omitting two participants from the psychotherapy treatment and four from the drug one, this would be a waste of valuable data and so is not recommended.

There are four main ways of analysing the results of factorial designs with SPSS. The first method, referred to as *Type I* in SPSS and previously known as the *hierarchical* or *sequential* approach, allows the investigator to determine the order of the effects. If one factor is thought to precede another, then it can be placed first. This approach should be used in non-experimental designs where the factors can be ordered in some sequential manner. If, for example, we are interested in the effect of ethnic group and income on job satisfaction, then ethnic group would be entered first since income cannot determine the ethnic group to which we belong.

Type II, previously known as the *classic experimental* or *least squares* approach, can be used with balanced or unbalanced designs where there are some cases in all cells. Tabachnick and Fidell (2001) recommend that this method should be used for non-experimental designs where there are unequal numbers of cases in cells and where cells having larger numbers of cases are thought to be more important.

Type III, previously known as the *regression, unweighted means* or *unique* approach, is the default and can be used where there are an equal number of cases in each cell or where the design is balanced in that the cell frequencies are proportional in terms of their marginal distributions. Tabachnick and Fidell (2001) recommend that this method should also be used for true experimental designs where there are unequal numbers of cases in cells due to random drop-out and where all cells are considered to be equally important.

Type IV is applied with balanced or unbalanced designs where there are no cases in some cells.

All four methods produce the same result for analysis of variance designs when there are equal numbers of participants in cells. For an unbalanced two-way analysis of variance design they only differ in the way they handle main effects so the results for the interaction effects and the error are the same. Where the main effects are not independent, the component sums of squares do not add up to the total sum of squares.

In this chapter, we have followed the recommendation of Tabachnick and Fidell (2001) in using the Type III method for true experimental designs.

Factorial design

To determine the effect of treatment, gender and their interaction on post-test depression as seen by the patient, the following procedure is needed:

→**Analyze** →**General Linear Model** →**Univariate...** [opens **Univariate** dialog box shown in Box 9.1]

1. Select dependent variable (e.g. **patpost**) to put in **Dependent Variable:** box.

2. Select independent variable/s (e.g. **gender** and **treat**) to put in **Fixed Factor(s):** box.

3. Select **Options**....

```
Univariate                                                    [×]

 id                          Dependent Variable:           Model...
 age                    [▶]    patpost
 patpre                                                    Contrasts...
 infpre                      Fixed Factor(s):
 infpost                                                   Plots...
                              gender
                       [◀]    treat                        Post Hoc...

                                                           Save...
                            Random Factor(s):
                       [▶]                                 Options...


                            Covariate(s):
                       [▶]


                            WLS Weight:
                       [▶]


            OK    Paste    Reset    Cancel    Help
```

BOX 9.1   Univariate dialog box

→**patpost** →▶ button beside **Dependent Variable:** [puts **patpost** in this box] →**gender** →▶ button beside **Fixed Factor(s):** [puts **gender** in this box] →**treat** →▶ button beside **Fixed Factor(s):** [puts **treat** in this box]

→**Options...** [opens **Univariate: Options** subdialog box shown in Box 9.2]

→**Descriptive statistics** →**Homogeneity tests** →**Continue** [closes **Univariate: Options** subdialog box]

→**Plots...** [opens **Univariate: Profile Plots** subdialog box shown in Box 9.3]

→**gender** →▶ button beside **Horizontal Axis:** [puts **gender** in this box] →**treat** →▶ button beside **Separate Lines:** [puts **treat** in this box] →**Add** [puts **gender*treat** in box under **Plot:**] →**Continue** [closes **Univariate: Profile Plots** subdialog box]

→**OK**

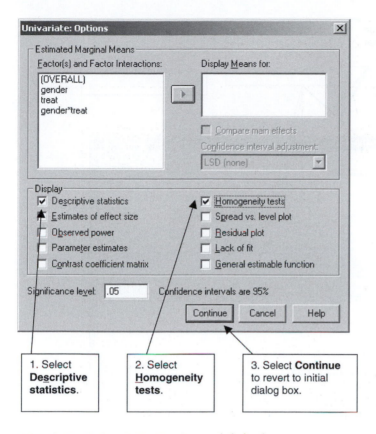

1. Select **Descriptive statistics**.

2. Select **Homogeneity tests**.

3. Select **Continue** to revert to initial dialog box.

BOX 9.2   Univariate: Options subdialog box

The means for the three treatments for women and men are shown in Table 9.2 and Figure 9.5.

Levene's test for homogeneity of variance is displayed in Table 9.3. It is not significant, which means there are no significant differences between the variances of the groups, an assumption on which this test is based. If the variances had been grossly unequal, then it may have been possible to reduce this through transforming the data by taking the log or square root of the dependent variable. This can easily be done with the **Compute** procedure on the **Transform** menu which displays the **Compute Variable** dialog box shown in Box 3.6. For example, the natural or Naperian log (base e) of **patpost** is produced by selecting the **Ln Functions and Special Variables** and inserting **patpost** as the numerical expression. The square root of **patpost** is created by selecting the **Sqrt Functions and Special Variables**. It is necessary to check that the transformations have produced the desired effect.

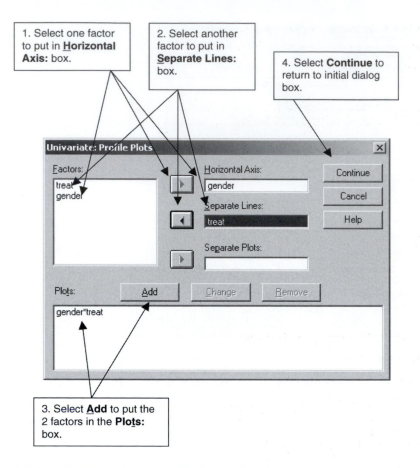

1. Select one factor to put in **Horizontal Axis:** box.

2. Select another factor to put in **Separate Lines:** box.

4. Select **Continue** to return to initial dialog box.

3. Select **Add** to put the 2 factors in the **Plots:** box.

BOX 9.3   Univariate: Profile Plots subdialog box

The tests of significance for determining the Type III sum of squares for each effect are shown in Table 9.4. These indicate that there is a significant effect for the treatment factor ($p < 0.0005$) and a significant interaction effect for treatment and gender ($p = 0.016$). If we plot this interaction, we can see that depression after the drug treatment is higher for women than men, while after psychotherapy it is higher for men than women. The mean square of an effect is its sum of squares divided by its degrees of freedom. Thus, for example, the mean square of the treatment effect is 767.942 divided by 2 which is 383.971. The F value for an effect is its mean square divided by that of the within-cells and residual term. So, for the treatment effect this would be 383.971 divided by 16.163 which is 23.756.

Having found that there is an overall significant difference in depression for the three treatments, we need to determine where this difference lies. One

TABLE 9.2 Means of post-test depression (**patpost**) in the three treatments for men and women (Depression Project)

Descriptive Statistics

Dependent Variable: patpost

gender	treat	Mean	Std. Deviation	N
1	1	25.50	4.796	4
	2	10.80	2.490	5
	3	25.33	4.761	6
	Total	20.53	8.096	15
2	1	25.25	2.630	4
	2	15.40	4.037	5
	3	19.17	4.355	6
	Total	19.53	5.330	15
Total	1	25.38	3.583	8
	2	13.10	3.985	10
	3	22.25	5.413	12
	Total	20.03	6.754	30

TABLE 9.3 **Homogeneity tests** output (Depression Project)

Levene's Test of Equality of Error Variances[a]

Dependent Variable: patpost

F	df1	df2	Sig.
1.213	5	24	.333

Tests the null hypothesis that the error variance of the dependent variable is equal across groups.

a. Design: Intercept+gender+treat+gender * treat.

TABLE 9.4 Tests of significance for main and interaction effects in an unrelated factorial design (Depression Project)

Tests of Between-Subjects Effects

Dependent Variable: patpost

Source	Type III Sum of Squares	df	Mean Square	F	Sig.
Corrected Model	935.050[a]	5	187.010	11.570	.000
Intercept	11959.543	1	11959.543	739.924	.000
gender	2.676	1	2.676	.166	.688
treat	767.942	2	383.971	23.756	.000
gender * treat	159.608	2	79.804	4.937	.016
Error	387.917	24	16.163		
Total	13363.000	30			
Corrected Total	1322.967	29			

a. R Squared = .707 (Adjusted R Squared = .646).

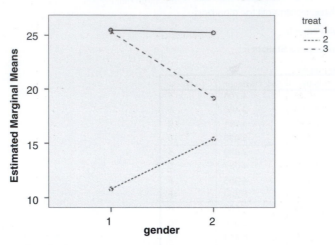

FIGURE 9.5 Plot of post-test patient depression of men and women (Depression Project) for SPSS 13 (which differs slightly from SPSS 10, 11 and 12). This plot has been edited with Chart Editor to vary the style of line by clicking on each numbered line in the legend.

way of doing this is to test for differences between two treatments at a time. If we had not anticipated certain differences between treatments, we would apply post hoc tests such as Scheffé to determine their statistical significance, whereas if we had predicted them we would use unrelated *t* tests (see Chapter 7).

Covariate design

If the patients' pre-test depression scores differ for gender, treatment or their interaction and if the pre-test scores are related to the post-test ones, then the results of the previous test will be biased by this. To determine if there are such differences, we need to run a factorial analysis on the patients' pre-test depression scores. If we do this, we find that there is a significant effect for treatments (see the output in Table 9.5), which means that the pre-test depression scores differ between treatments.

Covariate analysis is based on the same assumptions as the previous factorial analysis plus three additional ones. First, there must be a linear relationship between the dependent variable and the covariate. If there is no such relationship, then there is no need to conduct a covariate analysis. This assumption can be tested by plotting a scatter diagram (see Chapter 8) to see if the relationship appears non-linear. If the correlation is statistically

TABLE 9.5 Tests of significance for effects on pre-test depression (Depression Project)

Tests of Between-Subjects Effects

Dependent Variable: patpre

Source	Type III Sum of Squares	df	Mean Square	F	Sig.
Corrected Model	693.283[a]	5	138.657	13.387	.000
Intercept	26119.676	1	26119.676	2521.779	.000
gender	4.227	1	4.227	.408	.529
treat	686.475	2	343.237	33.139	.000
gender * treat	3.475	2	1.737	.168	.847
Error	248.583	24	10.358		
Total	28424.000	30			
Corrected Total	941.867	29			

a. R Squared = .736 (Adjusted R Squared = .681).

significant, then it is appropriate to carry out a covariate analysis. The statistical procedure **Univariate...** also provides information on this (see pp. 264–6). If the relationship is non-linear, it may be possible to transform it so that it becomes linear using a logarithmic transformation of one variable. The procedure for effecting such a transformation with SPSS has been described on page 259.

The second assumption is that the slope of the regression lines is the same in each group or cell. If they are the same, this implies that there is no interaction between the independent variable and the covariate and that the average within-cell regression can be used to adjust the scores of the dependent variable. This information is also provided by **Univariate....** If this condition is not met, then the Johnson–Neyman technique should be considered. This method is not available on SPSS but a description of it may be found elsewhere (Huitema, 1980).

The third assumption is that the covariate should be measured without error. For some variables such as gender and age, this assumption can usually be justified. For others, however, such as measures of depression, this needs to be checked. This can be done by computing the alpha reliability coefficient for multi-item variables (such as job satisfaction) or test–retest correlations where this information is available. A coefficient of 0.8 or above is usually taken as indicating a reliable measure. This assumption is more important in non- than in true-experimental designs, where its violation may lead to either Type I or II errors. In true-experimental designs, the violation of this assumption only leads to loss of power. As there are no agreed or simple procedures for adjusting covariates for unreliability, these will not be discussed.

The following procedure is necessary to test whether the regression lines are the same in each of the cells for the analysis of covariance in which the effect of treatment on the patients' post-test depression scores controlling for their pre-test ones is examined:

→**Analyze** →**General Linear Model** →**Univariate...** [opens **Univariate** dialog box shown in Box 9.1]

→**patpost** →▶ button beside **Dependent Variable:** [puts **patpost** in this box] →**treat** →▶ button beside **Fixed Factor(s):** [puts **treat** in this box] →**patpre** →button beside **Covariate(s):** [puts **patpre** in this box]

→**Model...** [opens **Univariate: Model** subdialog box shown in Box 9.4]

→**Custom** →**treat** →▶ button [puts **treat** under **Model:**]

→**patpre** →▶ button [puts **patpre** under **Model:**]

→**Interaction** →**patpre** →**treat** →▶ button [puts **patpre*treat** under **Model:**] →**Continue** [closes **Univariate: Model** subdialog box]

→**OK**

The output for this procedure is presented in Table 9.6. The interaction between the independent variable of treatment and the covariate of **patpre** is not significant since p is 0.793. This means that the slope of the regression line in each of the cells is similar and therefore the second assumption is met.

Consequently we can proceed with the main analysis of covariance using the following procedure:

→**Analyze** →**General Linear Model** →**Univariate...** [opens **Univariate** dialog box shown in Box 9.1]

→**patpost** →▶ button beside **Dependent Variable:** [puts **patpost** in this box] →**treat** →▶ button beside **Fixed Factor(s):** [puts **treat** in this box] →**patpre** →▶ button beside **Covariate(s):** [puts **patpre** in this box]

→**Model...** [opens **Univariate: Model** subdialog box shown in Box 9.4]

→**Full factorial** →**Continue** [closes **Univariate: Model** subdialog box]

→**Options...** [opens **Univariate: Options** subdialog box shown in Box 9.2]

→**treat** →▶ button [puts **treat** under **Display Means for:**]

→**Continue** [closes **Univariate: Options** subdialog box]

→**OK**

2. Select terms (e.g. **treat**, **patpre** and **patpre*treat**) to put in **Model:** box.

1. Select **Custom**.

Univariate: Model ☒

Specify Model
○ Full factorial   ◉ Custom

Factors & Covariates: Model:
treat(F)   treat
patpre(C)   patpre
                                         patpre*treat

Build Term(s)
▶
Interaction ▼

Sum of squares: [Type III ▼]   ☑ Include intercept in model

[Continue]   [Cancel]   [Help]

3. Select **Continue** to return to initial dialog box.

BOX 9.4   Univariate: Model subdialog box

The analysis of covariance table in Table 9.7 shows that the relationship between the covariate (**patpre**) and the dependent variable (**patpost**) is significant. Consequently, it is appropriate to proceed with the interpretation of the covariate analysis. This table also shows there is a significant treatment effect when pre-treatment depression is covaried out.

An inspection of the adjusted means for the three treatments presented in Table 9.8 with the observed means in Table 9.2 shows that controlling for pre-treatment depression has little effect on the mean for the control group, which remains at about 25. However, it makes a considerable difference to the means of the two treatment conditions, reversing their order so that patients who received psychotherapy report themselves as being more depressed than those given the drug treatment. The means have been adjusted using the

TABLE 9.6 Analysis of covariance table showing test of homogeneity of slope of regression line within cells (Depression Project)

Tests of Between-Subjects Effects

Dependent Variable: patpost

Source	Type III Sum of Squares	df	Mean Square	F	Sig.
Corrected Model	1071.498[a]	5	214.300	20.453	.000
Intercept	43.642	1	43.642	4.165	.052
treat	16.905	2	8.453	.807	.458
patpre	299.436	1	299.436	28.578	.000
treat * patpre	4.907	2	2.454	.234	.793
Error	251.468	24	10.478		
Total	13363.000	30			
Corrected Total	1322.967	29			

a. R Squared = .810 (Adjusted R Squared = .770).

TABLE 9.7 Analysis of covariance table (Depression Project)

Tests of Between-Subjects Effects

Dependent Variable: patpost

Source	Type III Sum of Squares	df	Mean Square	F	Sig.
Corrected Model	1066.591[a]	3	355.530	36.056	.000
Intercept	41.426	1	41.426	4.201	.051
patpre	298.650	1	298.650	30.287	.000
treat	339.161	2	169.580	17.198	.000
Error	256.375	26	9.861		
Total	13363.000	30			
Corrected Total	1322.967	29			

a. R Squared = .806 (Adjusted R Squared = .784).

TABLE 9.8 Adjusted means of post-test depression in the three treatments (Depression Project)

treat

Dependent Variable: patpost

treat	Mean	Std. Error	95% Confidence Interval	
			Lower Bound	Upper Bound
1	25.528[a]	1.111	23.245	27.811
2	19.660[a]	1.551	16.471	22.849
3	16.681[a]	1.359	13.888	19.474

a. Covariates appearing in the model are evaluated at the following values: patpre = 30.27.

weighted rather than the unweighted covariate grand mean (Cramer, 1998). The Bryant–Paulson post hoc test for determining whether this difference is significant is described in Stevens (1996).

Multiple measures design

So far, we have analysed only one of the two dependent measures, the patient's self-report of depression. Analysing the two dependent measures together has certain advantages. First, it reduces the probability of making Type I errors (deciding there is a difference when there is none) when making a number of comparisons. The probability of making this error is usually set at 0.05 when comparing two groups on one dependent variable. If we made two such independent comparisons, then the p level would increase to about 0.10. Since the comparisons are not independent, this probability is higher. Second, analysing the two dependent measures together provides us with a more sensitive measure of the effects of the independent variables.

The following procedure is necessary to test the effect of treatment on both the patient's and the informant's post-test assessment of the patient's depression:

→**Analyze** →**General Linear Model** → **Multivariate…** [opens **Multivariate** dialog box shown in Box 9.5]

→**patpost** →▶ button beside **Dependent Variable:** [puts **patpost** in this box] →**infpost** →▶ button beside **Dependent Variables:** [puts **infpost** in this box] →**treat** →▶ button beside **Fixed Factor(s):** [puts **treat** in this box]

→**Options…** [opens **Multivariate: Options** subdialog box shown in Box 9.6]

→**Descriptive statistics** →**Residual SSCP matrix** [gives Bartlett's test of sphericity] →**Homogeneity tests** [gives Box's M and Levene's test] →**Continue** [closes **Multivariate: Options** subdialog box]

→**OK**

The means and standard deviations for **patpost** and **infpost** for the three treatment conditions are shown in Table 9.9.

The results for Box's M and Levene's test are presented in Tables 9.10 and 9.11 respectively. Box's M test determines whether the covariance matrices of the two dependent variables are similar while Levene's test assesses whether

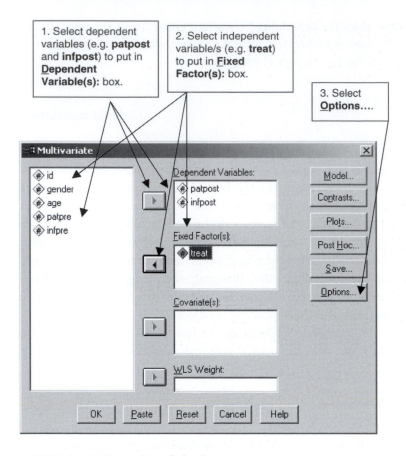

BOX 9.5 Multivariate dialog box

their variances are similar. For this example, both tests are not significant which means that the covariance matrices and the variances do not differ significantly across the three conditions.

Table 9.12 shows the output for Bartlett's test of sphericity which assesses whether the dependent measures are correlated. If the test is significant, as it is here, it means the two dependent measures are related. In this situation, it is more appropriate to use the multivariate test of significance to determine whether there are significant differences between the treatments. The result of this test is presented in Table 9.13 and shows the treatment effect to be significant when the two measures are taken together.

The univariate F tests for the treatment effect, which are presented in Table 9.14, show that the treatments differ on both the dependent measures when they are analysed separately. To determine which treatments differ

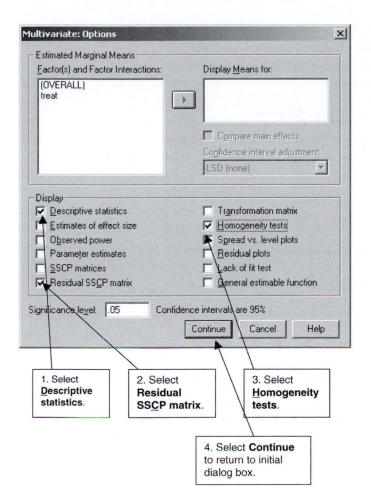

1. Select **Descriptive statistics**.

2. Select **Residual SSCP matrix**.

3. Select **Homogeneity tests**.

4. Select **Continue** to return to initial dialog box.

BOX 9.6   Multivariate: Options subdialog box

significantly from one another, it would be necessary to carry out a series of unrelated *t* tests or post hoc tests as discussed previously.

Mixed between–within design

The procedure for determining if there is a significant difference between the three conditions in improvement in depression as assessed by the patient before (**patpre**) and after (**patpost**) treatment is:

→**Analyze** →**General Linear Model** →**Repeated Measures...** [opens **Repeated Measures Define Factor(s)** dialog box shown in Box 9.7]

TABLE 9.9 Means and standard deviations of post-test depression scores for patients (**patpost**) and informants (**infpost**) for the three treatments (Depression Project)

Descriptive Statistics

	treat	Mean	Std. Deviation	N
patpost	1	25.38	3.583	8
	2	13.10	3.985	10
	3	22.25	5.413	12
	Total	20.03	6.754	30
infpost	1	26.38	3.420	8
	2	14.80	4.541	10
	3	22.75	6.730	12
	Total	21.07	6.992	30

TABLE 9.10 Box's M test (Depression Project)

Box's Test of Equality of Covariance Matrices[a]

Box's M	7.985
F	1.182
df1	6
df2	9324.416
Sig.	.313

Tests the null hypothesis that the observed covariance matrices of the dependent variables are equal across groups.

a. Design: Intercept+treat.

TABLE 9.11 Levene's test (Depression Project)

Levene's Test of Equality of Error Variances[a]

	F	df1	df2	Sig.
patpost	.456	2	27	.638
infpost	2.540	2	27	.098

Tests the null hypothesis that the error variance of the dependent variable is equal across groups.

a. Design: Intercept+treat.

➔highlight **factor1** and type **time** in **Within-Subject Factor Name:** box ➔**Number of Levels:** box and type **2** ➔**Add** ➔**Define** [opens **Repeated Measures** subdialog box shown in Box 9.8]

➔**patpre** ➔▶ button beside **Within-Subjects Variables [time]:** [puts **patpre** in this box] ➔**patpost** ➔▶ button beside **Within-Subjects Variables [time]:** [puts **patpost** in this box] ➔**treat** ➔▶ button beside **Between-Subjects Factor(s):** [puts **treat** in this box]

TABLE 9.12   Bartlett's test of sphericity
(Depression Project)

Bartlett's Test of Sphericity[a]

Likelihood Ratio	.000
Approx. Chi-Square	44.656
df	2
Sig.	.000

Tests the null hypothesis that the residual covariance matrix is proportional to an identity matrix.

a. Design: Intercept+treat.

TABLE 9.13   Multivariate tests of significance for the treatment effect
(Depression Project)

Multivariate Tests[c]

Effect		Value	F	Hypothesis df	Error df	Sig.
Intercept	Pillai's Trace	.956	280.195[a]	2.000	26.000	.000
	Wilks' Lambda	.044	280.195[a]	2.000	26.000	.000
	Hotelling's Trace	21.553	280.195[a]	2.000	26.000	.000
	Roy's Largest Root	21.553	280.195[a]	2.000	26.000	.000
treat	Pillai's Trace	.618	6.032	4.000	54.000	.000
	Wilks' Lambda	.393	7.724[a]	4.000	52.000	.000
	Hotelling's Trace	1.513	9.456	4.000	50.000	.000
	Roy's Largest Root	1.494	20.169[b]	2.000	27.000	.000

a. Exact statistic.

b. The statistic is an upper bound on F that yields a lower bound on the significance level.

c. Design: Intercept+treat.

TABLE 9.14   Univariate tests of significance for the two dependent measures
(Depression Project)

Tests of Between-Subjects Effects

Source	Dependent Variable	Type III Sum of Squares	df	Mean Square	F	Sig.
Corrected Model	patpost	767.942[a]	2	383.971	18.679	.000
	infpost	652.142[b]	2	326.071	11.497	.000
Intercept	patpost	11959.543	1	11959.543	581.789	.000
	infpost	13253.207	1	13253.207	467.317	.000
treat	patpost	767.942	2	383.971	18.679	.000
	infpost	652.142	2	326.071	11.497	.000
Error	patpost	555.025	27	20.556		
	infpost	765.725	27	28.360		
Total	patpost	13363.000	30			
	infpost	14732.000	30			
Corrected Total	patpost	1322.967	29			
	infpost	1417.867	29			

a. R Squared = .580 (Adjusted R Squared = .549).

b. R Squared = .460 (Adjusted R Squared = .420).

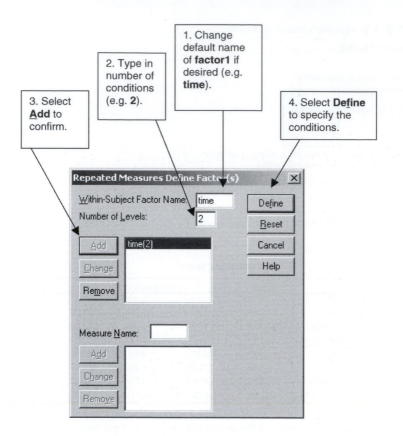

1. Change default name of **factor1** if desired (e.g. **time**).

2. Type in number of conditions (e.g. **2**).

3. Select **Add** to confirm.

4. Select **Define** to specify the conditions.

BOX 9.7 Repeated Measures Define Factor(s) dialog box

→**Options...** [opens **Repeated Measures: Options** subdialog box shown in Box 9.9]

→**Descriptive statistics** →**Continue** [closes **Repeated Measures: Options** subdialog box]

→**Plots...** [opens **Repeated Measures: Profile Plots** subdialog box shown in Box 9.10]

→**time** →▶ button beside **Horizontal Axis:** [puts **time** in this box] →**treat** →▶ button beside **Separate Lines:** [puts **treat** in this box] →**Add** [puts **time*treat** in box under **Plots**] →**Continue** [closes **Repeated Measures: Profile Plots** subdialog box]

→**OK**

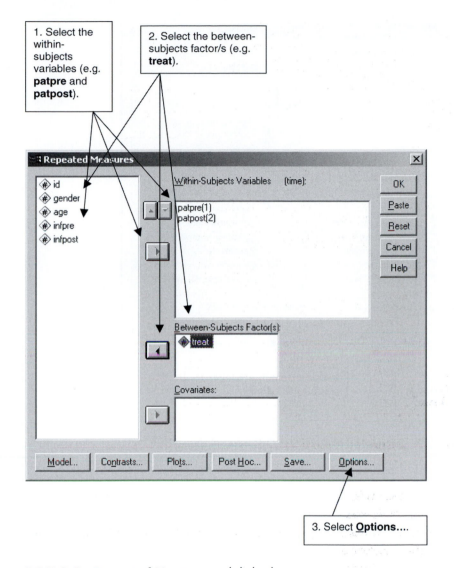

1. Select the within-subjects variables (e.g. **patpre** and **patpost**).

2. Select the between-subjects factor/s (e.g. **treat**).

3. Select **Options....**

BOX 9.8 **Repeated Measures** subdialog box

There is a significant effect for the interaction between treatment and time (i.e. the change between the pre- and the post-treatment scores), as indicated in the output in Table 9.15.

If we look at the means of the patients' pre-test and post-test depression scores in Table 9.16 and Figure 9.6, we can see that the amount of improvement shown by the three groups of patients is not the same. Least improvement has occurred in the group receiving no treatment (30.13 − 25.38 = 4.75),

1. Select **Descriptive statistics**.

2. Select **Continue** to return to previous dialog box.

BOX 9.9   Repeated Measures: Options subdialog box

while patients being administered the drug treatment exhibit the most improvement (35.42 − 22.25 = 13.17).

Statistical differences in the amount of improvement shown in the three treatments could be further examined using **One-Way ANOVA** where the dependent variable is the computed difference between pre- and post-test patient depression.

Combined design

As pointed out earlier on, it is possible to combine some of the above analyses. To show how this can be done, we shall look at the effect of two between-subjects factors (treatment and gender) and one within-subjects factor (pre- to post-test or time) on two dependent variables (depression as assessed by the

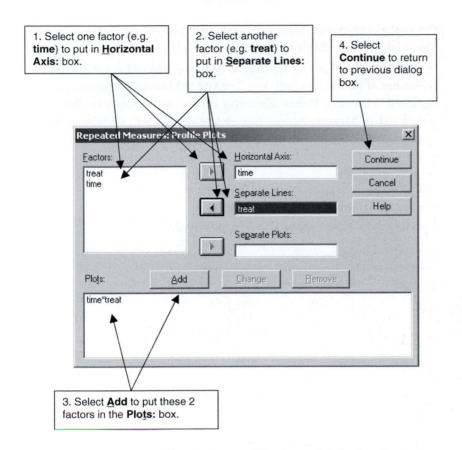

1. Select one factor (e.g. **time**) to put in **Horizontal Axis:** box.

2. Select another factor (e.g. **treat**) to put in **Separate Lines:** box.

4. Select **Continue** to return to previous dialog box.

3. Select **Add** to put these 2 factors in the **Plots:** box.

BOX 9.10 Repeated Measures: Profile Plots subdialog box

TABLE 9.15 Test of significance for interaction between time and treatment (Depression Project)

Tests of Within-Subjects Contrasts

Measure: MEASURE_1

Source	time	Type III Sum of Squares	df	Mean Square	F	Sig.
time	Linear	1365.352	1	1365.352	285.697	.000
time * treat	Linear	175.650	2	87.825	18.377	.000
Error(time)	Linear	129.033	27	4.779		

patient and an informant), covarying out the effects of age which we think might be related to the pre- and post-test measures. The following procedure would be used to carry this out:

→**Analyze** →**General Linear Model** →**Repeated Measures…** [opens **Repeated Measures Define Factor(s)** dialog box shown in Box 9.7]

→highlight **factor1** and type **time** in **Within-Subject Factor Name:** box →**Number of Levels:** box and type **2** →**Add** →**Measure>>** [opens more of **Repeated Measures Define Factor(s)** dialog box shown in Box 9.11] →type **pat** in **Measure Name:** box →**Add** →type **inf** in **Measure Name:** box →**Add**→**Define** [opens **Repeated Measures** subdialog box shown in Box 9.12]

TABLE 9.16 Means and standard deviations of patient pre-test (**patpre**) and post-test (**patpost**) depression in the three treatments (Depression Project)

Descriptive Statistics

	treat	Mean	Std. Deviation	N
patpre	1	30.13	3.720	8
	2	24.20	2.781	10
	3	35.42	2.843	12
	Total	30.27	5.699	30
patpost	1	25.38	3.583	8
	2	13.10	3.985	10
	3	22.25	5.413	12
	Total	20.03	6.754	30

Estimated Marginal Means of MEASURE_1

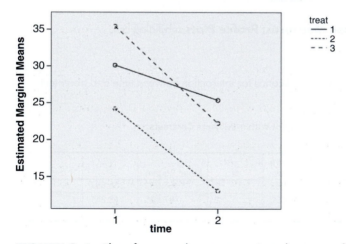

FIGURE 9.6 Plot of pre- and post-test patient depression for the three treatments (Depression Project) for SPSS 13 (which differs slightly for SPSS 10, 11 and 12). This plot has been edited with Chart Editor to vary the style of line by clicking on each numbered line in the legend.

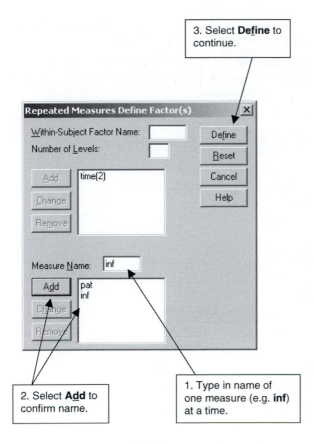

3. Select **Define** to continue.

Repeated Measures Define Factor(s)

Within-Subject Factor Name:

Number of Levels:

Add   time(2)

Change

Remove

Define

Reset

Cancel

Help

Measure Name: inf

Add   pat
        inf

Change

Remove

2. Select **Add** to confirm name.

1. Type in name of one measure (e.g. **inf**) at a time.

BOX 9.11 Repeated Measures Define Factor(s) extended dialog box

→**patpre** →▶ button beside **Within-Subjects Variables [time]:** [puts **patpre** in this box] →**patpost** →▶ button beside **Within-Subjects Variables [time]:** [puts **patpost** in this box] →**infpre** →▶ button beside **Within-Subjects Variables [time]:** [puts **infpre** in this box] →**infpost** →▶ button beside **Within-Subjects Variables [time]:** [puts **infpost** in this box] →**treat** →▶ button beside **Between-Subjects Factor(s):** [puts **treat** in this box] →**gender** →▶ button beside **Between-Subjects Factor(s):** [puts **gender** in this box] →**age** →▶ button beside **Covariate(s):** [puts **age** in this box]

→**Options...** [opens **Repeated Measures: Options** subdialog (box) shown in Box 9.9]

→**Descriptive statistics** →**Transformation matrix**

→**Continue** [closes **Repeated Measures: Options** subdialog box]

→**OK**

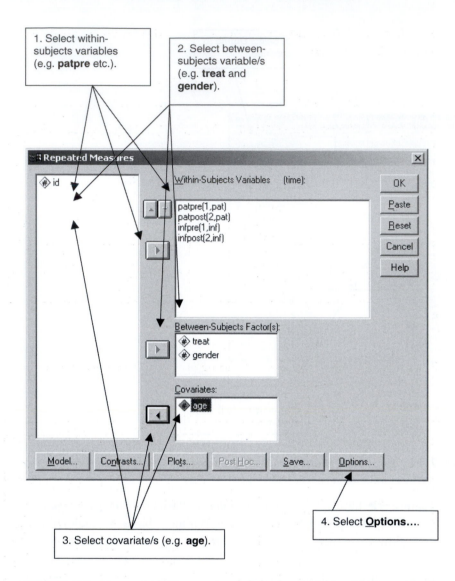

1. Select within-subjects variables (e.g. **patpre** etc.).

2. Select between-subjects variable/s (e.g. **treat** and **gender**).

3. Select covariate/s (e.g. **age**).

4. Select **Options**....

BOX 9.12   Repeated Measures subdialog box (combined design analysis)

In conducting a multivariate analysis of covariance, it is necessary to check that the covariate (**age**) is significantly correlated with the two dependent variables, which it is as the output in Table 9.17 shows.

The output for the multivariate tests is reproduced in Table 9.18. This shows a significant effect for the time by treatment by gender interaction effect.

TABLE 9.17   Relationship between the covariate of age and the two transformed variables (Depression Project)

Tests of Between-Subjects Effects

Transformed Variable: Average

Source	Measure	Type III Sum of Squares	df	Mean Square	F	Sig.
Intercept	pat	200.217	1	200.217	16.471	.000
	inf	322.787	1	322.787	19.914	.000
age	pat	298.580	1	298.580	24.562	.000
	inf	192.043	1	192.043	11.848	.002
treat	pat	549.908	2	274.954	22.619	.000
	inf	531.276	2	265.638	16.389	.000
gender	pat	9.063	1	9.063	.746	.397
	inf	8.461	1	8.461	.522	.477
treat * gender	pat	100.978	2	50.489	4.153	.029
	inf	324.974	2	162.487	10.025	.001
Error	pat	279.587	23	12.156		
	inf	372.799	23	16.209		

TABLE 9.18   Multivariate tests for the interaction between time, treatment and gender (Depression Project)

Multivariate[c,d]

Within Subjects Effect		Value	F	Hypothesis df	Error df	Sig.
time	Pillai's Trace	.364	6.305[a]	2.000	22.000	.007
	Wilks' Lambda	.636	6.305[a]	2.000	22.000	.007
	Hotelling's Trace	.573	6.305[a]	2.000	22.000	.007
	Roy's Largest Root	.573	6.305[a]	2.000	22.000	.007
time * age	Pillai's Trace	.009	.097[a]	2.000	22.000	.908
	Wilks' Lambda	.991	.097[a]	2.000	22.000	.908
	Hotelling's Trace	.009	.097[a]	2.000	22.000	.908
	Roy's Largest Root	.009	.097[a]	2.000	22.000	.908
time * treat	Pillai's Trace	.781	7.364	4.000	46.000	.000
	Wilks' Lambda	.241	11.423[a]	4.000	44.000	.000
	Hotelling's Trace	3.066	16.099	4.000	42.000	.000
	Roy's Largest Root	3.037	34.927[b]	2.000	23.000	.000
time * gender	Pillai's Trace	.098	1.196[a]	2.000	22.000	.321
	Wilks' Lambda	.902	1.196[a]	2.000	22.000	.321
	Hotelling's Trace	.109	1.196[a]	2.000	22.000	.321
	Roy's Largest Root	.109	1.196[a]	2.000	22.000	.321
time * treat * gender	Pillai's Trace	.576	4.653	4.000	46.000	.003
	Wilks' Lambda	.439	5.606[a]	4.000	44.000	.001
	Hotelling's Trace	1.245	6.537	4.000	42.000	.000
	Roy's Largest Root	1.217	13.998[b]	2.000	23.000	.000

a. Exact statistic.

b. The statistic is an upper bound on F that yields a lower bound on the significance level.

c. Design: Intercept+age+treat+gender+treat * gender.
   Within Subjects Design: time.

d. Tests are based on averaged variables.

TABLE 9.19 Univariate tests for the interaction effect between time, treatment and gender (Depression Project)

Tests of Within-Subjects Contrasts

Source	Measure	time	Type III Sum of Squares	df	Mean Square	F	Sig.
time	pat	Linear	32.706	1	32.706	12.916	.002
	inf	Linear	31.259	1	31.259	4.244	.051
time * age	pat	Linear	.091	1	.091	.036	.851
	inf	Linear	.218	1	.218	.030	.865
time * treat	pat	Linear	174.857	2	87.428	34.526	.000
	inf	Linear	185.773	2	92.886	12.610	.000
time * gender	pat	Linear	6.274	1	6.274	2.478	.129
	inf	Linear	6.758	1	6.758	.917	.348
time * treat * gender	pat	Linear	60.289	2	30.144	11.904	.000
	inf	Linear	27.641	2	13.820	1.876	.176
Error(time)	pat	Linear	58.242	23	2.532		
	inf	Linear	169.423	23	7.366		

TABLE 9.20 Transformed variables (Depression Project)

Average

Transformed Variable: AVERAGE

Dependent Variable	Measure	
	pat	inf
patpre	.707	.000
patpost	.707	.000
infpre	.000	.707
infpost	.000	.707

The univariate tests in Table 9.19 demonstrate the interaction effect to be significant ($p < 0.0005$) for the patient measure only (**pat**). It is not significant ($p = 0.176$) for the informant measure (**inf**). **Pat** refers to the transformed score which is the difference between the patient's pre- and post-test measure as can be seen in Table 9.20. **Inf** represents the difference between the informant's pre- and post-test score. To interpret these results, it would be necessary to compute the mean pre- and post-treatment patient depression scores, adjusted for age, for men and women in the three treatments. Additional analyses would have to be conducted to test these interpretations, as described previously.

Exercises

1   What are the two main advantages in studying the effects of two independent variables rather than one?
2   What is meant when two variables are said to interact?

3   How would you determine whether there was a significant interaction between two independent variables?

4   A colleague is interested in the relationship between alcohol, anxiety and gender on performance. Participants are randomly assigned to receiving one of four increasing dosages of alcohol. In addition, they are divided into three groups of low, moderate, and high anxiety. Which is the dependent variable?

5   How many factors are there in this design?

6   How many levels of anxiety are there?

7   How would you describe this design?

8   If there are unequal numbers of participants in each group and if the variable names for alcohol, anxiety, gender, and performance are **alcohol**, **anxiety**, **gender**, and **perform** respectively, what is the appropriate SPSS procedure for examining the effect of the first three variables on performance?

9   You are interested in examining the effect of three different methods of teaching on learning to read. Although participants have been randomly assigned to the three methods, you think that differences in intelligence may obscure any effects. How would you try to control statistically for the effects of intelligence?

10   What is the appropriate SPSS procedure for examining the effect of three teaching methods on learning to read, covarying out the effect of intelligence when the names for these three variables are **methods**, **read**, and **intell** respectively?

11   You are studying what effect physical attractiveness has on judgements of intelligence, likeability, honesty, and self-confidence. Participants are shown a photograph of either an attractive or an unattractive person and are asked to judge the extent to which this person has these four characteristics. How would you describe the design of this study?

12   If the names of the five variables in this study are **attract**, **intell**, **likeable**, **honesty**, and **confid** respectively, what is the appropriate SPSS procedure you would use for analysing the results of this study?

Chapter 10

Multivariate analysis: exploring relationships among three or more variables

IN THIS CHAPTER we will be concerned with a variety of approaches to the examination of relationships when more than two variables are involved. Clearly, these concerns follow on directly from those of Chapter 8, in which we focused upon bivariate analysis of relationships. In the present chapter, we will be concerned to explore the reasons for wanting to analyse three or more variables in conjunction; that is, why multivariate analysis is an important aspect of the examination of relationships among variables.

The basic rationale for multivariate analysis is to allow the researcher to discount the alternative explanations of a relationship that can arise when a survey/correlational design has been employed. The experimental researcher can discount alternative explanations of a relationship through the combination of having a control group as well as an experimental group (or through a number of experimental groups) and random assignment (see Chapter 1). The absence of these characteristics, which in large part derives from the failure or inability to manipulate the independent variable in a survey/correlational study, means that a number of potentially confounding factors may exist. For example, we may find a relationship between people's self-assigned social class (whether they describe themselves as middle or working class) and their voting preference (Conservative or Labour). But there are a number of problems that can be identified with interpreting such a relationship as causal. Could the relationship be spurious? This possibility could arise because people of higher incomes are both more likely to consider themselves middle class and to vote Conservative. Also, even if the relationship is not spurious, does the relationship apply equally to young and old? We know that age affects voting preferences, so how does this variable interact with self-assigned social class in regard to voting behaviour? Such a finding would imply that the class–voting relationship is moderated by age. The problem of spuriousness arises because we cannot make some people think they are middle class and others working class and then randomly assign subjects to the two categories. If we wanted to establish whether a moderated relationship exists whereby age moderated the class–voting relationship with an experimental study, we would use a factorial design (see Chapter 9). Obviously, we are not able to create such experimental conditions, so when we investigate this kind of issue through surveys, we have to recognise the limitations of inferring causal relationships from our data. In each of the two questions about the class–voting relationship, a third variable – income and age respectively – potentially contaminates the relationship and forces us to be sceptical about it.

The procedures to be explained in this chapter are designed to allow such contaminating variables to be discounted. This is done by imposing 'statistical controls' which allow the third variable to be 'held constant'. In this way we can examine the relationship between two variables by partialling out and thereby controlling the effect of a third variable. For example, if we believe that income confounds the relationship between self-assigned social class and voting, we examine the relationship between social class and voting for each income level in our sample. The sample might reveal four income levels, so we examine the class–voting relationship for each of these four income levels. We can then ask whether the relationship between class and voting persists for each income level or whether it has been eliminated for all or some of these levels. The third variable (i.e. the one that is controlled) is often referred to as the test factor (e.g. Rosenberg, 1968), but the term test variable is preferred in the following discussion.

The imposition of statistical controls suffers from a number of dis-advantages. In particular, it is only possible to control for those variables which occur to you as potentially important and which are relatively easy to measure. Other variables will constitute further contaminating factors, but the effects of these are unknown. Further, the time order of variables collected by means of a survey/correlational study cannot be established through multi-variate analysis, but has to be inferred. In order to make inferences about the likely direction of cause and effect, the researcher must look to probable directions of causation (e.g. education precedes current occupation) or to theories which suggest that certain variables are more likely to precede others. As suggested in Chapter 1, the generation of causal inferences from survey/correlational research can be hazardous, but in the present chapter we will largely sidestep these problems which are not capable of easy resolution in the absence of a panel study.

The initial exposition of multivariate analysis will solely emphasise the examination of three variables. It should be recognised that many examples of mutivariate analysis, particularly those involving correlation and regression techniques, go much further than this. Many researchers refer to the relation-ship between two variables as the *zero-order relationship*; when a third variable is introduced, they refer to the *first-order relationship*, that is the relationship between two variables when one variable is held constant; and when two extra variables are introduced, they refer to the *second-order relationship*, when two variables are held constant.

Multivariate analysis through contingency tables

In this section, we will examine the potential of contingency tables as a means of exploring relationships among three variables. Four contexts in which such analysis can be useful are provided: testing for spuriousness, testing for intervening variables, testing for moderated relationships, and examining multiple causation. Although these four notions are treated in connection with contingency table analysis, they are also relevant to the correlation and regression techniques which are examined later.

Testing for spuriousness

The idea of spuriousness was introduced in Chapter 1 in the context of a discussion about the nature of causality. In order to establish that there exists a relationship between two variables it is necessary to show that the relationship is non-spurious. A spurious relationship exists when the relationship between two variables is not a 'true' relationship, in that it only appears because a third variable (often called an extraneous variable – see Rosenberg, 1968) causes each of the variables making up the pair. In Table 10.1 a bivariate contingency table is presented which derives from an imaginary study of 500 manual workers in twelve firms. The table seems to show a relationship between the presence of variety in work and job satisfaction. For example, 80 per cent of those performing varied work are satisfied, as against only 24 per cent of those whose work is not varied. Thus there is a difference (d_1) of 56 per cent (i.e. $80 - 24$) between those performing varied work and

TABLE 10.1 Relationship between work variety and job satisfaction (imaginary data)

	Work variety		
	Varied work	*Not varied work*	
		1		2
	(200)	(60)	
Satisfied	80%	24%	
	$d_1 =$	56%	
Job satisfaction			
		3		4
	(50)	(190)	
Not satisfied	20%	76%	
	$d_2 =$	56%	

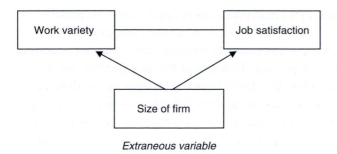

Extraneous variable

FIGURE 10.1 Is the relationship between work variety and job satisfaction spurious?

those not performing varied work in terms of job satisfaction. Contingency tables are not normally presented with the differences between cells inserted, but since these form the crux of the multivariate contingency table analysis, this additional information is provided in this and subsequent tables in this section.

Could the relationship between these two variables be spurious? Could it be that the size of the firm (the test variable) in which each respondent works has 'produced' the relationship (see Figure 10.1)? It may be that size of the firm affects both the amount of variety of work reported and levels of job satisfaction. In order to examine this possibility, we partition our sample into those who work in large firms and those who work in small firms. There are 250 respondents in each of these two categories. We then examine the relationship between amount of variety in work and job satisfaction for each category. If the relationship is spurious we would expect the relationship between amount of variety in work and job satisfaction largely to disappear. Table 10.2

TABLE 10.2 A spurious relationship: the relationship between work variety and job satisfaction, controlling for size of firm (imaginary data)

		Large firms				Small firms			
		Varied work		Not varied work		Varied work		Not varied work	
Job satisfaction	Satisfied	1 (190) 95% $d_1 =$	85% 10%	2 (42)		3 (10) 20% $d_2 =$	9% 11%	4 (18)	
	Not satisfied	5 (10) 5% $d_3 =$	15% 10%	6 (8)		7 (40) 80% $d_4 =$	91% 11%	8 (182)	

presents such an analysis. In a sense, what one is doing here is to present two separate tables: one examining the relationship between amount of variety in work and job satisfaction for respondents from large firms and one examining the same relationship for small firms. This notion is symbolised by the double line separating the analysis for large firms from the analysis for small firms.

What we find is that the relationship between amount of variety in work and job satisfaction has largely disappeared. Compare d_1 in Table 10.1 with both d_1 and d_2 in Table 10.2. Whereas d_1 in Table 10.1 is 56 per cent, implying a large difference between those whose work is varied and those whose work is not varied in terms of job satisfaction, the corresponding percentage differences in Table 10.2 are 10 and 11 per cent for d_1 and d_2 respectively. This means that when size of firm is controlled, the difference in terms of job satisfaction between those whose work is varied and those whose work is not varied is considerably reduced. This analysis implies that there is not a true relationship between variety in work and job satisfaction, because when size of firm is controlled the relationship between work variety and job satisfaction is almost eliminated. We can suggest that size of firm seems to affect both variables. Most respondents reporting varied work come from large firms ([cell1 + cell5] − [cell3 + cell7]) and most respondents who are satisfied come from large firms ([cell1 + cell2] − [cell3 + cell4]).

What would Table 10.2 look like if the relationship between variety in work and job satisfaction was not spurious when size of firm is controlled? Table 10.3 presents the same analysis but this time the relationship is not spurious. Again, we can compare d_1 in Table 10.1 with both d_1 and d_2 in Table 10.3. In Table 10.1, the difference between those who report variety in their work and those who report no variety is 56 per cent (i.e. d_1), whereas in

TABLE 10.3 A non-spurious relationship: the relationship between work variety and job satisfaction, controlling for size of firm (imaginary data)

		Large firms		Small firms	
		Varied work	Not varied work	Varied work	Not varied work
Job satisfaction	Satisfied	1 (166) 83% $d_1 =$	2 (14) 28% 55%	3 (34) 68% $d_2 =$	4 (46) 23% 45%
	Not satisfied	5 (34) 17% $d_3 =$	6 (36) 72% 55%	7 (16) 32% $d_4 =$	8 (154) 77% 45%

Table 10.3 the corresponding differences are 55 per cent for large firms (d_1) and 45 per cent for small firms (d_2) respectively. Thus, d_1 in Table 10.3 is almost exactly the same as d_1 in Table 10.1, but d_2 is 11 percentage points smaller (i.e. 56 − 45). However, this latter finding would not be sufficient to suggest that the relationship is spurious because the difference between those who report varied work and those whose work is not varied is still large for both respondents in large firms and those in small firms. We do not expect an exact replication of percentage differences when we carry out such controls. Similarly, as suggested in the context of the discussion of Table 10.2, we do not need percentage differences to disappear completely in order to infer that a relationship is spurious. When there is an in-between reduction in percentage differences (for example, to around half of the original difference), the relationship is probably partially spurious, implying that part of it is caused by the third variable and the other part is indicative of a 'true' relationship. This would have been the interpretation if the original d_1 difference of 56 per cent had fallen to around 28 per cent for respondents from both large firms and small firms.

Testing for intervening variables

The quest for intervening variables is different from the search for potentially spurious relationships. An intervening variable is one that is both a product of the independent variable and a cause of the dependent variable. Taking the data examined in Table 10.1, the sequence depicted in Figure 10.2 might be imagined. The analysis presented in Table 10.4 strongly suggests that the level of people's interest in their work is an intervening variable. As with Tables 10.2 and 10.3, we partition the sample into two groups (this time those who report that they are interested and those reporting no interest in their work) and examine the relationship between work variety and job satisfaction for each group. Again, we can compare d_1 in Table 10.1 with d_1 and d_2 in Table 10.4. In Table 10.1 d_1 is 56 per cent, but in Table 10.4 d_1 and d_2 are 13 per cent and 20

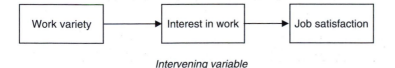

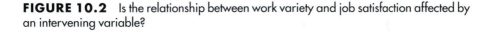

Intervening variable

FIGURE 10.2 Is the relationship between work variety and job satisfaction affected by an intervening variable?

289

TABLE 10.4 An intervening variable: the relationship between work variety and job satisfaction, controlling for interest in work (imaginary data)

	Interested		Not interested	
	Varied work	Not varied work	Varied work	Not varied work
Satisfied	1 (185) 93% $d_1 =$	2 (40) 80% 13%	3 (15) 30% $d_2 =$	4 (20) 10% 20%
Not satisfied	5 (15) 7% $d_3 =$	6 (10) 20% 13%	7 (35) 70% $d_4 =$	8 (180) 90% 20%

(left axis label: Job satisfaction)

per cent respectively. Clearly, d_1 and d_2 in Table 10.3 have not been reduced to zero (which would suggest that the whole of the relationship was through interest in work), but they are also much lower than the 56 per cent difference in Table 10.1. If d_1 and d_2 in Table 10.4 had remained at or around 56 per cent, we would conclude that interest in work is not an intervening variable.

The sequence in Figure 10.2 suggests that variety in work affects the degree of interest in work that people experience, which in turn affects their level of job satisfaction. This pattern differs from that depicted in Figure 10.1 in that, if the analysis supported the hypothesised sequence, it suggests that there is a relationship between amount of variety in work and job satisfaction, but the relationship is not direct. The search for intervening variables is often referred to as explanation, and it is easy to see why. If we find that a test variable acts as an intervening variable, we are able to gain some explanatory leverage on the bivariate relationship. Thus, we find that there is a relationship between amount of variety in work and job satisfaction and then ask why that relationship might exist. We speculate that it may be because those who have varied work become more interested in their work, which heightens their job satisfaction.

It should be apparent that the computation of a test for an intervening variable is identical to a test for spuriousness. How, then, do we know which is which? If we carry out an analysis like those shown in Tables 10.2, 10.3 and 10.4, how can we be sure that what we are taking to be an intervening variable is not in fact an indication that the relationship is spurious? The answer is that there should be only one logical possibility, that is, only one that makes sense. If we take the trio of variables in Figure 10.1, to argue that the test variable – size of firm – could be an intervening variable would mean that we would have to suggest that a person's level of work variety affects the size of the firm in which he or she works – an unlikely scenario. Similarly, to argue that the trio in Figure 10.2 could point to a test for spuriousness, would mean that we would have to accept that the test variable – interest in work – can affect the amount of variety in a person's work. This too makes much less sense than to perceive it as an intervening variable.

One further point should be registered. It is clear that controlling for interest in work in Table 10.4 has not totally eliminated the difference between those reporting varied work and those whose work is not varied in terms of job satisfaction. It would seem, therefore, that there are aspects of the relationship between amount of variety in work and job satisfaction that are not totally explained by the test variable, interest in work.

Testing for moderated relationships

A moderated relationship occurs when a relationship is found to hold for some categories of a sample but not others. Diagrammatically this can be displayed as in Figure 10.3. We may even find the character of a relationship can differ for categories of the test variable. We might find that for one category those who report varied work exhibit greater job satisfaction, but for another category of people the reverse may be true (i.e. varied work seems to engender lower levels of job satisfaction than work that is not varied).

Table 10.5 looks at the relationship between variety in work and job satisfaction for men and women. Once again, we can compare d_1 (56 per cent) in Table 10.1 with d_1 and d_2 in Table 10.5, which are 85 per cent and 12 per cent respectively. The bulk of the 56 percentage point difference between those

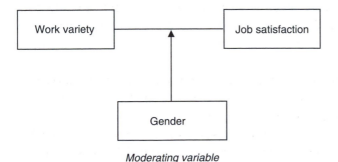

Moderating variable

FIGURE 10.3   Is the relationship between work variety and job satisfaction moderated by gender?

TABLE 10.5 A moderated relationship: the relationship between work variety and job satisfaction, controlling for gender (imaginary data)

		Men			Women		
		Varied work	Not varied work		Varied work	Not varied work	
Job satisfaction	Satisfied	1 (143) 95% $d_1 =$	2 (15) 10% 85%		3 (57) 57% $d_2 =$	4 (45) 45% 12%	
	Not satisfied	5 (7) 5% $d_3 =$	6 (135) 90% 85%		7 (43) 43% $d_4 =$	8 (55) 55% 12%	

reporting varied work and those reporting that work is not varied in Table 10.1 appears to derive from the relationship between variety in work and job satisfaction being far stronger for men than women and there being more men (300) than women (200) in the sample. Table 10.5 demonstrates the importance of searching for moderated relationships in that they allow the researcher to avoid inferring that a set of findings pertains to a sample as a whole, when in fact it only really applies to a portion of that sample. The term 'interaction effect' is often employed to refer to the situation in which a relationship between two variables differs substantially for categories of the test variable. This kind of occurrence was also addressed in Chapter 9. The discovery of such an effect often inaugurates a new line of inquiry in that it stimulates reflection about the likely reasons for such variations.

The discovery of moderated relationships can occur by design or by chance. When they occur by design, the researcher has usually anticipated the possibility that a relationship may be moderated (though he or she may be wrong of course). They can occur by chance when the researcher conducts a test for an intervening variable or a test for spuriousness and finds a marked contrast in findings for different categories of the test variable.

Multiple causation

Dependent variables in the social sciences are rarely determined by one variable alone, so that two or more potential independent variables can usefully be considered in conjunction. Figure 10.4 suggests that whether someone is allowed participation in decision-making at work also affects their level of job satisfaction. It is misleading to refer to participation in decision-making as

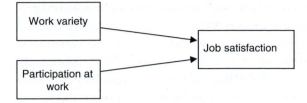

FIGURE 10.4 *Multiple causation*

a test variable in this context, since it is really a second independent variable. What, then, is the impact of amount of variety in work on job satisfaction when we control the effects of participation?

Again, we compare d_1 in Table 10.1 (56 per cent) with d_1 and d_2 in Table 10.6. The latter are 19 per cent and 18 per cent respectively. This suggests that, although the effect of amount of variety in work has not been reduced to zero or nearly zero, its impact has been reduced considerably. Participation in decision-making appears to be a more important cause of variation in job satisfaction. For example, compare the percentages in cells 1 and 3 in Table 10.6: among those respondents who report that they perform varied work, 93 per cent of those who experience participation exhibit job satisfaction, whereas only 30 per cent of those who do not experience participation are satisfied.

One reason for this pattern of findings is that most people who experience participation in decision-making also have varied jobs, that is (cell1 + cell5) − (cell2 + cell6). Likewise, most people who do not experience participation have work which is not varied, that is (cell4 + cell8) − (cell3 + cell7). Could this mean that the relationship between variety in work and job

TABLE 10.6 Multiple causation: the relationship between work variety and job satisfaction, controlling for participation at work (imaginary data)

		Participation		Little or no participation	
		Varied work	*Not varied work*	*Varied work*	*Not varied work*
Job satisfaction	Satisfied	1 (185) 93% $d_1 =$	2 (37) 74% 19%	3 (15) 30% $d_2 =$	4 (23) 12% 18%
	Not satisfied	5 (15) 7% $d_3 =$	6 (13) 26% 19%	7 (35) 70% $d_4 =$	8 (177) 88% 18%

satisfaction is really spurious, when participation in decision-making is employed as the test variable? The answer is that this is unlikely, since it would mean that participation in decision-making would have to cause variation in the amount of variety in work, which is a less likely possibility (since technological conditions tend to be the major influence on variables like work variety). Once again, we have to resort to a combination of intuitive logic and theoretical reflection in order to discount such a possibility. We will return to this kind of issue in the context of an examination of the use of multivariate analysis through correlation and regression.

Using SPSS to perform multivariate analysis through contingency tables

Taking the Job Survey data, we might want to examine the relationship between **skill** and **ethnicgp**, holding **gender** constant (i.e. as a test variable). Assuming that we want cell frequencies and column percentages, the following sequence would be followed:

→**Analyze** →**Descriptive Statistics** →**Crosstabs...** [opens **Crosstabs** dialog box shown in Box 8.1]

→**skill** →▶button [puts **skill** in **Row[s]:** box] →**ethnicgp** →▶button by **Column[s]:** [puts **ethnicgp** in box] →**gender** →▶button by bottom box [puts **gender** in box] ▶**Cells. . .** [opens **Crosstabs: Cell Display** subdialog box shown in Box 8.3]

[Ensure **Observed** in the **Counts** box has been selected and under **Percentages** ensure **Column:** has been selected] →**Continue** [closes **Crosstabs: Cell Display** subdialog box]

→**OK**

Two contingency tables crosstabulating **skill** by **ethnicgp** will be produced – one for men and one for women. Each table will have **ethnicgp** going across (i.e. as columns) and **skill** going down (i.e. as rows).

Multivariate analysis and correlation

Although the use of contingency tables provides a powerful tool for multivariate analysis, it suffers from a major limitation, namely that complex analyses with more than three variables require large samples, especially when the variables include a large number of categories. Otherwise, there is the likelihood of very small frequencies in many cells (and indeed the likelihood of many empty cells) when a small sample is employed. By contrast, correlation and regression can be used to conduct multivariate analyses on fairly small samples, although their use in relation to very small samples is limited. Further, both correlation and regression provide easy-to-interpret indications of the relative strength of relationships. On the other hand, if one or more variables are nominal, multivariate analysis through contingency tables is probably the best way forward for most purposes.

The partial correlation coefficient

One of the main ways in which the multivariate analysis of relationships is conducted in the social sciences is through the partial correlation coefficient. This test allows the researcher to examine the relationship between two variables while holding one other or more variables constant. It allows tests for spuriousness, tests for intervening variables, and multiple causation to be investigated. The researcher must stipulate the anticipated logic that underpins the three variables in question (for example, test for spuriousness) and can then investigate the effect of the test variable on the original relationship. Moderated relationships are probably better examined by computing Pearson's *r* for each category of the test variable (for example, for both men and women, or young, middle-aged, and old) and then comparing the *r*s.

The partial correlation coefficient is computed by first calculating the Pearson's *r* for each of the pairs of possible relationships involved. Thus, if the two variables concerned are *x* and *y*, and *t* is the test variable (or second independent variable in the case of investigating multiple causation), the partial correlation coefficient computes Pearson's *r* for *x* and *y*, *x* and *t*, and *y* and *t*. Because of this, it is necessary to remember that all the restrictions associated with Pearson's *r* apply to variables involved in the possible computation of the partial correlation coefficient (for example, variables must be interval).

There are three possible effects that can occur when partial correlation is undertaken: the relationship between *x* and *y* is unaffected by *t*; the relationship between *x* and *y* is totally explained by *t*; and the relationship between *x* and *y* is partially explained by *t*. Each of these three possibilities can be illustrated with Venn diagrams (see Figure 10.5). In the first case (a), *t* is only related to *x*, so the relationship between *x* and *y* is unchanged, because *t* can only have an impact on the relationship between *x* and *y* if it affects *both*

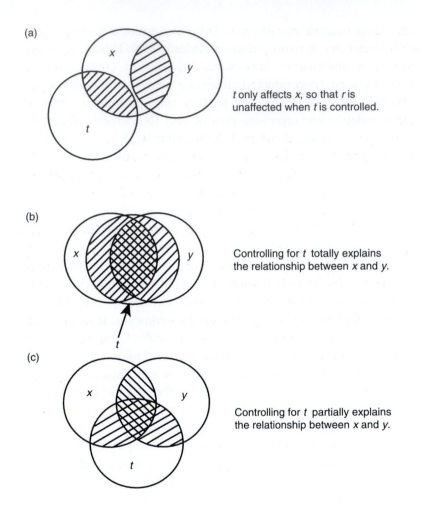

(a)

t only affects *x*, so that *r* is unaffected when *t* is controlled.

(b)

Controlling for *t* totally explains the relationship between *x* and *y*.

(c)

Controlling for *t* partially explains the relationship between *x* and *y*.

FIGURE 10.5   The effects of controlling for a test variable

variables. In the second case (b), all of the relationship between *x* and *y* (the shaded area) is encapsulated by *t*. This would mean that the relationship between *x* and *y* when *t* is controlled would be zero. What usually occurs is that the test variable, *t*, partly explains the relationship between *x* and *y*, as in the case of (c) in Figure 10.5. In this case, only part of the relationship between *x* and *y* is explained by *t* (the shaded area which is overlapped by *t*). This would mean that the partial correlation coefficient will be lower than the Pearson's *r* for *x* and *y*. This is the most normal outcome of calculating the partial correlation coefficient. If the first-order correlation between *x* and *y* when *t* is controlled is considerably less than the zero-order correlation between x and y, the researcher must decide (if he or she has not already done so) whether: (a) the x–y relationship is spurious, or at least largely so; or (b) whether t is an intervening variable between x and y; or (c) whether t is best thought of as a causal variable which is related to x and which largely eliminates the effect of x on y. These are the three possibilities represented in Figures 10.1, 10.2 and 10.4 respectively.

As an example, consider the data in Table 10.7. We have data on eighteen individuals relating to three variables: age, income and a questionnaire scale measuring support for the market economy, which goes from a minimum of 5 to a maximum of 25. The correlation between income and support for the market economy is 0.64. But could this relationship be spurious? Could it be that age should be introduced as a test variable, since we might anticipate that older people are both more likely to earn more and to support the market economy? This possibility can be anticipated because age is related to income (0.76) and to support (0.83). When we compute the partial correlation

TABLE 10.7 Income, age and support for the market economy (imaginary data)

Case number	Age	Income (£)	Support for market economy
1	20	9,000	11
2	23	8,000	9
3	28	12,500	12
4	30	10,000	14
5	32	15,000	10
6	34	12,500	13
7	35	13,000	16
8	37	14,500	14
9	37	14,000	17
10	41	16,000	13
11	43	15,500	15
12	47	14,000	14
13	50	16,500	18
14	52	12,500	17
15	54	14,500	15
16	59	15,000	19
17	61	17,000	22
18	63	16,500	18

coefficient for income and support controlling the effects of age, the level of correlation falls to 0.01. This means that the relationship between income and support for the market economy is spurious. When age is controlled, the relationship falls to nearly zero. A similar kind of reasoning would apply to the detection of intervening variables and multiple causation.

Partial correlation with SPSS

Imagine that we want to correlate **absence**, **autonom** and **satis** with each other, but controlling for **income**. We might think, for example, that the correlation of 0.733 between **autonom** and **satis** (see Table 8.7) might be due to **income**: if people have more autonomy, they are more likely to be given higher incomes, and this may make them more satisfied with their jobs. The following sequence would be followed:

→**Analyze** →**Correlate** →**Partial** . . . [opens **Partial Correlations** dialog box shown in Box 10.1]

→**absence** →►button by **Variables:** box [puts **absence** in **Variables:** box]

→**autonom** →►button by **Variables:** box [puts **autonom** in **Variables:** box]

→**satis** →►button by **Variables:** box [puts **satis** in **Variables:** box]

→**income** →►button by **Controlling for:** box [puts **income** in **Controlling for:** box] →**Two-tailed** or **One-tailed** [depending on which form of **Test of Significance** you want *and* ensure box by **Display actual significance level** has been selected]

→**Options...** [opens **Partial Correlations: Options** subdialog box shown in Box 10.2]

→*either* **Exclude cases listwise** *or* **Exclude cases pairwise** [depending on which way of handling missing cases you prefer] →**Continue** [closes **Partial Correlations: Options** subdialog box]

→**OK**

The output from this sequence is presented in Table 10.8. Listwise deletions of missing cases was selected in this instance. A useful facility within the **Partial** procedure is that Pearson's *r* can also be computed for all the possible pairs of variables listed in the **Partial Correlations** dialog box. In the **Partial Correlations: Options** subdialog box, simply select **Zero-order correlations** so that a tick appears in the box (if one is not there already).

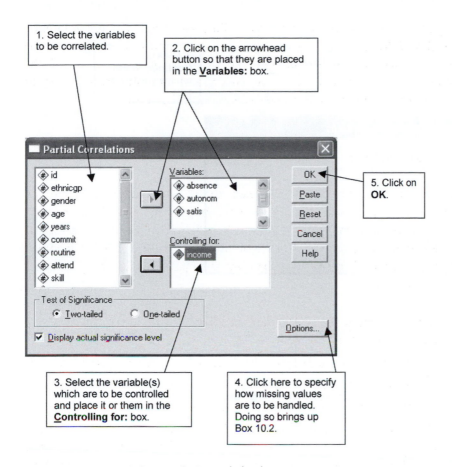

1. Select the variables to be correlated.

2. Click on the arrowhead button so that they are placed in the **Variables:** box.

5. Click on **OK**.

3. Select the variable(s) which are to be controlled and place it or them in the **Controlling for:** box.

4. Click here to specify how missing values are to be handled. Doing so brings up Box 10.2.

BOX 10.1   Partial Correlations dialog box

In fact, there is almost no difference between the correlation of 0.73 between **autonom** and **satis** and the 0.70 when these same variables are correlated with **income** held constant (see Table 10.8). This suggests that the correlation between **autonom** and **satis** is unaffected by **income**. The original bivariate correlation is often referred to as a *zero-order correlation* (i.e. with no variables controlled); when one variable is controlled, as in the case of **income** in this instance, the resulting correlation is known as a *first-order correlation*. Still higher order correlations can be obtained. For example, a *second-order correlation* would entail controlling for *two* variables, perhaps **age** and **income**. To do this within SPSS, simply add the additional variable(s) that you want to control for to the **Controlling for:** box in the **Partial Correlations** dialog box (Box 10.1).

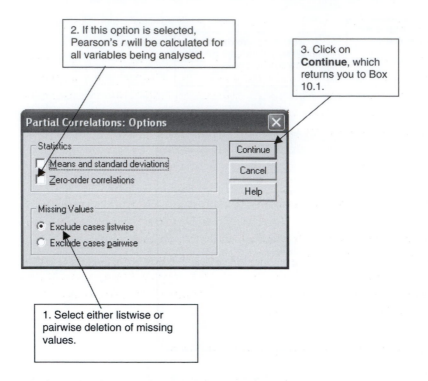

2. If this option is selected, Pearson's *r* will be calculated for all variables being analysed.

3. Click on **Continue**, which returns you to Box 10.1.

1. Select either listwise or pairwise deletion of missing values.

BOX 10.2   Partial Correlations: Options subdialog box

Regression and multivariate analysis

Nowadays regression, in the form of multiple regression, is the most widely used method for conducting multivariate analysis, particularly when more than three variables are involved. In Chapter 8 we previously encountered regression as a means of expressing relationships among pairs of variables. In

TABLE 10.8 Matrix of partial correlation coefficients (Job Survey data)

Correlations

Control Variables			absence	autonom	satis
income	absence	Correlation	1.000	-.038	-.165
		Significance (2-tailed)	.	.764	.192
		df	0	62	62
	autonom	Correlation	-.038	1.000	.696
		Significance (2-tailed)	.764	.	.000
		df	62	0	62
	satis	Correlation	-.165	.696	1.000
		Significance (2-tailed)	.192	.000	.
		df	62	62	0

this chapter, the focus will be on the presence of two or more independent variables.

Consider first of all, a fairly simple case in which there are three variables, that is two independent variables. The nature of the relationship between the dependent variable and the two independent variables is expressed in a similar manner to the bivariate case explored in Chapter 8. The analogous equation for mutivariate analysis is

$$y = a + b_1 x_1 + b_2 x_2 + e$$

where x_1 and x_2 are the two independent variables, a is the intercept, b_1 and b_2 are the regression coefficients for the two independent variables, and e is an error term which points to the fact that a proportion of the variance in the dependent variable, y, is unexplained by the regression equation. As in Chapter 8, the error term is ignored since it is not used for making predictions.

In order to illustrate the operation of multiple regression consider the data in Table 10.7. The regression equation for these data is

$$\text{support} = 5.913 + 0.21262\text{age} + 0.000008\text{income}$$

where 5.913 is the intercept (a), 0.21262 is the regression coefficient for the first independent variable, age (x_1), and 0.000008 is the regression coefficient for the second independent variable, income (x_2). Each of the two regression coefficients estimates the amount of change that occurs in the dependent variable (support for the market economy) for a one unit change in the independent variable. Moreover, the regression coefficient expresses the amount of change in the dependent variable with the effect of all other independent variables in the equation partialled out (i.e. controlled). Thus, if we had an equation with four independent variables, each of the four regression co-efficients would express the unique contribution of the relevant variable to the dependent variable (with the effect in each case of the three other variables removed). This feature is of considerable importance, since the independent variables in a multiple regression equation are almost always related to each other.

Thus, every extra year of a person's age increases support for the market economy by 0.21262, and every extra £1,000 increases support by 0.000008. Moreover, the effect of age on support is with the effect of income removed, and the effect of income on support is with the effect of age removed. If we wanted to predict the likely level of support for the market economy of someone aged 40 with an income of £17,500, we would substitute as follows:

$$y = 5.913 + (0.21262)(40) + (0.000008)(17500)$$
$$= 5.913 + 8.5048 + 0.014$$
$$= 14.56$$

Thus, we would expect that someone with an age of 40 and an income of £17,500 would have a score of 14.56 on the scale of support for the market economy.

While the ability to make such predictions is of some interest to social scientists, the strength of multiple regression lies primarily in its use as a means of establishing the relative importance of independent variables to the dependent variable. However, we cannot say that, simply because the regression coefficient for age is larger than that for income, this means that age is more important to support for the market economy than age. This is because age and income derive from different units of measurement that cannot be directly compared. In order to effect a comparison it is necessary to standardise the units of measurement involved. This can be done by multiplying each regression coefficient by the product of dividing the standard deviation of the relevant independent variable by the standard deviation of the dependent variable. The result is known as a *standardised regression coefficient* or *beta weight*. This coefficient is easily computed through SPSS. Standardised regression coefficients in a regression equation employ the same standard of measurement and therefore can be compared to determine which of two or more independent variables is the more important in relation to the dependent variable. They essentially tell us by how many standard deviation units the dependent variable will change for a one standard deviation change in the independent variable.

We can now take an example from the Job Survey data to illustrate some of these points. In the following example we will treat **satis** as the dependent variable and **routine**, **autonom**, **age** and **income** as the independent variables. These four independent variables were chosen because they are all known to be related to **satis**, as revealed by the relevant correlation coefficients. However, it is important to ensure that the independent variables are not too highly related to each other. The Pearson's *r* between each pair of independent variables should not exceed 0.80; otherwise the independent variables that show a relationship at or in excess of 0.80 may be suspected of exhibiting *multicollinearity*. Multicollinearity is usually regarded as a problem because it means that the regression coefficients may be unstable. This implies that they are likely to be subject to considerable variability from sample to sample. In any case, when two variables are very highly correlated, there seems little point in treating them as separate entities. Multicollinearity can be quite difficult to detect where there are more than two independent variables, but SPSS provides some diagnostic tools that will be examined below.

We can now take an example from the Job Survey data in order to illustrate some of these points. When the previous multiple regression analysis is carried out, the following equation is generated:

satis = −1.936 + 0.573**autonom** + 0.001**income** − 0.168**routine**

The variable **age** was eliminated from the equation by the procedure chosen for including variables in the analysis (the *stepwise* procedure described below), because it failed to meet the program's statistical criteria for inclusion. If it had been 'forced' into the equation, the impact of **age** on **satis** would have been almost zero. Thus, if we wanted to predict the likely **satis** score of someone with an **autonom** score of 16, an **income** of £16,000, and a **routine** score of 8, the calculation would proceed as follows:

$$\textbf{satis} = -1.936 + (0.573)(16) + (0.001)(16000) - (0.168)(8)$$
$$= -1.936 + 9.168 + 16 - 1.344$$
$$= 21.888$$

However, it is the *relative* impact of each of these variables on **satis** that provides the main area of interest for many social scientists. Table 10.9 presents the regression coefficients for the three independent variables remaining in the equation and the corresponding standardised regression coefficients. Although **autonom** provides the largest unstandardised and standardised regression coefficients, the case of **income** demonstrates the hazardousness of

TABLE 10.9 Comparison of unstandardised and standardised regression coefficients with **satis** as the dependent variable

Independent variables	Unstandardised regression coefficients	Standardised regression coefficients
autonom	0.573	0.483
income	0.001	0.383
routine	−0.168	−0.217
[intercept]	−1.936	—

using unstandardised coefficients in order to infer the magnitude of the impact of independent variables on the dependent variable. The variable **income** provides the smallest unstandardised coefficient (0.001), but the second-largest standardised coefficient (0.383). As pointed out earlier, the magnitude of an unstandardised coefficient is affected by the nature of the measurement scale for the variable itself. The variable **income** has a range from 11,800 to 21,000, whereas a variable like **routine** has a range of only 4 to 20. When we examine the standardised regression coefficients, we can see that **autonom** has the greatest impact on **satis** and **income** the next highest. The variable **routine** has the smallest impact which is negative, indicating that more **routine** engenders less **satis**. Finally, in spite of the fact that the Pearson's *r* between **age** and **satis** is moderate (0.38), when the three other variables are controlled, it does not have a sufficient impact on **satis** to avoid its exclusion through the program's default criteria for elimination.

We can see here some of the strengths of multiple regression and the use of standardised regression coefficients. In particular, the latter allow us to examine the effects of each of a number of independent variables on the dependent variable. Thus, the standardised coefficient for **autonom** means that for each one unit change in **autonom**, there is a standard deviation change in **satis** of 0.483, with the effects of **income** and **routine** on **satis** partialled out.

Although we cannot compare unstandardised regression coefficients within a multiple regression equation, we can compare them across equations when the same measures are employed. We may, for example, want to divide a sample into men and women and to compute separate multiple-regression equations for each gender. To do this, we would make use of the **Select Cases...** procedure. Thus, for example, in the case of the multiple regression analysis we have been covering, the equation for men is:

satis = −6.771 + 0.596**autonom** + 0.001**income**

and for women

satis = −1.146 + 0.678**autonom** + 0.001**income** −0.179**routine**

Two features of this contrast are particularly striking. First, for men **routine** has not met the statistical criteria of the stepwise procedure and therefore is removed from the equation (in addition to **age** which failed to meet the statistical criteria for both men and women). Second, the negative constant is much larger for men than for women. Such contrasts can provide a useful springboard for further research. Also, it is potentially important to be aware of such subsample differences, since they may have implications for the kinds of conclusion that are generated. However, it must be borne in mind that variables must be identical for such contrasts to be drawn. An alternative approach would be to include gender as a third variable in the equation, since dichotomous variables can legitimately be employed in multiple regression. The decision about which option to choose will be determined by the points that the researcher wishes to make about the data.

One of the questions that we may ask is how well the independent variables explain the dependent variable. In just the same way that we were able to use r^2 (the coefficient of determination) as a measure of how well the line of best fit represents the relationship between the two variables, we can compute the multiple coefficient of determination (R^2) for the collective effect of all of the independent variables. The R^2 value for the equation as a whole is 0.716, implying that only 28 per cent of the variance in **satis** (i.e. $100 - 716$) is not explained by the three variables in the equation. In addition, SPSS will produce an adjusted R^2. The technical reasons for this variation should not overly concern us here, but the basic idea is that the adjusted version provides a more conservative estimate than the ordinary R^2 of the amount of variance in **satis** that is explained. The adjusted R^2 takes into account the number of subjects and the number of independent variables involved. The magnitude of R^2 is bound to be inflated by the number of independent variables associated with the regression equation. The adjusted R^2 corrects for this by adjusting the level of R^2 to take account of the number of independent variables. The adjusted R^2 for the equation as a whole is 0.702, which is just a little smaller than the non-adjusted value.

Another aspect of how well the regression equation fits the data is the *standard error of the estimate*. This statistic allows the researcher to determine the limits of the confidence that he or she can exhibit in the prediction from a regression equation. A statistic that is used more frequently (and which is also generated in SPSS output) is the *standard error of the regression coefficient*. The standard error of each regression coefficient reflects on the accuracy of the equation as a whole and of the coefficient itself. If successive similar-sized samples are taken from the population, estimates of each regression coefficient will vary from sample to sample. The standard error of the regression co-efficient allows the researcher to determine the band of confidence for each coefficient. Thus, if b is the regression coefficient and s.e. is the standard error, we can be 95 per cent certain that the population regression coefficient will lie between $b + (1.96 \times \text{s.e.})$ and $b - (1.96 \times \text{s.e.})$. This confidence band can be established because of the properties of the normal distribution that were discussed in Chapter 6 and if the sample has been selected randomly. The confidence intervals for each regression coefficient can be generated by SPSS by making the appropriate selection, as in the illustration below. Thus, the confidence band for the regression coefficient for **autonom** will be between $0.573 + (1.96 \times 0.096)$ and $0.573 - (1.96 \times 0.096)$, that is, between 0.76 and 0.38. This confidence band means that we can be 95 per cent confident that the population regression coefficient for **autonom** will lie between 0.76 and 0.38. This calculation can be extremely useful when the researcher is seeking to make predictions and requires a sense of their likely accuracy.

Statistical significance and multiple regression

A useful statistical test that is related to R^2 is the F ratio. The F ratio test generated by SPSS is based on the multiple correlation (R) for the analysis. The multiple correlation, which is of course the square root of the coefficient of determination, expresses the correlation between the dependent variable (**satis**) and all of the independent variables collectively (i.e. **autonom**, **routine**, **age**, and **income**). The multiple R for the multiple regression analysis under consideration is 0.846. The F ratio test allows the researcher to test the null hypothesis that the multiple correlation is zero in the population from which the sample (which should be random) was taken. For our computed equation, $F = 51.280$ (see Table 10.10, ANOVA table bottom row) and the significance level is 0.000 (which means $p < 0.0005$), suggesting that it is extremely improbable that R in the population is zero.

The calculation of the F ratio is useful as a test of statistical significance for the equation as a whole, since R reflects how well the independent variables collectively correlate with the dependent variable. If it is required to test the statistical significance of the individual regression coefficients, a different test must be used. A number of approaches to this question can be found. Two approaches which can be found within SPSS will be proffered. First, a statistic that is based on the F ratio calculates the significance of the change in the value of R^2 as a result of the inclusion of each additional variable in an equation. Since each variable is entered into the equation in turn, the individual contribution of each variable to R^2 is calculated and the statistical significance of that contribution can be assessed. In the computation of the multiple-regression equation, a procedure for deciding the sequence of the entry of variables into the equation called *stepwise* was employed. An explanation of this procedure will be given in the next section, but in the meantime it may be noted that it means that each variable is entered according to the magnitude of its contribution to R^2. Thus an examination of the SPSS output (Table 10.10) shows that the variables were entered in the sequence: **autonom**, **income**, **routine** (**age** was not entered). The contribution of **autonom** to R^2 was 0.524 (see Model Summary section of Table 10.10). When **income** was entered the R^2 became 0.682, suggesting that this variable added 0.158 (0.682 − 0.524) to R^2. The variable **routine** added a further 0.034 (0.716 − 0.682). Clearly, **autonom** was by far the major contributor to R^2. In each case, an F test of the change in R^2 shows that the change was statistically significant. The significance levels for the R^2 changes as a result of the inclusion of **autonom** and **income** were 0.000 in each case; the significance level for the R^2 change as a result of the inclusion of **routine** was 0.009.

SPSS will produce a test of the statistical significance of individual regression coefficients through the calculation of a t value for each coefficient and an associated two-tailed significance test. As the output in Table 10.10 indicates (see Coefficients section of the table, bottom row), the significance levels for **autonom** and **income** were 0.000, and for **routine** 0.009. These are consistent with the previous analysis using the F ratio and suggest that the coefficients for **income**, **autonom** and **routine** are highly unlikely to be zero in the population.

Multiple regression and SPSS

The regression program within SPSS has quite a large range of options and can generate a large amount of output. In this section it is proposed to simplify these elements as far as possible by dealing with the multiple-regression equation that was the focus of the preceding section and to show how this was generated with SPSS. The output is presented in Table 10.10. The sequence of actions to generate this output is as follows:

> **Analyze** → **Regression** → **Linear...** [opens **Linear Regression** dialog box shown in Box 10.3]
>
> → **satis** → ▶ button [puts **satis** in **Dependent:** box] → **autonom** → ▶ button [puts **autonom** in **Independent[s]:** box] → **routine** → ▶ button [puts **routine** in **Independent[s]:** box] → **age** → ▶ button [puts in **age** **Independent[s]:** box] → **income** → ▶ button [puts **income** in **Independent[s]:** box] → downward pointing arrow in box by **Method:** → **Stepwise** → **Statistics...** [opens **Linear Regression: Statistics** subdialog box shown in Box 10.4]

1. Place the variable that is likely to be the dependent variable in this box.

2. Place the variables that are likely to be the independent variables in this box.

3. Click on the downward-pointing arrowhead to select stepwise or any other method of including variables in the regression equation.

Linear Regression

Dependent:
satis

5. When the variables have been selected, click on **OK**.

Block 1 of 1

Previous   Next

Independent(s):
autonom
routine
age

Method: Stepwise

Selection Variable:

Rule...

Case Labels:

WLS Weight:

id
ethnicgp
gender
income
age
years
commit
autonom
routine
attend
skill
prody
qual
absence
incomegp

OK
Paste
Reset
Cancel
Help

Statistics...   Plots...   Save...   Options...

4. Select **Statistics...** in order to generate additional regression information such as tests of multicollinearity and the change in *R* squared.

BOX 10.3   Linear Regression dialog box

under **Regression Coefficients → Confidence intervals → Collinearity diagnostics** [*if* not already selected] **→ R squared change → Continue** [closes **Linear Regression: Statistics** subdialog box]

→ OK

1. Select these additional items of information to provide all of the information found in Table 10.10. **Estimates** and **Model fit** are default selections. The others must be made. **Confidence intervals** provides the confidence intervals for each regression coefficient. **R squared change** shows how much R^2 changes as each variable is included in the equation. **Collinearity diagnostics** gives information about multicollinearity through the calculations of 'tolerance'.

2. Click on **Continue** to return to Box 10.3.

Linear Regression: Statistics

Regression Coefficients
- ☑ Estimates
- ☑ Confidence intervals
- ☐ Covariance matrix

- ☑ Model fit
- ☑ R squared change
- ☐ Descriptives
- ☐ Part and partial correlations
- ☑ Collinearity diagnostics

Residuals
- ☐ Durbin-Watson
- ☐ Casewise diagnostics
  - ⦿ Outliers outside: 3 standard deviations
  - ○ All cases

Continue | Cancel | Help

BOX 10.4   Linear Regression: Statistics subdialog box

In this sequence of actions, **R squared** change was selected because it provides information about the statistical significance of the R^2 change as a result of the inclusion of each variable in the equation. **Collinearity diagnostics** was selected because it generates helpful information about multicollinearity. **Confidence intervals** was selected because it provides the confidence interval for each regression coefficient. **Model fit** is a default selection in SPSS and should *not* normally be deselected.

The output in Table 10.10 was produced with cases with missing values being omitted on a *listwise* basis, which is the default within SPSS. Thus, a case is excluded if there is a missing value for any one of the five variables involved in the equation. Missing values can also be dealt with on a *pairwise* basis or the mean for the variable can be substituted for a missing value. To change the basis for excluding missing values, click on **Options...** in the **Linear Regression** dialog box. The **Linear Regression: Options** subdialog box opens. In the

Missing Values box click on whichever approach to handling missing values is preferred and then click on **Continue**. You will then be back in the **Linear Regression** dialog box.

The output in Table 10.10 provides a large amount of regression information. The table with the heading 'Variables Entered/Removed' outlines the order in which the variables were included in the analysis. Model 1 includes just **autonom**, Model 2 includes both **autonom** and **income**, and Model 3 includes all the variables that fulfilled the statistical criteria of the stepwise procedure. By implication, **age** did not meet the criteria. The following elements in the output relate to aspects of multiple regression that have been covered below:

TABLE 10.10 SPSS multiple regression output (Job Survey data)

Variables Entered/Removed[a]

Model	Variables Entered	Variables Removed	Method
1	autonom		Stepwise (Criteria: Probability-of-F-to-enter <= .050, Probability-of-F-to-remove >= .100).
2	income		Stepwise (Criteria: Probability-of-F-to-enter <= .050, Probability-of-F-to-remove >= .100).
3	routine		Stepwise (Criteria: Probability-of-F-to-enter <= .050, Probability-of-F-to-remove >= .100).

This section of the regression output provides information about the sequence in which variables were entered into the equation and the criteria for their inclusion. The sequence is determined by each variable's contribution to explaining the variance of the dependent variable.

a. Dependent Variable: satis

Model Summary

Model	R	R Square	Adjusted R Square	Std. Error of the Estimate	R Square Change	F Change	df1	df2	Sig. F Change
1	.724[a]	.524	.516	2.270	.524	69.357	1	63	.000
2	.826[b]	.682	.672	1.869	.158	30.890	1	62	.000
3	.846[c]	.716	.702	1.782	.034	7.254	1	61	.009

Change Statistics

a. Predictors: (Constant), autonom

The calculations for Model 3 show the R^2 and adjusted R^2 for the equation at the end of the stepwise procedure.

This column shows how much R^2 changes as each variable enters the equation.

These columns show the change in the F ratio and the statistical significance of each change.

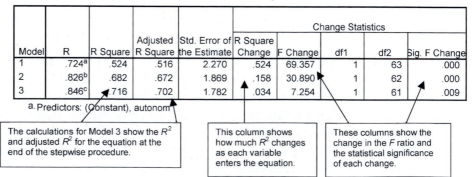

TABLE 10.10—*continued*

ANOVA[d]

Model		Sum of Squares	df	Mean Square	F	Sig.
1	Regression	357.346	1	357.346	69.357	.000[a]
	Residual	324.593	63	5.152		
	Total	681.938	64			
2	Regression	465.288	2	232.644	66.577	.000[b]
	Residual	216.650	62	3.494		
	Total	681.938	64			
3	Regression	488.315	3	162.772	51.280	.000[c]
	Residual	193.624	61	3.174		
	Total	681.938	64			

a. Predictors: (Constant), autonom.

b. Predictors: (Constant), autonom, income.

c. Predictors: (Constant), autonom, income, routine.

d. Dependent Variable: satis.

The values in these cells present an *F* test for the whole equation and a test of statistical significance of the *F* ratio.

Coefficients[a]

Model		Unstandardized Coefficients B	Std. Error	Standardized Coefficients Beta	t	Sig.	95% Confidence Interval for B Lower Bound	Upper Bound	Collinearity Statistics Tolerance	VIF
1	(Constant)	2.815	1.019		2.763	.007	.779	4.851		
	autonom	.859	.103	.724	8.328	.000	.653	1.065	1.000	1.000
2	(Constant)	-6.323	1.846		-3.425	.001	-10.012	-2.633		
	autonom	.685	.091	.577	7.569	.000	.504	.866	.881	1.136
	income	.001	.000	.424	5.558	.000	.000	.001	.881	1.136
3	(Constant)	-1.936	2.397		-.807	.423	-6.730	2.858		
	autonom	.573	.096	.483	5.974	.000	.381	.764	.713	1.402
	income	.001	.000	.383	5.148	.000	.000	.001	.843	1.186
	routine	-.168	.063	-.217	-2.693	.009	-.294	-.043	.716	1.397

a. Dependent Variable: satis.

These cells provide details of the intercept and the regression coefficient and standard error of each independent variable.	This cell provides the standardised regression coefficient (beta weight) for each independent variable.	These cells provide a *t* test and significance level for each regression coefficient.	These cells show the confidence intervals of each regression coefficient.	This cell provides information about multicollinearity for each independent variable.

Excluded Variables[d]

Model		Beta In	t	Sig.	Partial Correlation	Collinearity Statistics Tolerance	VIF	Minimum Tolerance
1	income	.424[a]	5.558	.000	.577	.881	1.136	.881
	routine	-.303[a]	-3.234	.002	-.380	.748	1.338	.748
	age	.194[a]	2.244	.028	.274	.947	1.056	.947
2	routine	-.217[b]	-2.693	.009	-.326	.716	1.397	.713
	age	-.079[b]	-.861	.392	-.110	.606	1.649	.564
3	age	.006[c]	.061	.951	.008	.529	1.891	.483

a. Predictors in the Model: (Constant), autonom.

b. Predictors in the Model: (Constant), autonom, income.

c. Predictors in the Model: (Constant), autonom, income, routine.

d. Dependent Variable: satis.

1   Information about the **Multiple R**, **R Square**, **Adjusted R Square**, and the **Standard Error of the Estimate** are given in the table headed 'Model Summary'. This tells us, for example, that the **R Square** is 0.716 once **routine** has followed **autonom** and **income** into the equation, suggesting that around 72 per cent of the variance in **satis** is explained by these three variables.

2   Also in the 'Model Summary' table is information about the **R Square Change**, showing the amount that each variable contributes to **R Square**, the F test value of the change, and the associated level of statistical significance.

3   In the table with the heading 'ANOVA' is an analysis of variance table, which can be interpreted in the same way as the ANOVA procedure described in Chapter 7. The analysis of variance table has not been discussed in the present chapter because it is not necessary to an understanding of regression for our current purposes. The information in the table that relates to Model 3 provides the **F** ratio for the whole equation (51.280) which is shown to be significant at 0.0005 (**Sig** = .000).

4   In the table with the heading 'Coefficients', are the following important bits of summary information for the equation as a whole (Model 3): **B** (the unstandardised regression coefficient) for each of the three variables and the constant; **Std. Error** (the standard error of the regression co-efficient) for each of the three variables and the constant; **Beta** (the standardised regression coefficient) for each of the three variables; the t value (**t**) for each unstandardised regression coefficient; the significance of the t value (**Sig.**); and the 95 per cent confidence interval for each of the unstandardised coefficients. The information in Table 10.9 was extracted from this section of the output.

5   Information about multicollinearity is given in the table with the heading 'Coefficients'. This information can be sought in the column **Tolerance** for Model 3. The **Tolerance** statistic is derived from 1 minus the multiple R for each independent variable. The multiple R for each independent variable is made up of its correlation with all of the other independent variables. When the tolerance is low, the multiple correlation is high and there is the possibility of multicollinearity. The tolerances for **autonom**, **routine**, and **income** are 0.713, 0.716, and 0.843 respectively, suggesting that multicollinearity is unlikely. If the tolerance figures had been close to zero, multicollinearity would have been a possibility and in fact likely. SPSS will produce other ways of diagnosing multicollinearity, which are called **collinearity diagnostics**. These include the *variance inflation factor*

(**VIF**) for each independent variable. The VIF is calculated as 1 divided by the tolerance level for that independent variable and is especially useful for assessing the impact of multicollinearity on the precision of estimates (such as confidence intervals) from the regression equation. However, this kind of consideration constitutes a more advanced issue and readers will typically find that the tolerance calculations will meet their needs.

As we have seen, **age** never enters the equation because it failed to con-form to the criteria for inclusion operated by the *stepwise* procedure. This is one of a number of approaches that can be used in deciding how and whether independent variables should be entered in the equation and is probably the most commonly used approach. Although popular, the stepwise method is none the less controversial because it affords priority to statistical criteria for inclusion rather than theoretical ones. Independent variables are entered only if they meet the package's statistical criteria (though these can be adjusted) and the order of inclusion is determined by the contribution of each variable to the explained variance. The variables are entered in steps, with the variable that exhibits the highest correlation with the dependent variable being entered at the first step (i.e. **autonom**). This variable must also meet the program's criteria for inclusion in terms of the required *F* ratio value. The variable that exhibits the largest partial correlation with the dependent variable (with the effect of the first independent variable partialled out) is then entered (i.e. **income**). This variable must then meet the *F* ratio default criteria. The variable **age** does not meet the necessary criteria and is therefore not included in the equation. In addition, as each new variable is entered, variables that are already in the equation are reassessed to determine whether they still meet the necessary statistical criteria. If they do not, they are removed from the equation.

Path analysis

The final area to be examined in this chapter, path analysis, is an extension of the multiple regression procedures explored in the previous section. In fact, path analysis entails the use of multiple regression in relation to explicitly formulated causal models. Path analysis cannot establish causality; it cannot be used as a substitute for the researcher's views about the likely causal linkages among groups of variables. All it can do is examine the pattern of relationships between three or more variables; but it can neither confirm nor reject the hypothetical causal imagery.

The aim of path analysis is to provide quantitative estimates of the causal connections between sets of variables. The connections proceed in one direction and are viewed as making up distinct paths. These ideas can best be explained with reference to the central feature of a path analysis – the path diagram. The path diagram makes explicit the likely causal connections between variables. An example is provided in Figure 10.6 which takes four variables employed in the Job Survey: **age**, **income**, **autonom** and **satis**. The arrows indicate expected causal connections between variables. The model moves from left to right implying causal priority to those variables closer to the left. Each p denotes a causal path and hence a path coefficient that will need to be computed. The model proposes that **age** has a direct effect on **satis** (p_1). But indirect effects of **age** on **satis** are also proposed: **age** affects **income** (p_5) which in turn affects **satis** (p_6); **age** affects **autonom** (p_2) which in turn affects **satis** (p_3); and **age** affects **autonom** (p_2) again, but this time affects **income** (p_4) which in turn affects **satis** (p_6). In addition, **autonom** has a direct effect on **satis** (p_3) and an indirect effect whereby it affects **income** (p_4) which in turn affects **satis** (p_6). Finally, **income** has a direct effect on **satis** (p_6), but no indirect effects. Thus, a direct effect occurs when a variable has an effect on

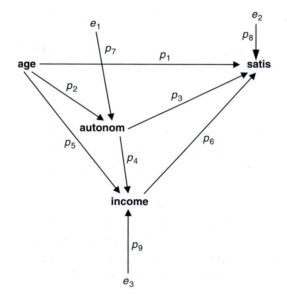

FIGURE 10.6 Path diagram for **satis**

another variable without a third variable intervening between them; an indirect effect occurs when there is a third intervening variable through which two variables are connected.

In addition, **income**, **autonom** and **satis** have further arrows directed to them from outside the nexus of variables. These refer to the amount of unexplained variance for each variable respectively. Thus, the arrow from e_1 to **autonom** (p_7) refers to the amount of variance in **autonom** that is not accounted for by **age**. Likewise, the arrow from e_2 to **satis** (p_8) denotes the amount of error arising from the variance in **satis** that is not explained by **age**, **autonom** and **income**. Finally, the arrow from e_3 to **income** (p_9) denotes the amount of variance in **income** that is unexplained by **age** and **autonom**. These error terms point to the fact that there are other variables that have an impact on **autonom** and **satis**, but which are not included in the path diagram.

In order to provide estimates of each of the postulated paths, path coefficients are computed. A path coefficient is a standardised regression coefficient. The path coefficients are computed by setting up three *structural equations*, that is equations which stipulate the structure of hypothesised relationships in a model. In the case of Figure 10.6, three structural equations will be required – one for **autonom**, one for **satis** and one for **income**. The three equations will be:

$$\textbf{autonom} = x_1\textbf{age} + e_1 \tag{10.1}$$

$$\textbf{satis} = x_1\textbf{age} + x_2\textbf{autonom} + x_3\textbf{income} + e_2 \tag{10.2}$$

$$\textbf{income} = x_1\textbf{age} + x_2\textbf{autonom} + e_3 \tag{10.3}$$

The standardised coefficient for **age** in (10.1) will provide p_2. The coefficients for **age**, **autonom** and **income** in (10.2) will provide p_1, p_3 and p_6 respectively. Finally, the coefficients for **age** and **autonom** in (10.3) will provide p_5 and p_4 respectively.

Thus, in order to compute the path coefficients, it is necessary to treat the three equations as multiple regression equations and the resulting standardised regression coefficients provide the path coefficients. The intercepts in each case are ignored. The three error terms are calculated by taking the R^2 for each equation away from 1 and taking the square root of the result of this subtraction.

In order to complete all the paths in Figure 10.6, all the path coefficients will have to be computed. The stepwise procedure should therefore not be used because if certain variables do not enter the equation due to the program's default criteria for inclusion and exclusion, no path coefficients can be computed for them. In SPSS, instead of choosing **Stepwise** in the **Method:** box (see Box 10.3), choose **Enter**, which will force all variables into the equation.

Therefore, to compute equation (10.1) the following steps would need to be followed (assuming that listwise deletion of missing cases has already been selected):

→**Statistics** →**Regression** →**Linear…** [opens **Linear Regression** dialog box shown in Box 10.3]

→**autonom** →▶ button [puts **autonom** in **Dependent:** box] →**age** →▶ button [puts **age** in **Independent[s]:** box] →downward-pointing arrow in box by **Method:** →**Enter** →**OK**

For equation (10.2):

→**Statistics** →**Regression** →**Linear…** [opens **Linear Regression** dialog box shown in Box 10.3)]

→**satis** →▶ button [puts **satis** in **Dependent:** box] →**age** →▶ button [puts **age** in **Independent[s]:** box] →**autonom** →▶ button [puts **autonom** in **Independent[s]:** box] →**income** →▶ button [puts **income** in **Independent[s]:** box] →downward-pointing arrow in box by **Method:** →**Enter** →**OK**

For equation (10.3):

→**Statistics** →**Regression** →**Linear…** [opens **Linear Regression** dialog box shown in Box 10.3]

→**income** →▶ button [puts **income** in **Dependent:** box] →**age** →▶ button [puts **age** in **Independent[s]:** box] →**autonom** →▶ button [puts **autonom** in **Independent[s]:** box] →downward-pointing arrow in box by **Method:** →**Enter** →**OK**

When conducting a path analysis the critical issues to search for in the SPSS output are the standardised regression coefficient for each variable (under the heading **Beta** in the last section of the table) and the R^2 (for the error term paths). If we take the results of the third equation, we find that the standardised coefficients for **autonom** and **age** are 0.215 and 0.567 respectively and the R^2 is 0.426. Thus for p_4, p_5 and p_9 in the path diagram (Figure 10.7) we substitute 0.22, 0.57 and 0.76 (the latter being the square root of $1 - 0.426$). All of the relevant path coefficients have been inserted in Figure 10.7.

Since the path coefficients are standardised, it is possible to compare them directly. We can see that **age** has a very small negative direct effect on **satis**, but it has a number of fairly pronounced positive indirect effects on **satis**. In particular, there is a strong sequence that goes from **age** to **income** ($p_5 = 0.57$) to **satis** ($p_6 = 0.47$).

Many researchers recommend calculating the overall impact of a variable like **age** on **satis**. This would be done as follows. We take the direct effect of **age** (-0.08) and add to it the indirect effects. The indirect effects are gleaned by multiplying the coefficients for each path from **age** to **satis**. The paths from **age** to **income** to **satis** would be calculated as $(0.57)(0.47) = 0.27$. For the paths from **age** to **autonom** to **satis** we have $(0.28)(0.58) = 0.16$. Finally, the sequence from **age** to **autonom** to **income** to **satis** yields $(0.28)(0.22)(0.47) = 0.03$. Thus the total indirect effect of **age** on **satis** is $0.27 + 0.16 + 0.03 = 0.46$. For the total effect of **age** on **satis**, we add the direct effect and the total indirect effect, that is, $-0.08 + 0.46 = 0.38$. This exercise suggests that the indirect effect of **age** on **satis** is inconsistent with its direct effect, since the former is slightly negative

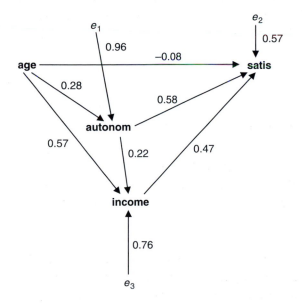

FIGURE 10.7   Path diagram for **satis** with path coefficients

and the indirect effect is positive. Clearly, an appreciation of the intervening variables **income** and **autonom** is essential to an understanding of the relationship between **age** and **satis**.

The effect of **age** on **satis** could be compared with the effect of other variables in the path diagram. Thus, the effect of **autonom** is made up of the direct effect (0.57) plus the indirect effect of **autonom** to **income** to **satis**, that is, $0.58 + (0.22)(0.47)$, which equals 0.68. The effect of **income** on **satis** is made up only of the direct effect, which is 0.47, since there is no indirect effect from **income** to **satis**. Thus, we have three effect coefficients as they are often called (e.g. Pedhazur, 1982) – 0.38, 0.68 and 0.47 for **age**, **autonom** and **income** respectively – implying that **autonom** has the largest overall effect on **satis**.

Sometimes, it is not possible to specify the causal direction between all of the variables in a path diagram. In Figure 10.8 **autonom** and **routine** are deemed to be correlates; there is no attempt to ascribe causal priority to one or the other. The link between them is indicated by a curved arrow with two heads. Each variable has a direct effect on **absence** (p_5 and p_4). In addition, each variable has an indirect effect on **absence** through **satis**: **autonom** to **satis** (p_1) and **satis** to **absence** (p_3); **routine** to **satis** (p_2) and **satis** to **absence** (p_3). In order to generate the necessary coefficients, we would need the Pearson's r for **autonom** and **routine** and the standardised regression coefficients from two equations:

$$\textbf{satis} = a + x_1\textbf{autonom} + x_2\textbf{routine} + e_1 \tag{10.4}$$

$$\textbf{absence} = a + x_1\textbf{autonom} + x_2\textbf{routine} + x_3\textbf{satis} + e_2 \tag{10.5}$$

We could then compare the total causal effects of **autonom**, **routine** and **satis**. The total effect would be made up of the direct effect plus the total

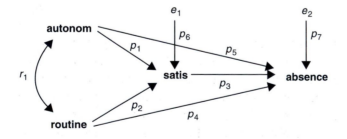

FIGURE 10.8 Path diagram for **absence**

indirect effect. The total effect of each of these three variables on **absence** would be:

Total effect of **autonom** = $(p_5) + (p_1)(p_3)$
Total effect of **routine** = $(p_4) + (p_2)(p_3)$
Total effect of **satis** = p_3

These three total effects can then be compared to establish which has the greater overall effect on absence. However, with complex models involving a large number of variables, the decomposition of effects using the foregoing procedures can prove unreliable and alternative methods have to be employed (Pedhazur, 1982).

Path analysis has become a popular technique because it allows the relative impact of variables within a causal network to be estimated. It forces the researcher to make explicit the causal structure that is believed to underpin the variables of interest. On the other hand, it suffers from the problem that it cannot confirm the underlying causal structure. It tells us what the relative impact of the variables upon each other is, but cannot validate that causal structure. Since a cause must precede an effect, the time order of variables must be established in the construction of a path diagram. We are forced to rely on theoretical ideas and our common-sense notions for information about the likely sequence of the variables in the real world. Sometimes these conceptions of time ordering of variables will be faulty and the ensuing path diagram will be misleading. Clearly, while path analysis has much to offer, its potential limitations should also be appreciated. In this chapter, it has only been feasible to cover a limited range of issues in relation to path analysis and the emphasis has been upon the use of examples to illustrate some of the relevant procedures, rather than a formal presentation of the issues. Readers requiring more detailed treatments should consult Land (1969), Pedhazur (1982) and Davis (1985).

Exercises

1   A researcher hypothesises that women are more likely than men to support legislation for equal pay between the sexes. The researcher decides to conduct a social survey and draws a sample of 1,000 individuals among whom men and women are equally represented. One set of questions asked directs the respondent to indicate whether he or she approves of such legislation. The findings are provided in Table 10.11:

TABLE 10.11 The relationship between approval of equal pay legislation and gender

	Men %	Women %
Approve	58	71
Disapprove	42	29
Total	100	100
n =	500	500

Is the researcher's belief that women are more likely than men to support equal pay legislation confirmed by the data in Table 10.11?

2   Following on from question 1, the researcher controls for age and the results of the analysis are provided in Table 10.12. What are the implications of this analysis for the researcher's view that men and women differ in support for equal pay legislation?

3   What SPSS procedure would be required to examine the relationship between **ethnicgp** and **commit**, controlling for **gender**? Assume that you want **ethnicgp** going across that table and that you need both frequency counts and column percentages.

4   A researcher is interested in the correlates of the number of times that people attend religious services during the course of a year. On the basis of a sample of individuals, he finds that income correlates fairly well with frequency of attendance (Pearson's $r = 0.59$). When the researcher

TABLE 10.12 The relationship between approval of equal pay legislation and gender, controlling for age

	Under 35 (%)		35 and over (%)	
	Men	*Women*	*Men*	*Women*
Approve	68	92	48	54
Disapprove	32	8	52	46
Total	100	100	100	100
n =	250	250	250	250

controls for the effects of age the partial correlation coefficient is found to be 0.12. Why has the size of the correlation fallen so much?

5   What SPSS procedure would you need to correlate **income** and **satis**, controlling for **age**? Assume that you want to display actual significance levels and that missing cases are to be deleted listwise.

6   Consider the following regression equation and other details:

$$y = 7.3 + 2.3x_1 + 4.1x_2 - 1.4x_3 \quad R^2 = 0.78 \quad F = 21.43, p < 0.01$$

(a) What value would you expect y to exhibit if $x_1 = 9$, $x_2 = 22$ and $x_3 = 17$?

(b) How much of the variance in y is explained by x_1, x_2 and x_3?

(c) Which of the three independent variables exhibits the largest effect on y?

(d) What does the negative sign for x_3 mean?

7   What SPSS procedure would you need to provide the data for the multiple regression equations on p. 319 In considering the commands, you should bear in mind that the information is required for a path analysis.

8   Turning to the first of the two equations referred to in question 7 (i.e. the one with **satis** as the dependent variable):

(a) How much of the variance in **satis** do the two variables account for?

(b) Are the individual regression coefficients for **autonom** and **routine** statistically significant?

(c) What is the standardised regression coefficient for **routine**?

9   Examine Figure 10.8. Using the information generated for questions 7 and 8, which variable has the largest overall effect on **absence** – is it **autonom, routine** or **satis**?

Chapter 11

Aggregating variables: exploratory factor analysis

MANY OF THE concepts we use to describe human behaviour seem to consist of a number of different aspects. Take, for example, the concept of job satisfaction. When we say we are satisfied with our job, this statement may refer to various feelings we have about our work, such as being keen to go to it every day, not looking for other kinds of jobs, being prepared to spend time and effort on it, and having a sense of achievement about it. If these different components contribute to our judgement of how satisfied we are with our job, we would expect them to be interrelated. In other words, how eager we are to go to work should be correlated with the feeling of accomplishment we gain from it and so on. Similarly, the concept of job routine may refer to a number of interdependent characteristics such as how repetitive the work is, how much it makes us think about what we are doing, the number of different kinds of tasks we have to carry out each day and so on. Some people may enjoy repetitive work while others may prefer a job which is more varied. If this is the case, we would expect job satisfaction to be unrelated to job routine. To determine this, we could ask people to describe their feelings about their job in terms of these characteristics and see to what extent those aspects which reflect satisfaction are correlated with one another and are unrelated to those which represent routine. Characteristics which go together constitute a *factor* and *factor analysis* refers to a number of related statistical techniques which help us to determine them.

These techniques are used for three main purposes. First, as implied above, they can assess the degree to which items, such as those measuring job satisfaction and routine, are tapping the same concept. If people respond in similar ways to questions concerning job satisfaction as they do to those about job routine, this implies that these two concepts are not seen as being conceptually distinct by these people. If, however, their answers to the job-satisfaction items are unrelated to their ones to the job-routine items, this suggests that these two feelings can be distinguished. In other words, factor analysis enables us to assess the *factorial validity* of the questions which make up our scales by telling us the extent to which they seem to be measuring the same concepts or variables.

Second, if we have a large number of variables, factor analysis can determine the degree to which they can be reduced to a smaller set. Suppose, for example, we were interested in how gender and ethnic group are related to †titudes towards work. To measure this, we generate from our own experience twelve questions similar to those used in the Job Survey to reflect the different feelings we think people hold towards their job. At this stage, we have no idea that they might form three distinct concepts (i.e. job satisfaction, autonomy and routine). To analyse the relationship of gender and ethnic group to these items, we would have to conduct twelve separate analyses. There would be two major disadvantages to doing this. First, it would make it more difficult to understand the findings since we would have to keep in mind the results of twelve different tests. Second, the more statistical tests we carry out, the more likely we are to find that some of them will be significant by chance. It is not possible to determine the likelihood of this if the data come from the same sample.

The third use to which factor analysis has been put is related to the previous one but is more ambitious in the sense that it is aimed at trying to make sense of the bewildering complexity of social behaviour by reducing it to a more limited number of factors. A good example of this is the factor analytic approach to the description of personality by psychologists such as Eysenck and Cattell (for example, Eysenck and Eysenck, 1969; Cattell, 1973). There are a large number of ways in which the personality of people varies. One indication of this is the hundreds of words describing personality characteristics which are listed in a dictionary. Many of these terms seem to refer to similar aspects. For example, the words 'sociable', 'outwardgoing', 'gregarious', and 'extraverted' all describe individuals who like the company of others. If we ask people to describe themselves or someone they know well in terms of these and other words, and we factor analyse this information, we will find that these characteristics will group themselves into a smaller number of factors. In fact, a major factor that emerges is one called sociability or extraversion. Some people, then, see factor analysis as a tool to bring order to the way we see things by determining which variables are related and which variables are not.

Two uses of factor analysis can be distinguished. The one most commonly reported is the *exploratory* kind in which the relationships between various variables are examined without determining the extent to which the results fit a particular model. *Confirmatory* factor analysis, on the other hand, compares the solution found against a hypothetical one. For example, if we expected the four items measuring job satisfaction in the Job Survey to form one factor, then we could assess the degree to which they did so by comparing the results of our analysis with a hypothetical solution in which this was done perfectly. Although there are techniques for making these kinds of statistical comparisons (for example, Bentler, 1995; Jöreskog and Sörbom, 1996), they are only available as a separate program. Consequently, we shall confine our discussion to the exploratory use of factor analysis. We will illustrate its use with an analysis of the job satisfaction and routine items in the Job Survey, in which we will describe the decisions to be made, followed by the commands to carry them out.

Correlation matrix

The initial step is to compute a correlation matrix for the eight items which make up the two scales of job satisfaction and routine. If there are no significant correlations between these items, then this means that they are unrelated and that we would not expect them to form one or more factors. In other words, it would not be worthwhile to go on to conduct a factor analysis. Consequently, this should be the first stage in deciding whether to carry one out. The correlation matrix for these items, together with their significance levels, is presented in Table 11.1. All but one of the items are significantly correlated at less than the 0.05 level, either positively or negatively, with one another, which suggests that they may constitute one or more factors.

Sample size

Second, the reliability of the factors emerging from a factor analysis depends on the size of the sample, although there is no consensus on what the size should be. There is agreement, however, that there should be more participants than variables. Gorsuch (1983), for example, has proposed an absolute

TABLE 11.1 Correlation and significance level matrices for satisfaction and routine items (Job Survey)

Correlation Matrix

		satis1	satis2	satis3	satis4	routine1	routine2	routine3	routine4
Correlation	satis1	1.000	-.439	.439	-.442	-.468	-.465	-.393	-.351
	satis2	-.439	1.000	-.312	.474	.522	.472	.433	.463
	satis3	.439	-.312	1.000	-.567	-.289	-.193	-.287	-.229
	satis4	-.442	.474	-.567	1.000	.422	.417	.415	.300
	routine1	-.468	.522	-.289	.422	1.000	.692	.794	.725
	routine2	-.465	.472	-.193	.417	.692	1.000	.620	.496
	routine3	-.393	.433	-.287	.415	.794	.620	1.000	.636
	routine4	-.351	.463	-.229	.300	.725	.496	.636	1.000
Sig. (1-tailed)	satis1		.000	.000	.000	.000	.000	.000	.002
	satis2	.000		.005	.000	.000	.000	.000	.000
	satis3	.000	.005		.000	.008	.057	.009	.030
	satis4	.000	.000	.000		.000	.000	.000	.007
	routine1	.000	.000	.008	.000		.000	.000	.000
	routine2	.000	.000	.057	.000	.000		.000	.000
	routine3	.000	.000	.009	.000	.000	.000		.000
	routine4	.002	.000	.030	.007	.000	.000	.000	

minimum of five participants per variable and not less than 100 individuals per analysis. Although factor analysis can be carried out on samples smaller than this to describe the relationships between the variables, not much confidence should be placed on these same factors emerging in a second sample. Consequently, if the main purpose of a study is to find out what factors underlie a group of variables, it is essential that the sample should be sufficiently large to enable this to be done reliably.

Principal components or factors?

The two most widely used forms of factor analysis are *principal components* and *factor* analysis (called *principal-axis factoring* in SPSS). There are also other kinds of methods which are available on SPSS such as alpha, image, and maximum likelihood factoring, but these are used much less frequently. Because of this and the need to keep the discussion brief, we will only outline the first two techniques. When talking about both these methods we shall refer to them collectively as factor analysis, as is the usual convention. However, when specifically discussing the method of factor analysis we shall call it principal-axis factoring, as SPSS does, to distinguish it from the general method.

Factor analysis is primarily concerned with describing the variation or variance which is shared by the scores of people on three or more variables. This variance is referred to as *common variance* and needs to be distinguished from two other kinds of variance. *Specific variance* describes the variation which is specific or unique to a variable and which is not shared with any other variable. *Error variance*, on the other hand, is the variation due to the fluctuations which inevitably result from measuring something. If, for example, you weigh yourself a number of times in quick succession, you will find that the readings will vary somewhat, despite the fact that your weight could not have changed in so short a time. These fluctuations in measurement are known as error variance. So the total variation that we find in the scores of an instrument (such as an item or test) to assess a particular variable can be divided or partitioned into common, specific and error variance.

Total variance = Common variance + Specific variance + Error variance

Since factor analysis cannot distinguish specific from error variance, they are combined to form *unique variance*. In other words, the total variance of a test consists of its common and its unique variance.

This idea may be illustrated with the relationship between three variables, x, y, and z, as displayed in the Venn diagram in Figure 11.1. The overlap between any two of the variables and all three of them represents common variance (the shaded areas), while the remaining unshaded areas constitute the unique variance of each of the three variables.

The difference between principal-components analysis and principal-axis factoring lies essentially in how they handle unique variance. In principal-components analysis, all the variance of a score or variable is analysed, including its unique variance. In other words, it is assumed that the test used to assess the variable is perfectly reliable and without error. In principal-axis factoring, only the variance which is common to or shared by the tests is analysed – that is to say, an attempt is made to exclude unique variance from the analysis. Since principal-components analysis examines the total variance of a test, this is set at 1, while for principal-axis factoring it varies between 0 and 1. The variance of a test to be explained is known as its *communality*. Tables 11.2 and 11.3 show the SPSS output for the communalities of the principal-components and principal-axes analyses respectively. The values of the communalities for the principal components are 1s while those for the principal axes vary from 0.381 (for the first item) to 0.765 (for the fifth item).

In both these methods, the first component or axis that is extracted accounts for the largest amount of variance shared by the tests. The second factor consists of the next largest amount of variance which is not related to or explained by the first one. In other words, these two factors are unrelated or *orthogonal* to one another. The third factor extracts the next largest amount of variance, and so on. There are as many factors as variables,

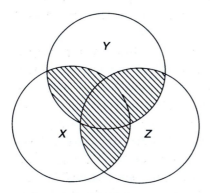

FIGURE 11.1   Common and unique variance

TABLE 11.2 Communalities of principal components (Job Survey)

Communalities

	Initial	Extraction
satis1	1.000	.546
satis2	1.000	.506
satis3	1.000	.752
satis4	1.000	.706
routine1	1.000	.859
routine2	1.000	.653
routine3	1.000	.749
routine4	1.000	.686

Extraction Method: Principal Component Analysis.

TABLE 11.3 Communalities of principal axes (Job Survey)

Communalities

	Initial	Extraction
satis1	.381	.419
satis2	.394	.415
satis3	.389	.514
satis4	.468	.621
routine1	.765	.905
routine2	.545	.546
routine3	.655	.682
routine4	.550	.560

Extraction Method: Principal Axis Factoring.

although the degree of variance which is explained by successive factors becomes smaller and smaller. In other words, the first few factors are the most important ones.

The SPSS output showing the initial factors produced by a principal-components analysis of the job satisfaction and routine items and the amount of the variance they account for (their *eigenvalue*) is presented in Table 11.4. The variance accounted for by the first factor is 4.248 or 53.1 per cent of the total variance. The total variance explained by the eight factors is simply the sum of their eigenvalues, which in this case is 8. The proportion of variance accounted for by any one factor is its eigenvalue divided by the sum of the eigenvalues, which is multiplied by 100 to convert it to a percentage. Thus, for example, the proportion of variance due to the first factor is about 4.25/8 or 0.531, which multiplied by 100 equals 53.1.

TABLE 11.4 Initial principal components and their variance (Job Survey)

Total Variance Explained

Component	Initial Eigenvalues			Extraction Sums of Squared Loadings			Rotation Sums of Squared Loadings		
	Total	% of Variance	Cumulative %	Total	% of Variance	Cumulative %	Total	% of Variance	Cumulative %
1	4.248	53.106	53.106	4.248	53.106	53.106	3.263	40.794	40.794
2	1.208	15.105	68.211	1.208	15.105	68.211	2.193	27.417	68.211
3	.628	7.851	76.062						
4	.579	7.240	83.302						
5	.524	6.548	89.849						
6	.334	4.177	94.026						
7	.305	3.812	97.838						
8	.173	2.162	100.000						

Extraction Method: Principal Component Analysis.

Number of factors to be retained

Since the object of factor analysis is to reduce the number of variables we have to handle, this would not be achieved if we used all of them. Consequently, the next step is to decide how many factors we should keep. This really is a question of how many of the smaller factors we should retain, since we would obviously keep the first few which explain most of the variance. There are two main criteria used for deciding which factors to exclude. The first, known as *Kaiser's criterion*, is to select those factors which have an eigenvalue of greater than one. SPSS does this by default unless it receives instructions to do otherwise. Since the total variance that any one variable can have has been standardised as 1, what this means, in effect, is that a factor which explains less variance than a single variable is excluded.

The second method is the graphical *scree test* proposed by Cattell (1966). In this method, a graph is drawn of the descending variance accounted for by the factors initially extracted. The one produced by SPSS for the factors described in Table 11.2 or 11.3 is depicted in Figure 11.2. The plot typically shows a break between the steep slope of the initial factors and the gentle one of the later factors. The term 'scree', in fact, is a geological one for describing the debris found at the bottom of a rocky slope and implies that these factors are not very important. The factors to be retained are those which lie before the point at which the eigenvalues seem to level off. This occurs after the first two factors in this case, both of which incidentally have eigenvalues of greater than 1. In other words, both criteria suggest the same number of factors in this example. The choice of criterion may depend on the size of the average communalities and the number of variables and participants. The Kaiser criterion has been recommended for situations where the number of variables is less than 30 and the average communality is greater than 0.70 or when the number of participants is greater than 250 and the mean communality is greater than

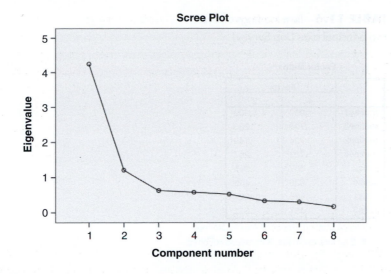

Scree Plot

FIGURE 11.2 Scree test of eigenvalues (Job Survey) from SPSS 13 (which differs slightly from SPSS 10, 11 and 12)

or equal to 0.60 (Stevens, 1996). If the number of factors to be extracted differs from that suggested by the Kaiser criterion, then this has to be specified with the appropriate SPSS option.

The two principal-components factors are shown in Table 11.5, while the two principal-axis ones are displayed in Table 11.6. The relationship between each item or test and a factor is expressed as a correlation or *loading*.

The items have been listed, by request, in terms of the size of their

TABLE 11.5 Item loadings on first two principal components (Job Survey)

Component Matrix[a]

	Component	
	1	2
routine1	.873	.310
routine3	.814	.296
routine2	.771	.242
routine4	.744	.364
satis2	.706	-.087
satis1	-.673	.306
satis4	.671	-.506
satis3	-.524	.691

Extraction Method: Principal Component Analysis.

a. 2 components extracted.

TABLE 11.6 Item loadings on first
two principal axes (Job Survey)

Factor Matrix[a]

	Factor	
	1	2
routine1	.900	.309
routine3	.793	.230
routine2	.724	.149
routine4	.703	.257
satis2	.637	-.095
satis4	.636	-.465
satis1	-.606	.227
satis3	-.481	.531

Extraction Method: Principal Axis Factoring.
a. 2 factors extracted. 8 iterations required.

loadings on the factor to which they are most closely related. For example, the item **routine1** loads most highly on the first of the two factors in both analyses, although its correlation with them varies somewhat. In other words, the two analyses produce somewhat different solutions. All but one (**satis3**) of the eight items correlate most highly with the first factor.

Rotation of factors

The first factors extracted from an analysis are those which account for the maximum amount of variance. As a consequence, what they represent might not be easy to interpret since items will not correlate as highly with them as they might. In fact, most of the items will fall on the first factor, although their correlations with it may not be that high. In order to increase the interpretability of factors, they are rotated to maximise the loadings of some of the items. These items can then be used to identify the meaning of the factor. A number of ways have been developed to rotate factors, some of which are available on SPSS. The two most commonly used methods are *orthogonal* rotation, which produces factors which are unrelated to or independent of one another, and *oblique* rotation, in which the factors are correlated.

There is some controversy as to which of these two kinds of rotation is the more appropriate. The advantage of orthogonal rotation is that the information the factors provide is not redundant, since a person's score on one factor is unrelated to their score on another. For example, if we found two orthogonal factors which we interpreted as being job satisfaction and routine, then what this means is that in general how satisfied people are with their job is not related to how routine they see it as being. The disadvantage of orthogonal rotation, on the other hand, is that the factors may have been forced to be unrelated, whereas in real life they may be related. In other words, an orthogonal solution may be more artificial and not necessarily an accurate reflection of what occurs naturally in the world. This may be less likely with oblique rotation, although it should be borne in mind that the original factors in an analysis are made to be orthogonal.

Orthogonal rotation

An orthogonal rotation of the two principal-components factors is shown in Table 11.7. The method for doing this was *varimax*. In terms of the orthogonally rotated solution, five and not seven items load on the first factor, while three of them correlate most highly with the second one. The items which load most strongly on the first factor are listed or grouped together first and are ordered in terms of the size of their correlations. The items which correlate most strongly with the second factor form the second group on the second factor. If there had been a third factor, then the items which loaded most highly on it would constitute the third group on the third factor, and so on. Although the data are made up, if we obtained a result like this with real data it would suggest that the way in which people answered the job routine items was not related to the way they responded to the job satisfaction ones,

TABLE 11.7 Item loadings on orthogonally rotated first two principal components (Job Survey)

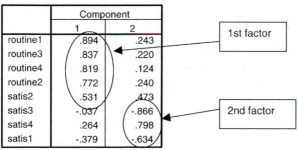

Rotated Component Matrix[a]

	Component 1	Component 2
routine1	.894	.243
routine3	.837	.220
routine4	.819	.124
routine2	.772	.240
satis2	.531	.473
satis3	-.037	-.866
satis4	.264	.798
satis1	-.379	-.634

Extraction Method: Principal Component Analysis.
Rotation Method: Varimax with Kaiser Normalization.
a. Rotation converged in 3 iterations.

with the exception of **satis2**. In other words, the two groups of items seem to be factorially distinct. The loadings of items on factors can be positive or negative: for example, the **satis2** item has a negative correlation with the first factor while the four job routine items are positively related to it.

In general, the meaning of a factor is determined by the items which load most highly on it. Which items to ignore when interpreting a factor is arguable. It may not be appropriate to use the significance level of the factor loading since this depends on the size of the sample. In addition, the appropriate level to use is complicated by the fact that a large number of correlations have been computed on data which come from the same participants. Conventionally, items or variables which correlate less than 0.3 with a factor are omitted from consideration since they account for less than 9 per cent of the variance and so are not very important. An alternative criterion to use is the correlation above which no item correlates highly with more than one factor. The advantage of this rule is that factors are interpreted in terms of items unique to them. Consequently, their meaning should be less ambiguous. According to these two rules, factor 1 comprises all four of the routine items and **satis2** whereas factor 2 contains **satis3**, **satis4** and **satis1**. However, the use of these two conventions in conjunction engenders a highly stringent set of criteria for deciding which variables should be included on which factors. Many researchers ignore the second convention and emphasise all loadings in excess of 0.3 regardless of whether any variables are thereby implicated in more than one factor.

The amount or percentage of variance that each of the orthogonally rotated factors accounts for is shown in the penultimate column of Table 11.4. It is about 41 per cent for the first factor and 27 per cent for the second.

Oblique rotation

Oblique rotation produced by the *oblimin* method in SPSS gives three matrices. The first, a *pattern* matrix, consists of correlations between the variables and the factors. The second, the *structure* matrix, is made up of weights which reflect the unique variance each factor contributes to a variable. This is the matrix which is generally used to interpret the factors. The oblique factors shown in Table 11.8 are from this matrix for the principal-components analysis. The results are similar to the orthogonal rotation except that the loadings between the items and factors are higher.

TABLE 11.8   Item loadings on obliquely rotated first
two components (Job Survey)

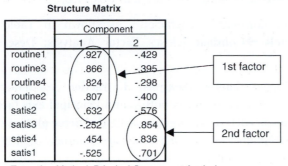

Structure Matrix

	Component	
	1	2
routine1	.927	-.429
routine3	.866	-.395
routine4	.824	-.298
routine2	.807	-.400
satis2	.632	-.576
satis3	-.252	.854
satis4	.454	-.836
satis1	-.525	.701

1st factor

2nd factor

Extraction Method: Principal Component Analysis.
Rotation Method: Oblimin with Kaiser Normalization.

TABLE 11.9   Correlations between obliquely
rotated first two principal components (Job Survey)

Component Correlation Matrix

Component	1	2
1	1.000	-.451
2	-.451	1.000

Extraction Method: Principal Component Analysis.
Rotation Method: Oblimin with Kaiser Normalization.

The third matrix shows the correlations between the factors and is
presented in Table 11.9. Since they are moderately intercorrelated (−0.45),
oblique rotation may be more appropriate in this case. It is difficult to estimate
the amount of variance accounted for by oblique factors since the variance is
shared between the correlated factors. Thus, for example, as the two factors
are correlated in this instance, part of the variance of the first factor would
also be part of the second.

SPSS factor analysis procedure

The following procedure was used to compute the output for the principal-
components analysis:

→**Analyze** →**Data Reduction** →**Factor...** [opens **Factor Analysis** dialog
box shown in Box 11.1]

→**satis1** to **satis4** →▶button [puts **satis1** to **satis4** under **Variables:**] →**routine1** to **routine4** →▶button →**Descriptives...** [opens **Factor Analysis: Descriptives** subdialog box shown in Box 11.2]

→**Coefficients** [for correlation coefficients as shown in Table 11.1] →**Significance levels** →**Continue** [closes **Factor Analysis: Descriptives** subdialog box]

→**Extraction...** [opens **Factor Analysis: Extraction** subdialog box shown in Box 11.3] →down-pointing button and **Principal axis factoring** if **Principal components** default option not wanted →**Scree plot** [as shown in Figure 11.1] →**Number of factors:** and type number of factors if

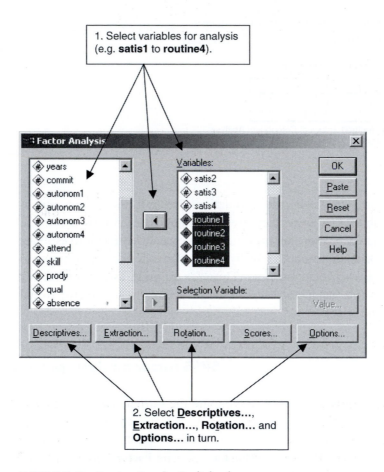

BOX 11.1 **Factor Analysis** dialog box

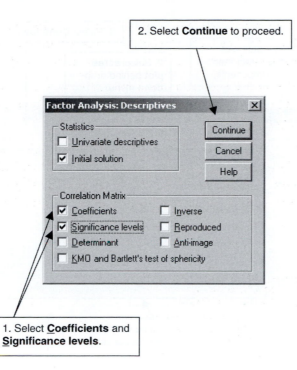

2. Select **Continue** to proceed.

1. Select **Coefficients** and **Significance levels**.

BOX 11.2 Factor Analysis: Descriptives subdialog box

different from default option of Kaiser's criterion →**Ma<u>x</u>imum Iterations for Convergence:** and type number if default of **25** not wanted →**Continue** [closes **Factor Analysis: Extraction** subdialog box]

→**Ro<u>t</u>ation. . .** [opens **Factor Analysis: Rotation** subdialog box shown in Box 11.4] →**Direct <u>O</u>blimin** or **<u>V</u>arimax** →**Continue** [closes **Factor Analysis: Rotation** subdialog box]

→**<u>O</u>ptions. . .** [opens **Factor Analysis: Options** subdialog box shown in Box 11.5] →**<u>S</u>orted by size** [highest loadings shown first] →**Continue** [closes **Factor Analysis: Options** subdialog box]

→**OK**

It is sometimes necessary to increase the number of iterations required to arrive at a factor solution. An *iteration* may be thought of as an attempt to estimate the total common variance of a variable or item to be accounted for by the main factors. Successive attempts are made (iterations) until the estimates change little. If we found that the default maximum number of 25

1. Select ▼ button of **Method** for other than principal components.

2. Select **scree plot** behind drop-down menu.

4. Select **Continue** to proceed.

Factor Analysis: Extraction

Method: Principal components

- Principal components
- Unweighted least squares
- Generalized least squares
- Maximum likelihood
- Principal axis factoring
- Alpha factoring

Analyze
- ● Correl...
- ○ Covar...

...rotated factor solution

...ree plot

Extract
- ● Eigenvalues over: 1
- ○ Number of factors:

Maximum Iterations for Convergence: 25

Continue
Cancel
Help

3. Increase maximum number of iterations if insufficient for convergence.

BOX 11.3   Factor Analysis: Extraction subdialog box

1. Select rotation method (e.g. **Varimax**).

3. Select **Continue** to proceed.

Factor Analysis: Rotation

Method
- ○ None
- ● Varimax
- ○ Direct Oblimin   Delta: 0
- ○ Quartimax
- ○ Equamax
- ○ Promax   Kappa: 4

Display
- ☑ Rotated solution   ☐ Loading plot(s)

Maximum Iterations for Convergence: 25

Continue
Cancel
Help

2. Increase number of iterations if convergence fails.

BOX 11.4   Factor Analysis: Rotation subdialog box

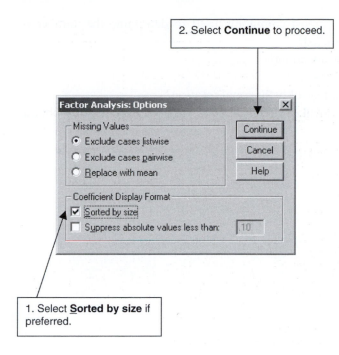

2. Select **Continue** to proceed.

1. Select **Sorted by size** if preferred.

BOX 11.5   **Factor Analysis: Options** subdialog box

iterations was insufficient to produce an acceptable solution, we could increase it to, say 50.

Exercises

1   You have developed a questionnaire to measure anxiety which consists of ten items. You want to know whether the items constitute a single factor. To find this out, would it be appropriate to carry out a factor analysis on the ten items?

2   If you were to carry out a factor analysis on ten items or variables, what would be the minimum number of participants or cases you would use?

3   What is the unique variance of a variable?

4   How does principal-components analysis differ from principal-axis factoring?

5   How many factors are there in a factor analysis?

6   Which factor accounts for most of the variance?

7   Why are not all the factors extracted?

8   Which criterion is most commonly used to determine the number of factors to be extracted?

9   What is meant by a loading?

10   Why are factors rotated?

11   What is the advantage of orthogonal rotation?

12   Is it possible to calculate the amount of variance explained by oblique factors?

Answers to exercises

Chapter 1

1   These forms of analysis concentrate upon one, two and three or more variables respectively.

2   It is necessary in order to ensure that members of experimental and control groups are as alike as possible. If members of the experimental and control groups are alike any contrasts that are found between the two groups cannot be attributed to differences in the membership of the two groups; instead, it is possible to infer that it is the experimental stimulus (Exp) that is the source of the differences between the two groups.

3   The reasoning is faulty. First, those who read the quality dailies and those who read the tabloids will differ from each other in ways other than the newspapers that they read. In other words, people cannot be treated as though they have been randomly assigned to two experimental treatments – qualities and tabloids. Second, the causal inference is risky because it is possible that people with a certain level of political knowledge are more likely to read certain kinds of newspaper, rather than the type of newspaper affecting the level of political knowledge.

Chapter 2

1   Since not all possible religious affiliations have been included (e.g. Baha'i, Zoroastrianism), it is important to have a further option in which these can be placed. This can be called 'Other'.

2   The most convenient way of coding this information is to assign a number to each option, such as 1 for Agnostic, 2 for Atheist, and so on.

3   This information should be coded as missing. In other words, you need to assign a number to data that are missing.

4   If this happened very infrequently, then one possibility would be to code this kind of response as missing. Since the answer is not truly missing, an alternative course of action would be to record one of the two answers. There are a number of ways this could be done. First, the most common category could be chosen. Second, one of the two answers could be selected at random. Third, using other information we could try to predict which of the two was the most likely one. If there were a large number of such multiple answers, then a separate code could be used to signify them.

5   If we provide an identification number for each participant and if Agnostics are coded as 1 and Atheists as 2, your data file should look something like this:

```
01    1   25
02    1   47
03    2   33
04    2   18
```

In other words, the information for the same participant is placed in a separate row, while the information for the same variable is placed in the same column(s).

6   Through the way they are defined in the Data Editor.

Chapter 3

1   →**Data** →**Select Cases...**
    → **If condition is satisfied** →**If...**
    →**ethnicgp** →▶ button →= →**4** →**Continue**
    →**OK**

2   **gender = 2 & age <= 25 & (ethnicgp = 2 | ethnicgp = 4)**

3   satis1 > 0 & satis2 > 0 & satis3 > 0 & satis4 > 0

4   →Transform →Recode →Into Same Variables…

    →skill →Old and New Values…

    →1 [in box entitled Value: in Old Value section] →box called Value: in New Value section and type 1 →Add →2 [in box entitled Value: in Old Value section] →box called Value: in New Value section and type 1 →Add →3 [in box entitled Value: in Old Value section] →box called Value: in the New Value section and type 2 →Add →4 [in box entitled Value: in Old Value section] →box called Value: in New Value section and type 2 →Add →Continue

    →OK

5   →Transform →Recode →Into Different Variables…

    →income [in box entitled Input Variables –> Output Variable:] →in box entitled Name: type incomec →Change →Old and New Values…

    →Range: and type 1 [in first box] →second box and type 4999 → box called Value: in New Value section and type 1

    →Add →Range: and type 5000 [in first box] →second box and type 9999 →box called Value: in New Value section and type 2 → Add →Range: and type 10000 →box called Value: in the New Value section and type 3 → Add →Copy old value[s] →Add →Continue

    →OK

6   →Transform →Compute…

    →in box entitled Target Variable: type days →weeks →► button [puts weeks into box entitled Numeric Expression:] →* →7 →OK

Chapter 4

1   (b)

2   It forces the researcher to think about the breadth of the concept and the possibility that it comprises a number of distinct components.

3   (a) dichotomous
    (b) nominal
    (c) ordinal
    (d) interval/ratio

4   Interval.

5   External reliability.

6 →**An<u>a</u>lyze** →**Sc<u>a</u>le** →**<u>R</u>eliability Analysis…**

→**autonom1**, **autonom2**, **autonom3** and **autonom4** while holding down Ctrl key →▶button [puts **autonom1**, **autonom2**, **autonom3** and **autonom4** in **Items:** box] →**<u>M</u>odel:** →**Alpha** in drop-down menu →**OK**

7 Internal reliability.

8 (a)

Chapter 5

1 →**<u>A</u>nalyze** →**<u>D</u>escriptive Statistics** →**<u>F</u>requencies…**

→**prody** →▶button →**OK**

2 17.4 per cent.

3 The value of 2,700 for case number 20 is an outlier and would distort the size of both the mean and the range.

4 (c)

5 →**<u>A</u>nalyze** →**<u>D</u>escriptive Statistics** →**<u>E</u>xplore…**

→**satis** →▶button by **<u>D</u>ependent List** →**OK**

6 6.

7 It takes all values in a distribution into account and is easier to interpret in relation to the mean which is more commonly employed as a measure of central tendency than the median.

Chapter 6

1 A representative sample is one which accurately mirrors the population from which it was drawn. A random sample is a type of sample which aims to enhance the likelihood of achieving a representative sample. However, due to a number of factors (such as sampling error or non-response), it is unlikely that a random sample will be a representative sample.

2 Because it enhances the likelihood that the groups (i.e strata) in the population will be accurately represented.

3 When a population is highly dispersed, the time and cost of interviewing can be reduced by multistage cluster sampling.

4 No. Quite aside from the problems of non-response and sampling error, it is unlikely that the Yellow Pages provide a sufficiently complete and accurate sampling frame.

5   Since there are only two possible outcomes (heads and tails) and the coin
    was flipped four times, the probability of finding the particular sequence
    you did would be one out of sixteen ($2 \times 2 \times 2 \times 2$) or 0.0625.

6   No. Even if the coin was unbiased, you would still have a one in sixteen
    chance that you would obtain four heads in a row.

7   The probability of obtaining any sequence of two heads and two tails is
    six out of sixteen or 0.375 since six such sequences are possible. In other
    words, this is the most likely outcome.

8   Since there are only two outcomes to each question (true and false), the
    most likely score for someone who has no general knowledge is 50 points
    (0.5×100), which is the mean of the probability distribution.

9   Once again, there are only two outcomes for each person (butter or
    margarine). The probability of guessing correctly is 0.5. Since fifty
    people took part, the mean or most likely number of people guessing
    correctly would be twenty-five.

10 The null hypothesis would be that there was no difference in talkative-
    ness between men and women.

11 The non-directional hypothesis would be that men and women differ in
    talkativeness. In other words, the direction of the difference is not stated.

12 The lower boundary is 36.23 and the upper boundary is 42.15. This
    means that there is a 95 per cent probability that the population mean
    will lie within this range.

Chapter 7

1   A chi-square test should be used since there are two unrelated categorical
    variables (i.e. shop and type of book) and the number of books sold in
    any one category is fixed. In other words, the number of books in this
    case is a frequency count.

2   The null hypothesis is that the number of books sold according to shop
    or type of book does not differ from that expected by chance.

3   →**Analyze** →**D̲escriptive Statistics** →**C̲rosstabs…**

    →**book** →►button [puts **book** under **R̲ow[s]:**] →**shop** →►button [puts
    shop under **C̲olumn[s]:**] →**Ce̲lls…**

    →**E̲xpected** [in **Counts** section] →**Continue**

    →**S̲tatistics…**

    →**Ch̲i-square** →**Continue**

    →**OK**

4   We would use a two-tailed level of significance in this case and in others involving a comparison of three or more cells since it is not possible to determine the direction of any differences as all differences have been made positive by being squared.

5   Since the value of 0.25 is greater than the conventional criterion or cut-off point of 0.05, we would conclude that the number of books sold did not differ significantly according to shop or type of book. A probability value of 0.25 means that we could expect to obtain this result by chance one out of four times. To be more certain that our result is not due to chance, it is customary to expect the finding to occur at or less than five times out of a hundred.

6   A finding with a probability level of 0.0001 would not mean that there had been a greater difference in the number of books sold than one with a probability level of 0.037. It would simply mean that the former finding was less likely to occur (once in 10,000 times) than the latter one (thirty-seven out of a thousand times).

7   A binomial test would be used to determine if there had been a significant difference.

8   If we specify the direction of the difference in the number of books sold between the two shops, we would use a one-tailed level of significance.

9   You would simply divide the two-tailed level by 2, which in this case would give a one-tailed level of 0.042.

10   It would be inappropriate to analyse these data with a binomial test since it does not take account of the number of men and women who reported not having this experience. In other words, it does not compare the proportion of men with the proportion of women reporting this experience. Consequently, it is necessary to use a chi-square test for two samples. Note, however, that it would have been possible to have used a binomial test if the proportion of people falling in love in one sample was compared with that in the other. However, it may be simpler to use chi-square.

11   Since the number of close friends a person has is a ratio measure and the data being compared come from two unrelated samples (men and women), an unrelated *t* test should be used.

12   The pooled variance estimate is used to interpret the results of a *t* test when the variances do not differ significantly from one another.

13   You would use a repeated-measure test since the average number of books sold is an interval/ratio measure which can vary between the ten shops, and the cases (i.e. the ten shops) are the same for the three time periods.

Chapter 8

1   (a) →<u>A</u>nalyze →<u>D</u>escriptive Statistics →<u>C</u>rosstabs...

      →**prody** →►button [puts **prody** in **R<u>o</u>w[s]:** box] →**gender** →►button [puts **gender** in **Column[s]:** box] →C<u>e</u>lls [Ensure there is a tick by **Observed** in the **Counts** box. Under **Percentages** ensure there is a tick by <u>C</u>olumn].

      →**Continue**

      →**OK**

    (b) Taking the sequence in 1(a) before clicking on **OK**,
      →<u>A</u>nalyze

      →**Ch<u>i</u>-square** →**Continue**

      →**OK**

    (c) With $\chi^2 = 1.183$ and $p > 0.05$, the relationship would be regarded as non-significant.

    (d) 35.5 per cent.

2   The reasoning is faulty. Chi-square cannot establish the strength of a relationship between two variables. Also, statistical significance is not the same as substantive significance, so that the researcher would be incorrect in believing that the presence of a statistically significant chi-square value indicates that the relationship is important.

3   (a) →<u>A</u>nalyze →<u>C</u>orrelate →<u>B</u>ivariate...

      →**income** →►button →**years** →►button →**satis** →►button →**age** →►button →**Pearso<u>n</u>** [if not already selected] →<u>D</u>isplay **actual significance level** [if not already selected] →**One ta<u>i</u>led** [*if* preferred to **T<u>w</u>o-tailed**] →**OK**

    (b) The correlation between **age** and **years** ($r = 0.81$, rounded up).

    (c) 66 per cent.

4   There is a host of errors. The researcher should not have employed r to assess the correlation, since social class is an ordinal variable. The amount of variance explained is 53.3 per cent, not 73 per cent. Finally, the causal inference (i.e. that social class explains the number of books read) is risky with a correlational/survey design of this kind.

5   The statistical significance of r is affected, not just by the size of r, but also by the size of the sample. As sample size increases, it becomes much easier for r to be statistically significant. The reason, therefore, for the contrast in the findings is that the sample size for the researcher's study,

in which $r = 0.55$ and $p > 0.05$, is smaller than the one which found a smaller correlation but was statistically highly significant.

6   (a) Since these two variables are ordinal, a measure of rank correlation will probably be most appropriate. Since there are quite a few tied ranks, Kendall's tau may be more appropriate than Spearman's rho.

      (b) →**Analyze** →**Correlate** →**Bivariate...**

→**prody** →▶button →**commit** →▶button →**Kendall's tau-b** [if not already selected] →**Display actual significance level** →**One-tailed** [*if* preferred to **Two-tailed**]

→**OK**

      (c) tau = 0.25, $p = 0.011$. This suggests that there is a weak correlation but we can be confident that a correlation of at least this size can be found in the population from which the sample was taken.

7   (a) The intercept.
      (b) The regression coefficient. For each extra year, **autonom** increases by 0.0623.
      (c) Not terribly well. Only 8 per cent of the variance in **autonom** is explained by **age**.
      (d) 10.33
      (e) →**Analyze** →**Regression** →**Linear...**

→**autonom** →▶button next to **Dependent:** box →**age** →▶button next to **Independent[s]:** box →**OK**

Chapter 9

1   One advantage is that a more accurate measure of error variance is provided. The other is to examine interaction effects between the two variables.

2   An interaction is when the effect of one variable is not the same under all the conditions of the other variable.

3   You would conduct an analysis of variance (ANOVA) to determine whether the interaction between the two variables was significant.

4   Performance is the dependent variable since the way in which it is affected by alcohol, anxiety and gender is being investigated.

5   There are three factors, that is, alcohol, anxiety and gender.

6   There are three levels of anxiety.

7   It can be described as a $4 \times 3 \times 2$ factorial design.

8   →**Analyze** →**General Linear Model** →**Univariate...**

→**perform** →▶ button beside **Dependent Variable:** →**alcohol** →▶ button beside **Fixed Factor(s):** →**anxiety** →▶ button beside **Fixed Factor(s):** →**gender** →▶ button beside **Fixed Factor(s):**

→**Options . . .** →**Descriptive statistics** →**Homogeneity tests**

→**Continue**

→**OK**

9   First, you would find out if there were any differences in intelligence between the three conditions, using one-way analysis of variance. If there were no significant differences, then you could assume that the effect of intelligence is likely to be equal in the three conditions and that there is no need to control for it statistically. If you had found that there were significant differences in intelligence between the three conditions, you would need to determine if there was any relationship between intelligence and the learning to read measure. If such a relationship existed, you could control for the effect of intelligence by conducting an analysis of covariance.

10 →**Analyze** →**General Linear Model** →**Univariate...**

→**read** →▶ button beside **Dependent Variable:** →**methods** →▶ button beside **Fixed Factor(s):** →**intell** →▶ button beside **Covariate(s):**

→**Options...**

→**methods** → button →**Continue**

→**OK**

11 It is a between-subjects design with multiple measures or a multivariate analysis of variant (MANOVA).

12 →**Analyze** →**General Linear Model** →**Multivariate...**

→**intell** →▶ button beside **Dependent Variables:** →**likeable** →▶ button beside **Dependent Variables:** →**honesty** →▶ button beside **Dependent Variables:** →**confid** →▶ button beside **Dependent Variables:** →**attract** →▶ button beside **Fixed Factor(s):**

→**Options...**

→**Descriptive statistics** →**Residual SSCP matrix**

→**Homogeneity tests** →**Continue**

→**OK**

Chapter 10

1   To a large extent, in that 71 per cent of women support equal pay legislation, as against 58 per cent of men.

2   Table 10E.2 suggests that the relationship between sex and approval for
equal pay legislation is moderated by age. For respondents under the age
of 35, there is greater overall support for legislation, and the difference
between men and women is greater than in Table 10E.1. Among
those who are 35 and over, the overall level of approval is lower and the
difference between men and women is much less than in Table 10E.1
Clearly, the relationship between sex and approval for equal pay legislation applies to the under-35s in this imaginary example, rather than
those who are 35 or over.

3   →**Analyze** →**Summarize** →**Crosstabs...**

→**commit** →▶button by **Row[s]:** →**ethnicgp** →▶button by **Column[s]:**
→**gender** →▶button by bottom box →**Cells** [Ensure there is a tick by
Observed in the **Counts** box. Under **Percentages** ensure there is a tick
by **Column**]

→**Continue**

→**OK**

4   The main possibility is that the relationship between income and
attendance at religious services is spurious. Age is probably related to
both income and attendance. However, it should also be noted that the
relationship between income and attendance does not disappear entirely
when age is controlled.

5   →**Analyze** →**Correlate** →**Partial...**

→**income** →▶button by **Variables:** box →**satis** →▶button by **Variables:**
box →**age** →▶button by **Controlling for:** box →**Two-tailed** or **One-tailed**
depending on which form of **Test of Significance** you want *and* ensure
Display actual significance level has been selected →**Options...**

→**Exclude cases listwise** →**Continue**

→**OK**

If you follow this sequence, the partial correlation between **income** and
satis (controlling for **age**) is 0.55. The zero-order correlation is 0.62,
suggesting that the relationship between **income** and **satis** is largely
unaffected by **age**.

6   (a) 94.4.

(b) 78 per cent. The multiple coefficient of determination (R^2) suggests that a large proportion of y is explained by the three variables (78 per cent) and the equation as a whole is statistically significant, suggesting that the multiple correlation between the three independent variables and y is unlikely to be zero in the population.

(c) This was a trick question. Since the three regression coefficients presented in the equation are unstandardised, it is not possible to compare them to determine which independent variable has the largest effect on y. In order to make such an inference, standardised regression coefficients would be required.

(d) For every one unit change in x_3, y decreases by 1.4.

7   Equation (10.4):
→**Analyze** →**Regression** →**Linear**…

→**satis** →▶button next to **Dependent:** box →**autonom** →▶button next to **Independent[s]:** box →**routine**→▶button next to **Independent[s]:** box →downward-pointing arrow in box by **Method:** →**Enter** →**OK**
Equation (10.5):
→**Analyze** →**Regression** →**Linear**…

→**absence** →▶button next to **Dependent:** box →**autonom** →▶button next to **Independent[s]:** box →**routine** →▶button next to **Independent[s]:** box →**satis** →▶button next to **Independent[s]:** box →downward-pointing arrow in box by **Method:** →**Enter** →**OK**

8   (a) According to the adjusted R^2, 59 per cent of the variance in **satis** is explained by **autonom** and **routine**.

(b) Yes. The t values for **autonom** and **routine** are significant at $p < 0.000$ and $p < 0.002$ respectively.

(c) −0.293.

9   The largest effect coefficient is for **satis** (−0.50). The effect coefficients for **autonom** and **routine** respectively were −0.115 and −0.02.

Chapter 11

1   No. If you were to do this, you would be examining the way in which your anxiety items were grouped together. In other words, you may be analysing the factor structure of anxiety itself. To find out if your ten items assessed a single factor of anxiety, you would need to include items which measured at least another variable such as sociability.

2   At least 50–100 cases.

3   This is the variance which is not shared with other variables.

4   Principal-components analysis analyses all the variance of a variable while principal-axis factoring analyses the variance it shares with the other variables.

5   There are as many factors as variables.

6   The first factor always accounts for the largest amount of variance.

7   This would defeat the aim of factor analysis which is to reduce the number of variables that need to be examined. The smaller factors may account for less variance than that of a single variable.

8   Kaiser's criterion, which extracts factors with an eigenvalue of greater than one.

9   A loading is a measure of association between a variable and a factor.

10   Factors are rotated to increase the loading of some items and to decrease that of others so as to make the factors easier to interpret.

11   The advantage of orthogonal rotation is that since the factors are uncorrelated with one another, they provide the minimum number of factors required to account for the relationships between the variables.

12   No. Since the variance may be shared between two or more factors, it is not possible to estimate it.

Appendix

Key Differences between SPSS 13 and recent earlier versions

SPSS 12

The major differences between SPSS 12 and SPSS 13 for the topics covered in this book concern **Compute Variable** . . . , **Scatter/Dot** . . . and the **Chart Editor**. In SPSS 12 the **Compute Variable** dialog box has a single **Functions** box from which options can be chosen. **Scatter/Dot** . . . is called **Scatter** . . . , the **Scatter/Dot** dialog box is called **Scatterplot** and there is no **Dot** option. To label the slices of a pie diagram and add the percentages of cases in each, double click anywhere in the **Chart Editor,** →double click on pie diagram (to open **Properties** dialog box) →**Data Value Labels** (in **Properties** dialog box) →**Count** in **Contents** box →**red X** (to put in **Available** box) →variable name (e.g. **ethnicgp**) →curved upward arrow (to put in **Contents** box) →**Percent** →curved upward arrow (to put in **Contents** box) →**Apply** →**Close**. To fit a regression line to a scatterplot, →on a circle in the chart of the **Chart Editor** so that the circles in the plot become highlighted →**Chart** →**Add Chart Element** →**Fit Line at Total** [opens the **Properties** dialog box]. Assuming that the **Fit Line** tab is active →**Linear** (this is usually the default) →**Close**.

SPSS 11

The major differences between SPSS 12 and SPSS 11 also apply to SPSS 10 and 9. They are relatively few. In these previous releases (that is, 11 and earlier) variable names cannot begin with a capital letter and are restricted to 8 characters. The **Data** and **Transform** options are not available in the **Viewer** or **Output** window. Some output is not organized into tables such as partial correlation and reliability. The **Chart Editor** works differently. To fit a regression line to a scatterplot, →double click anywhere in the scatterplot to open the **Chart Editor** →**Chart** →**Options** . . . [opens **Scatterplot Options** dialog box] →**Total** under **Fit Line** →**OK**.

SPSS 10

Changes between SPSS 10 and SPSS 11 are very minor and hardly noticeable.

Bibliography

Bentler, P.M. (1995) *EQS Structural Equations Program Manual*, Encino, CA: Multivariate.

Blauner, R. (1964) *Alienation and Freedom: The Factory Worker and His Industry*, Chicago: University of Chicago Press.

Bohrnstedt, G.W. and Knoke, D. (1982) *Statistics for Social Data Analysis*, Itasca, IL: F.E. Peacock.

Boneau, C. (1960) 'The effects of violations of assumptions underlying the *t* test', *Psychological Bulletin* 57: 49–64.

Brayfield, A. and Rothe, H. (1951) 'An index of job satisfaction', *Journal of Applied Psychology* 35: 307–11.

Bridgman, P.W. (1927) *The Logic of Modern Physics*, London: Macmillan.

Bryman, A. (1985) 'Professionalism and the clergy', *Review of Religious Research* 26: 253–60.

Bryman, A. (1986) *Leadership and Organizations*, London: Routledge.

Bryman, A. (1988a) *Quantity and Quality in Social Research*, London: Routledge.

Bryman, A. (1988b) 'Introduction: "inside" accounts and social research in organizations', in A. Bryman (ed.), *Doing Research in Organizations*, London: Routledge.

Bryman, A. (1989) *Research Methods and Organization Studies*, London: Routledge.

Bryman, A. and Cramer, D. (1990) *Quantitative Data Analysis for Social Scientists*. London: Routledge.

355

Bryman, A. and Cramer, D. (1994) *Quantitative Data Analysis for Social Scientists* (rev. edn), London: Routledge.

Bryman, A. and Cramer, D. (1997) *Quantitative Data Analysis with SPSS for Windows: A Guide for Social Scientists*, London: Routledge.

Bryman, A. and Cramer, D. (1999) *Quantitative Data Analysis with SPSS Release 8 for Windows: A Guide for Social Scientists*, London: Routledge.

Bryman, A. and Cramer, D. (2001) *Quantitative Data Analysis with SPSS Release 10 for Windows: A Guide for Social Scientists*, London: Routledge.

Campbell, D.T. and Fiske, D.W. (1959) 'Convergent and discriminant validation by the multitrait–multimethod index', *Psychological Bulletin* 56: 81–105.

Cattell, R.B. (1966) 'The meaning and strategic use of factor analysis', in R.B. Cattell (ed.), *Handbook of Multivariate Experimental Psychology*, Chicago: Rand McNally.

Cattell, R.B. (1973) *Personality and Mood by Questionnaire*, San Francisco: Jossey-Bass.

Child, J. (1973) 'Predicting and understanding organization structure', *Administrative Science Quarterly* 18: 168–85.

Cohen, L. and Holliday, M. (1982) *Statistics for Social Scientists*, London: Harper & Row.

Conover, W.J. (1980) *Practical Nonparametric Statistics* (2nd edn), New York: John Wiley.

Cramer, D. (1996) 'Job satisfaction and organizational continuance commitment: a two-wave panel study', *Journal of Organizational Behavior* 17: 389–400.

Cramer, D. (1998) *Fundamental Statistics for Social Research: Step-by-Step Calculations and Computer Techniques Using SPSS for Windows*, London: Routledge.

Cronbach, L.J. and Meehl, P.E. (1955) 'Construct validity in psychological tests', *Psychological Bulletin* 52: 281–302.

Davis, J.A. (1985) *The Logic of Causal Order*, Sage University Paper Series on Quantitative Applications in the Social Sciences, series no. 55, Beverly Hills, CA: Sage.

Durkheim, E. (1952 [1898]) *Suicide: A Study in Sociology*, London: Routledge & Kegan Paul.

Eysenck, H.J. and Eysenck, S.B.G. (1969) *Personality Structure and Measurement*, London: Routledge & Kegan Paul.

Freeman, L.C. (1965) *Elementary Applied Statistics: For Students of Behavioral Science*, New York: John Wiley.

Games, P. and Lucas, P. (1966) 'Power of the analysis of variance of independent groups on non-normal and normally transformed data', *Educational and Psychological Measurement* 26: 311–27.

Glock, C.Y. and Stark, R. (1965) *Religion and Society in Tension*, Chicago: Rand McNally.

Gorsuch, R.L. (1983) *Factor Analysis*, Hillsdale, NJ: Lawrence Erlbaum.

Gould, S.J. (1991) 'The median isn't the message', in *Bully for Brontosaurus: Reflections in Natural History*, London: Hutchison Radius.

Goyder, J. (1988) *The Silent Minority: Non-respondents on Social Surveys*, Oxford: Polity Press.

Hall, R.H. (1968) 'Professionalization and bureaucratization', *American Sociological Review* 33: 92–104.

Hirschi, T. (1969) *Causes of Delinquency*, Berkeley: University of California Press.

Huff, D. (1973) *How to Lie with Statistics*, Harmondsworth: Penguin.

Huitema, B. (1980) *The Analysis of Covariance and Alternatives*, New York: John Wiley.

Jenkins, G.D., Nadler, D.A., Lawler, E.E. and Cammann, C. (1975), 'Structured observations: an approach to measuring the nature of jobs', *Journal of Applied Psychology* 60: 171–81.

Jöreskog, K.G. and Sörbom, D. (1996) *LISREL 8: Users Reference Guide*, Hillsdale, NJ: Laurence Erlbaum Associates Inc.

Labovitz, S. (1970) 'The assignment of numbers to rank order categories', *American Sociological Review* 35: 515–24.

Labovitz, S. (1971) 'In defense of assigning numbers to ranks', *American Sociological Review* 36: 521–2.

Land, K.C. (1969) 'Principles of path analysis', in E.F. Borgatta and G.F. Bohrnstedt (eds), *Sociological Methodology 1969*, San Francisco: Jossey-Bass.

Lazarsfeld, P.F. (1958) 'Evidence and inference in social research', *Daedalus* 87: 99–130.

Levene, H. (1960) 'Robust tests for equality of variances', in I. Olkin (ed.), *Contributions to Probability and Statistics*, Stanford, CA: Stanford University Press.

Locke, E.A. and Schweiger, D.M. (1979) 'Participation in decision-making: one more look', in B.M. Staw (ed.), *Research in Organizational Behavior*, vol. 1, Greenwich, CT: JAI Press.

Lord, F.M. (1953) 'On the statistical treatment of football numbers', *American Psychologist* 8: 750–1.

McNemar, Q. (1969) *Psychological Statistics* (4th edn), New York: John Wiley.

Marshall, G., Newby, H., Rose, D. and Vogler, C. (1988) *Social Class in Modern Britain*, London: Unwin Hyman.

Maxwell, S.E. (1980) 'Pairwise multiple comparisons in repeated measures designs', *Journal of Educational Statistics* 5: 269–87.

Merton, R.K. (1967) *On Theoretical Sociology*, New York: Free Press.

Mitchell, T.R. (1985) 'An evaluation of the validity of correlational research conducted in organizations', *Academy of Management Review* 10: 192–205.

Mosteller, F. and Tukey, J.W. (1977) *Data Analysis and Regression*, Reading, MA: Addison-Wesley.

Murray, I. (1995) 'How your council rates in the efficiency league', *The Times* 30 March: 32.

O'Brien, R.M. (1979) 'The use of Pearson's *r* with ordinal data', *American Sociological Review* 44: 851–7.

Pedhazur, E.J. (1982) *Multiple Regression in Behavioral Research: Explanation and Prediction* (2nd edn), New York: Holt, Rinehart & Winston.

Rosenberg, M. (1968) *The Logic of Survey Analysis*, New York: Basic Books.

Siegel, S. and Castellan, N.J. Jr (1988) *Non-parametric Statistics for the Behavioral Sciences* (2nd edn), New York: McGraw-Hill.

Snizek, W.E. (1972) 'Hall's professionalism scale: an empirical reassessment', *American Sociological Review* 37: 10–14.

Stevens, J. (1996) *Applied Multivariate Statistics for the Social Sciences* (3rd edn), Mahwah, NJ: Lawrence Erlbaum.

Stevens, J.P. (1979) 'Comment on Olson: choosing a test statistic in multivariate analysis of variance', *Psychological Bulletin* 86: 728–37.

Stevens, S.S. (1946) 'On the theory of scales of measurement', *Science* 103: 677–80.

Tabachnick, B.G. and Fidell, L.S. (2001) *Using Multivariate Statistics* (4th edn), Boston: Allyn & Bacon.

Tukey, J.W. (1977) *Exploratory Data Analysis*, Reading, MA: Addison-Wesley.

Walker, H. (1940) 'Degrees of freedom', *Journal of Educational Psychology* 31: 253–69.

Wilcox, R.R. (1987) 'New designs in analysis of variance', *Annual Review of Psychology* 38: 29–60.

Index

Entries in **bold** are SPSS procedures and dialog boxes